CAMBRIDGE LIBRARY COLLECTION

Books of enduring scholarly value

MW01615018

Art and Architecture

From the middle of the eighteenth century, with the growth of travel at home and abroad and the increase in leisure for the wealthier classes, the arts became the subject of more widespread appreciation and discussion. The rapid expansion of book and periodical publishing in this area both reflected and encouraged interest in art and art history among the wider reading public. This series throws light on the development of visual culture and aesthetics. It covers topics from the Grand Tour to the great exhibitions of the nineteenth century, and includes art criticism and biography.

Palissy the Potter

This two-volume biography of the sixteenth-century French potter and natural scientist Bernard Palissy (*c.*1510–*c.*1590) was published in 1852, the year after the Great Exhibition, in which Palissy's extraordinary art had been brought before the Victorian public by Minton's highly decorated 'Palissy wares'. Henry Morley (1822–94) trained in medicine but later became an author and editor, writing for Charles Dickens among others. Here he gathers together all the material then available about Palissy, including the potter's own writings and a contemporary biography. Palissy was among the many European ceramicists who attempted to reproduce Chinese porcelain; his lack of success drove his family into poverty, but his highly ornamented wares, encrusted with sea creatures, came to the attention of Catherine de' Medici, who gave him her patronage and protection (he was a convinced Protestant); after her death he was sent to the Bastille, and died there.

Palissy the Potter

The Life of Bernard Palissy, of Saintes,
His Labours and Discoveries in Art and Science

VOLUME 1

HENRY MORLEY

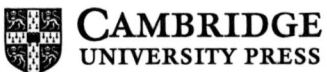

CAMBRIDGE
UNIVERSITY PRESS

University Printing House, Cambridge, CB2 8BS, United Kingdom

Cambridge University Press is part of the University of Cambridge.

It furthers the University's mission by disseminating knowledge in the pursuit of education, learning and research at the highest international levels of excellence.

www.cambridge.org
Information on this title: www.cambridge.org/9781108078061

© in this compilation Cambridge University Press 2015

This edition first published 1852
This digitally printed version 2015

ISBN 978-1-108-07806-1 Paperback

PALISSY THE POTTER.

PALISSY THE POTTER.

THE LIFE

OF

BERNARD PALISSY, OF SAINTES,

HIS LABOURS AND DISCOVERIES IN ART AND SCIENCE;

WITH AN OUTLINE OF

HIS PHILOSOPHICAL DOCTRINES,

AND A TRANSLATION OF

ILLUSTRATIVE SELECTIONS FROM HIS WORKS.

BY HENRY MORLEY.

" Je n'ai point eu d'autre liure que le ciel et la terre, lequel est conneu de tous,
et est donné à tous de connoistre et lire ce beau liure."   PALISSY.

IN TWO VOLUMES.

VOL. I.

LONDON:

CHAPMAN AND HALL, 193, PICCADILLY.

1852.

PREFACE.

In Chapters II. to VI. of the first volume of this book
I have feigned two or three simple incidents and dialogues, in order that so I might more easily describe the
character of the experience that must have been acquired
by Palissy during his early travels. Nothing else in
these volumes is fictitious; and in the chapters above
named the information given is in no case fanciful:
every point has been selected, as nearly as possible, from
contemporary writings, and the dialogues express opinions of the time as they were spoken by the men who
held them.

So much preface is made necessary by the romantic
character of many incidents in the life of a man who
laboured three centuries ago in turbulent times,

Voyaging through strange seas of thought, alone.

In his own day he was a man obscurely great among the prominently little; but the world, as it grows, improves its estimate of greatness, and the name of Palissy perhaps will not remain obscure.

London, *October*, 1852.

ERRATA.

On page 185, in the first volume, at the twelfth line, Leghorn is printed for Libourne. It is requested that the reader will be kind enough to make correction of this error with a pen.

Vol. I.—Page 26, last line, for *from*, read *to*; p. 38, l. 16, for *drive*, read *dive*; p. 64, l. 17, for 1649, read 1469; p. 65, l. 9, for *V.*, read *I.*; p. 102, l. 7, for *usually*, read *usual*; p. 175, l. 7, for *day*, read *days*; p. 180, l. 1, for *Saintonge*, read *Saintes*; p. 185, l. 12, for *Leghorn*, read *Libourne*; p. 203, l. 3, for *by*, read *from*; p. 231, l. 6, for *II.*, read *I.*; p. 273, l. 4, for *works*, read *work*; p. 282, l. 11, for *prosecuting*, read *persecuting*.

Vol. II.—Page 110, last line, for *passages*, read *passage*; p. 172, l. 7, for *tells*, read *tell*; p. 185, l. 26, for *Hieronoymus*, read *Hieronymus*.

CONTENTS OF VOL. I.

PALISSY THE POTTER.

CHAPTER I.

BIRTH, PARENTAGE, AND EARLY EDUCATION.

For the birth of Bernard Palissy we can assign no more precise date than the year 1509, with a concession that this may be wrong within a limit of six years on either side. The date assigned by his last editor is 1510.

Of the birthplace of Bernard Palissy we only know that it was somewhere in the diocese of Agen. The aforesaid editor does, indeed, undertake to be particular. He tells us that Palissy was born at Chapelle Biron, a poor hamlet near the small town of Biron, in Perigord.

The town of Biron lies so near the southern boundary of Perigord, upon the little river Lade, that to descend the Lade only so far as to Chapelle Biron, is to cross from Perigord into the Agenois. Chapelle Biron is placed about three-quarters of a mile over the border; but although politically situated in the diocese of Agen, it belongs, by virtue of its scenery, to Perigord.

Perigord is a province, in part hilly and mountainous, in part made up of barren plains. In the days of Palissy, it abounded more than it now does in forest tracts, containing many walnut-trees, and chestnuts in such great abundance that they formed the staple food of the poor natives. These chestnuts also aided in the fattening of herds of pigs, whose noses were at all times prompt to perceive where truffles were concealed under the light soil within the forest. The wealth of Perigord depended, at the time in which we are now interested, on its forests and its pigs; in an inferior degree, on oxen, upon vineyards, and the oil extracted from its nuts. Its truffles were then, as now, an appreciated luxury; and perhaps the notion of combining with these dainties in a pie the excellent pheasants which are fattened in the truffle-yielding woods, had already dawned upon men as the great idea which was hereafter to make Perigord illustrious.

Over the vast heaths, and through the woods, and by the numerous river-torrents which the mountains pour upon the province, walked a free-hearted, clever, lively race of men. Hard and energetic as their dialect was their war-loving character, and good recruits were yielded from their number to the many armies called for in that period of troubles. Many armies had been marching into and out of France, hither and thither, during the period preceding the birth of Palissy; moreover, since the consolidation of the monarchy, neglect had been suffered by districts distant from the central power—by Perigord and its neighbours among the rest. Therefore, in the beginning of the sixteenth century traces of former cultivation were already beginning to be defaced, and the internal wealth of Perigord was rapidly decreasing. The life-blood of France, then in a diseased condition (as it very often is, causing the body of the country to be frequently disfigured by eruptions)—the life-blood then gathering about the head, caused that to throb in a distressing manner, while it left a chill at the extremities.

Through Chapelle Biron flows the river Lade, a little tributary to the Lot; the waters of the Lot flow into the Garonne. By these rivers the Agenois, the district submitted to the diocese of Agen, is made fertile. Physically, the Agenois differs only from its northern neighbour, Perigord, in having larger rivers, more vines, fewer hills, and a soil more uniformly generous. The barren tract about Chapelle Biron is not a characteristic of the Agenois, but, as we said before, of Perigord. If, therefore, it was in Chapelle Biron ·that Palissy was born, it would please the fanciful to show how well he had been fitted with a birthplace. The variety of scene, the combinations of fertility and barrenness, would make a scrap of Perigord poetically fit to be the birthplace of a man who lived through scenes of intense contrast; who was free-hearted, clever, lively as men are who play upon the heaths when they are children; who was grandly energetic, and if not delighting in a war with men, warred

B 2

against difficulties in the way of knowledge with a heroism that communicates even to the baldest records of his life the colour of romance.

Unluckily, we are unable to attach much credit to the theory which has deposited the birthplace of Palissy upon the skirts of Perigord. That he was native of the fertile Agenois, all writers, on the assurance of his contemporaries, will of course agree. By simple misconception, he has now and then been chronicled in dictionaries as a native of the town of Agen. Some hamlet was probably his birthplace; but the evidence in favour of Chapelle Biron is insufficient. It is no more, I believe, than this: that there is at Chapelle Biron a kiln, bearing the name of Palissy; and that a family with that name, supposed to be descended from the Potter, had for some time resided on the spot. Now we know with certainty that the father of Palissy could not have been a potter. Bernard himself tells us, that when he commenced his own experiments in pottery, he " had never seen earth baked;"* therefore his father's livelihood could not have been drawn out of a kiln. The existence of a Palissy family upon the spot may make it probable, that among the descendants of the Potter, who had many children, one settled at Chapelle Biron, following in a rude way the calling which had made his family-name famous in the History of Art; but it does not prove that Bernard was born at that place. Still, therefore, the

---

* In *L'Art de Terre*, which will be found translated under the title of " The Artist in Earth," at the end of this biography.

doubt must be allowed to hang about this portion of our subject. Of some of the grandest rivers which fertilise our world, the source has been for ages undiscovered,—of many, even the existence was for centuries unknown, except to the few dwellers by their banks.

Concerning the parentage of Bernard Palissy, we shall need but little shrewdness to arrive at a satisfactory amount of knowledge. The business to which he was educated was that of a glass-painter,* and worker generally in painted glass. Painted windows were formed both after the manner of mosaic-work (which had originated the invention), by the artistic combination of fragments of glass differently coloured, and also by the fixing upon sheet-glass of pigments laid on with a brush. Glass-making, and all the processes connected with the shaping and colouring of glass, belonged to the art of *Verrerie*, which was accounted in the days of Palissy, and long before and afterwards, an honourable occupation. Not honourable or worshipful in the vague sense employed by our own trading corporations, but literally an occupation which a nobleman might follow without loss of caste in the eyes of a punctilious community.

There were two or three such noble trades, and there was need of them. Penny-needing nobles swarmed formerly in France, as they do now in Spain or Austria.

---

* "I for a long time practised glass-painting, until I was assured that I could earn bread by labour on earth." This and other passages to the same effect occur in *L'Art de Terre*.

They were born to the right of talking big and eating little. They received a birthright, and paid for it with their potage. For the benefit of such men, or rather for the benefit of the order to which they belonged, and to prevent these ragged nobles from breaking down the platform which elevates men noble by their birth above men noble by their honesty, it was from early times thought prudent to honour one or two trades, by allowing noblemen to get their bread in them without a loss of dignity. Thus glass and glory came to be akin. I mean, of course, the glory which consists in a nobility by right of calfskin, as separated from and lifted over a nobility by right of soul. Some satirist, no doubt, suggested glass as a fit substance to be paired with glory of this kind, since both were blown after the fashion of a bubble, both could be seen through by a man with healthy eyes, and both required forbearance in the handling.

The infusion of nobility into the glass trade was so complete, that a belief arose, and has been to this day maintained in many places, that nobles only were permitted to engage in this employment; that they transmitted the trade to their children, and allowed no new business to be opened by a stranger, unless he produced his patents of nobility. By law this never was the fact; by custom it appears to have been the case, however, in a few districts, while in others glass-working was practised by men who had not the immunities of the noble-class, and certainly did not acquire them by virtue of their occupation. The practice of *Verrerie* was in fact, as I before said, honourable; it might be practised by a noble without loss of caste, although it did not elevate men out of lower classes, otherwise than by associating them with what was thought to be a gentlemanly occupation.

Poor nobles, labouring for food as glass-workers, taught the trade to their sons; and as few who laboured would be willing to communicate their secrets to strangers, in whom they had not the interest of near relationship, it will be more especially true of glass-workers, as it was true very generally of most trades formerly, and is true rather generally now, that the occupation of the father comes to be the occupation of the son. Bernard Palissy we know to have been born poor, and to have received in his childhood no more than a peasant's education, except that he learned to draw* and paint on glass. We cannot err much in inferring, therefore, that his father was a glass-worker. Additional testimony is, however, furnished by the fact that Palissy, himself bred to *Verrerie*, apparently believes the art to be confined to nobles. He speaks at all times, not from books, but from experience. We may with certainty, perhaps, infer that he himself belonged to one of the innumerable families of petty nobles; and in that case, undoubtedly, the trade to which

---

* "God has gifted me with some knowledge of drawing."—*The Artist in Earth.* With Palissy's occupations from the first, drawing was associated, and it therefore has frequent mention in his works. From this passage we may suppose the taste to have been developed very early.

he was educated he acquired from the instructions of his
father. Writing in later life, Palissy says:

"I beg you to consider awhile our glasses, which,
through having been too common among men, have fallen
to so vile a price, that the greater part of those who make
them live more sordidly than Paris porters. The occupation is noble, and the men who work at it are nobles;
but several who exercise that art as gentlemen, would
gladly be plebeians, and possess wherewith to pay the
taxes."

Of these glass-workers, living more sordidly than Paris
porters, we have accounts somewhat more recent than the
time of Palissy, which do not indicate that they improved in their condition. The fine gentleman who
travelled out of town, found, buried in the gloom of a wild
forest, men whose sylvan solitude he celebrated in the
cant phrase of his day. The simplicity, the candour, the
remoteness from men and the propinquity to birds, enjoyed
by the glass-workers in the great wood, were duly
envied by the little gentleman, who nevertheless would
have felt, as against his own person, the suspicion of simplicity to be an insult, and who did not venture to be
candid even to himself. The gentleman to whom it was
a glorious birthright to be idle, professed to admire the
painful toil by which the rough men in the woods earned
their exemption from the vapours; and never could the
head under a wig forget the day when, for some festival,
wild hair was combed, and rugged beards were shaven, by

the mirror of a pool in the recesses of the forest,—when,
rudely accoutred and after an antique way, the knights
of the glade made holiday, and bowed, like creatures out
of Ariosto, at the feet of the wild beauties of the hamlet.
The forest-chase of a wild dinner, and the red glow of
the furnace after sunset upon moss and bark of trees,
supplied the traveller with themes for a sickly, tepid
eloquence, which leaves, after evaporation, a distinct trace
of nothing but the fact that the glass-workers were
miserably poor.

The furnaces and hamlets of these people were generally
to be found in the recesses of a forest, and for the choice
of a situation of this kind, good reasons existed.   At a
period when domestic buildings were much more combus-
tible than they now are, the existence of glass-furnaces
within a town was a decided source of risk.   It was the
banishment of glass-huts from the town itself, in the year
1291, which caused the establishment near Venice of the
famous glass-works of Murano.   Glass had been made in
Gaul from the remote time of the elder Pliny, and the
French did not neglect those measures of precaution
which were thought requisite in other countries, and of
which we find records at a later period in London also.
Moreover, to the glass-workers themselves, when wood
was their fuel, and the ashes of certain twigs, and of fern,
were used as an ingredient in their manufacture, it was
more convenient to build their workshops in the wood,
where articles of which they were in daily want sur-

rounded them, and they were saved much loss of time, or
much expense of carriage. For this reason, either scattered or singly, or collected with the dwellings of their
owners into little woodland hamlets, the fires of the French
glass-workers were lighted, in the days of Palissy, most
frequently in the recesses of a forest.

Very reasonably, therefore, we may suppose that in a
hamlet of the kind thus indicated Palissy was born ; that
as a child he rolled upon the moss, and ripened with the
chestnuts. Bits of coloured glass held a high place, no
doubt, among his early toys, and some of his first lessons
must have been those which taught him to distinguish
between certain minerals, by the burning of which upon
its surface, glass was coloured. Of the learning of his
day, none was communicated to the child. The invention of printing had revived letters, and created with the
power the desire to read. Italy excepted, little literature
had been then added by Europe to the stores of history,
philosophy, and poetry, bequeathed to us by ancient Greece
and Rome. Whatever folly may attach in our own day
to an exclusive study of the ancients, borrowed from our
forefathers, to the neglect of better things, that folly is not
to be ascribed to our forefathers themselves. Before they
had the minds of Shakspeare, Goethe, Molière, Cervantes,
Humboldt, and some thousand more, to study, it was in
Greek and Latin that they had to seek the highest, and,
with some obvious exceptions, the only literature which
tended to the education of the world. The degree of

familiarity with Greek and Latin was therefore the test of education in the time of Palissy, and fairly so.   It has continued until lately the test, even in our own day; because we idly followed an old rule, after the reason of it had for years departed.

Palissy afterwards, conscious of his innate strength, a little gloried in his want of Greek and Latin.*   But he has not yet learnt, perhaps, that languages so named exist.   For now he plays before us as a child, busy beside the forest-brook, or pondering upon the structure of a chestnut. The child, exchanging hours of reverie for madcap freaks and noisy pastimes, follows now the impulse of a mind created to be thoughtful, now the prompting of a lively laughter-loving temperament which works upon a body gifted with the fullest health.   Knowing what fatigues and what privations swept over that body, and left it in pos-session of a vigorous old age, we guess how the rich blood could tinge its cheeks in the first days when it still had few pursuits more troublesome than butterflies to chase. Knowing that, throughout life to the last, and at a time when others often sink into mechanical existence, Bernard Palissy retained a quick eye, a clear head and a clean

---

* "I have had no other books than Heaven and Earth, which are open to all."—"And how could you contradict so wise a person, you who are nothing.   We know that Cardan is a famous doctor, who has graduated at Toledo, and has composed many books in the Latin lan-guage; and you who have only the language of your mother, in what is it that you dare to contradict him?"   These passages are from the treatise "On Stones;" and many more might be adduced.

heart—keen to detect truth, and fearless to maintain it. simple as a child, and playful as a child, for fourscore years,—we guess that in his boyhood he could romp with vigour when he was not in the mood for reverie.

But it was not all holiday to Bernard in his youth. Whether the child learnt that lesson, escaped seldom, which is taught within the walls of home, when lips which have been shaped a thousand times to kisses, model in clay the last smile that can only rot, we have no means of knowing. But the knowledge of the father, that is to say, the knowledge of a glass-painter, was transmitted to the son. Bernard learnt to read and write. The minerals employed in staining glass, and some few of their properties, had to be learned also, and they made up the child's first lesson in chemistry, a science which he afterwards— in Nature, not in books—pursued with ardour. An unconquerable spirit of inquiry, and a determined freedom in obeying its dictates, were inborn elements which would display their rule over the child's mind as clearly as they asserted afterwards their sway over the man. We use our fancies very little, if we picture the boy Bernard fingering his father's drugs, and asking questions concerning them, which, since his father cannot give sufficient answers, he walks out into the wood to think over, or ask again of Nature, in whose language (richer than the Greek or Latin) he was then beginning to be versed. Digging, to ascertain what minerals his native earth can yield, combining, roasting, and experimenting, we may fancy the boy happy; and we cannot reasonably think that he omitted such amusements. Again, the business of the glass-painter requires that he should paint from certain patterns placed under the glass, or work according to a given plan, unless he should himself be able to originate designs. However the case may have been with Palissy the father, Palissy the son was not content to copy plans and drawings, without labouring on so that he might become himself an artist. The diligence with which young Bernard prac-tised drawing during these first years, had a marked influence over his career in after-life. Nature supplied him with his copies: the trees of his own wood, adjacent rocks, the birds, the lizards, or his mother's face, were at the same time the most convenient and the most welcome objects to a draughtsman whose appointed volumes were the works of Nature, and whose chief delight was a mi-nute observation of her ways.

Thus, then, it came to pass that Bernard Palissy, by the time he had grown lusty, and acquired a down upon his chin, was qualified not only to assist his father in the honourable trade of *Verrerie*, but was at the same time skilful to gratify the vanity or affection of his neighbours, by painting images of them, or of their houses, or what-ever other things they loved, on sheets of paper. But the trade of glass-painting, which had borne good fruit not long before, was at that time falling rapidly into the yellow leaf.* The son, upon the boundaries of manhood,

* This accords with the history of *Verrerie*. Before turning his

with the hopes of life before him, capable of independent
toil, was out of place as partner with his father, in a business that provided to a single household scanty sustenance.
Nor, in the present instance, did so listless an arrangement
suit the mind of a youth eager to see and learn.

So soon, therefore, as his limbs were duly knitted, and
his mind was strengthened into capability of separate
existence, Bernard Palissy, aged about eighteen years,
shouldered a scanty wallet, scattered his farewells through
the native hamlet, and marched out of it, to find his own
position in the world.

mind some years afterwards to pottery, Palissy says (*Artist in Earth*):
" I recalled to mind several suggestions that some people had made to
me in fun, when I was painting portraits. Then seeing that these were
falling out of request in the country where I dwelt, and that glass-
painting also was little patronised, I began to think" . . . . .

CHAPTER II.

PALISSY OBTAINS SOME KNOWLEDGE OF THE WORLD.

WATCHFUL of lizards—a warm friend to trees—a studious traveller in stony places, which to his eyes were not barren,—contemplative, cheerful, simple-hearted,—Bernard Palissy passed out of the cover of his native wood. He loitered to examine nettles by the wayside, or to put some oddly-fashioned stone into his wallet. The ambition of two princes, whom it is customary to call great—Francis I. of France, and Charles V. of Spain—had led to the tumult of an idle conflict, in which one half of Europe was involved. Two hundred thousand lives destroyed, and the ruin of a million of families, left to these two great men, when their rivalry was over, no gain but repentance. So Bernard, stout and vigorous, entered a world in which there was provided ample field for military glory. Was he a coward, that he should lie down under a chestnut-tree in times like these, and plan a journey over France, during which he would obtain funds—or so he thought—

by practising his skill as painter in the noble houses and
the towns? His mind dwelt most upon the study to be
done during those years of wandering by the wayside—
upon the woods, the rivers, and the mountains of all
France to be spread out as a heritage before his intellect.
He set his face towards the Pyrenees, and by the travel
of a few days entered Gascony.

It was the year 1528;* and here and there upon the
road were weary, footsore men, who had escaped to return
as they were able from the war in Italy. One Gascon,
who in that year returned among the rest, and who lived
afterwards to be a noted soldier, was Blaise de Montluc.
If we desire to know how coarse and jarring were the
elements of that world in which the simple-minded Palissy
desired to prosper, Blaise de Montluc is a communicative
man, and we may draw from his experience a little knowledge.

Blaise de Montluc was, in accordance with the spirit
of his day, a perfect soldier; he was nothing else. To him
a day of peace brought more vexation than a year of
trouble. Strife was his rest; and his religion—for in
his military way he was very religious—was the notion
that he had a God, whose business it was, if paid sufficient wages in the way of vows, to help him in the day

---

* Perhaps. The chronology is theoretical until about 1540; but it
seemed better to assume in the narrative the dates which I thought
probably correct, and afterwards to lay before the reader the conflicting
evidence on which they have to be established.

of battle. At the age of seventy-five, compelled to super-annuate himself, lame, as he says, in almost every limb with pike-wounds and the wounds of shot, the old man closed his life with the recital of his history. The face that bent over his paper was made ugly by a harquebuss, whose shot had left in it a running sore, apparently incurable. The stump of the man of battles having thus, at the age of seventy-five, superannuated itself, dictated or wrote the story of its past life, and has left complete those " Commentaries of Montluc" which Henri IV. styled " The Soldier's Bible."

Montluc was by eight or ten years older than Palissy, and had been at work in the great world, seeking joy and profit in its ferment, while Palissy yet dwelt as a child in the seclusion of the forest. Of the court politics Montluc knew little, Palissy much less; nor is it requisite that we should place ourselves at any distance from their point of view, in looking at the turmoils of society. The mean and wretched selfishness of kings in those old times concerns us only here in its effects. The royal motives, and the royal glories or disgraces, may be found by reference to any history of France. When Palissy sat down to gossip with the crippled soldier in his cottage, or trudged with him upon the road for company, so far as their two ways were one, what sort of narratives instructed him in the world's doings at that time and for the few preceding years? Montluc returned among the cripples, and what his tale would have been we know; therefore we need

feign nothing, but soberly relate Montluc's view of the
world, which Palissy had come forth to encounter.*

Montluc was, in 1528, a young soldier, aged perhaps
twenty-seven. His house was noble, but impoverished.
Bred as a page in the house of the Duke Antoine de
Lorraine, he had become, in the next place, archer of the
duke's company, having M. de Bayard for his lieutenant.
Rumour, however, brought him tidings of the noble
deeds that formed the daily run of military life in Italy,
and Montluc had a mania for laurels. He went, therefore, to Gascony, and obtained equipment from his father,
with a little money and a Spanish horse, on which he
galloped forth in search of fortune. He had not travelled
a day's journey from his father's house before he met the
Sieur de Castelnau, an old gentleman entitled by experience to give him copious information on Italian matters,
and communicative as old gentlemen are apt to be. Montluc spurred on and crossed the mountains, hurrying to
Milan. He was then seventeen, and had his career before
him, as now at the same age Bernard Palissy is entering
on his.

Two uncles by the mother's side, named Stillac, welcomed young Montluc ; and one of these two uncles

---

* The *Commentaires de Montluc* give a minute picture of war as it
was managed by France in the sixteenth century, but they are at the
same time very long and very tedious to any one who does not care to
read all the "did he's" and "did I's" of a garrulous old soldier. The
narrative in the text consists of the facts told in his first pages by
Montluc, reduced in scale very considerably.

serving M. de l'Escunt,* who was brother to M. de Lautrec, marshal of France, Blaise de Montluc was entered as an archer in his company. Among these common archers there were not a few born gentlemen. The French were not particularly fortunate, for they lost the duchy of Milan. Never mind that: we have here the smallest possible concern with gains and losses of that nature. The war on this occasion lasted twenty-two months, and young Blaise, who knew that it was necessary for a soldier to display as soon as possible his quality of stomach, fought so diligently that five horses were killed under him in ten days, besides that he was once made a prisoner and ransomed by his comrades. Montluc was in the battle of Bicoque, where he saw M. de Montmorenci, with whom afterwards, when constable of France, Palissy became acquainted, struggling on foot.

After the loss of Milan, Montluc returned to France as man-at-arms and archer in the army of Odet de Foix (Lautrec). The Spaniards soon formed a party for him, and Montluc's next day of pleasure was a battle at Saint Jean de Luz. In that battle, among others who were struck down was M. de la Faye of Saintonge, afterwards a friend to Palissy. The French had very much the worst of the entertainment at Saint Jean de Luz; they were routed, and would have suffered most severely from

---

* So Montluc calls Thomas de Foix, Sieur de *Lescun*, brother to Lautrec, and also to Françoise de Foix, Countess Chateaubriand, the king's mistress.

the Spanish cavalry, if Montluc had not, in the teeth of
cautious counsel, inspired a hundred cross-bowmen on
foot with readiness to follow him and check the fatal
movement. These hundred men took cross-bows; for at
that time (in the year 1523) there were no harquebusses
in the nation.* Six men with harquebusses, Gascons,
had however only a few days before deserted from the
enemy, and coming to Saint Jean de Luz, had found
Montluc on guard at the town gate, who impounded

* Cannons, the first artillery, were invented about the year 1336.
They were, at first, bars of iron hooped together, or plates of iron made
into a machine with hides ; great stones were the first cannon-balls,
and the first cannons usually burst and killed their friends after the
third time of firing. As they were also very heavy and cumbrous, the
ancient machines of war were for a century considered preferable.
With time, however, came improvement; in the course of a century
cannons were better made, and cured in a great measure of their vice of
bursting. But they were very large, and the loading, firing, and after-
cleansing, formed so tedious a business, that with diligence it was considered brisk to fire off the same cannon four times in a day. They
were used only against towns, and it was thought specially inhuman
when the English in France first turned them against men. When the
manufacture had improved, those barbarous old names, of which Mons
Meg is a sample, were set aside, and cannons had names according to
their size, borrowed from birds of prey. The smallest cannon then discharged a two-pound shot. The step from cannon towards musketry
was made by the harquebuss, first used in Germany. In 1471, it was
imported into England in the hands of three hundred Flemings. The
Spaniards also used it early. Its introduction into France was so late,
that there were in 1667 only four harquebusses to each company of
the French army. The harquebusses mentioned in the text were
very heavy, carried generally by attendants, and supported upon rests
when fired. The cumbrousness of the apparatus, the way in which the
ammunition was disposed, and the clumsiness of the matchlock, made
the process of reloading very tedious. The balls fired were never
lighter than twelve to the pound.

them for his own service. The cavalry was charging down on the small band of foot which interposed itself between the Spaniards and the routed French:—Montluc, when they were very close, ordered his archers to aim at the horses' heads, and fifty horses fell. The perilous retreat of Montluc's band, cut off from their friends and hunted by their enemy, was a notable affair. The young soldier performed his service and brought back his men, four only missing. Lautrec, who was a reserved man, too rarely given to praise, rewarded young Montluc with marked expressions of his favour.

The camp of the Spaniards having retired, part of Lautrec's army was disbanded, and Montluc, then twenty years of age, was put over the company of his late captain. The Spaniards, altering their minds, advanced, and took Fontarabia. As for Montluc, his duty making him a dweller in stone walls, to which life he was as hostile as the savages of old, he declined the ignoble life, and travelled off to Italy again, where the revolt of M. de Bourbon had lighted up the blaze of a more thoroughly delightful hell. Thither Montluc went, since he could get no regular engagement, as a volunteer, accompanied by five or six young blades whom he had picked up on his road; these all served under Captain Castille de Navarre. So Montluc was at the siege of Pavia, and at the battle on St. Matthew's-day. It was quite a pity that King Francis, just before this battle, had dismissed, through motives of economy, three thousand Swiss under their colonel, who was

called commonly " le Grand Diant." The aid of le Grand
Diant ought not to be dispensed with in such undertakings
as those which formed, three centuries ago, the foreign
policy of European states. The result of the battle was
the capture of King Francis, and with him, among other
gentlemen, of some whose names will occur elsewhere in
these pages—M. de Montmorenci, M. de Nevers, and M.
de Brion. Montluc, also a prisoner, aged twenty-three,
was ordered, with all others of his kind who were too poor
to provide ransom, to quit the camp and find his way to
France.

How King Francis went as prisoner to Madrid, what
he did there, and how he came to France again, are
questions in which we are not concerned—except to state,
that when he did get home, Montluc was soon emanci-
pated from the bonds of peace. Being required to raise
a troop of foot in Gascony, he marched at the head of eight
hundred men for Italy, having among his men four or five
hundred harquebusses, though there were still scarcely
any of those weapons used in France. The old man, when
memoir-writing, wipes his ulcerated face with the stump
of a hand, and abuses harquebusses heartily. The young
man, having got to Italy, was soon shot in the leg; and
being lamed for a season, was not at the siege of Pavia.
He followed the camp on a litter. His Gascons had been
divided, and himself left commander of four hundred.
Being recovered from his lameness, on a certain occasion
the French came before a small town named Capistrano,

situated on a mountain. Two breaches had been made in its walls, each of them only large enough for the admission of a single man. Montluc was ordered with his troop to force the town.

"This was a year ago," Montluc might have said, if he had been the soldier whom chance brought to sit upon a hill-side, and pour out his tale of war into the ear of Palissy. Assume that it was he, and that the young Bernard, with his eye intent upon the movements in a bird's-nest, endeavoured to keep out the images from which his soul recoiled. "This was a year ago. Count Pedro of Navarre bade us to storm the town. I had long panted for the day when I might be the first to enter by a breach. The time was come. I shouted to my men to follow closely, and rushed through the wall, with a coat of mail upon my body, such as the Germans wear, a sword in hand, a buckler on my left arm, and a morion on my head. The breach made entry into a house; and the enemy had torn up a number of the planks just overhead, and piled a mass of stones upon the upper floor. I leapt in quickly; but, as my lieutenant followed, the stones were shot down, hurting some men, and partly closing up the entrance. None could follow; but I did not notice that, as I ran on to the door leading to the street. That was defended by the enemy; and while I fought them, the men from above fired down upon me through the reft in the ceiling with their harquebusses. A shot pierced my buckler, and cracked my arm; the next shot splintered the bone at my shoulder,

on the same side. I dropped my buckler, and my arm
seemed to be gone; I could not feel it. Then, seeing that
I was alone, I fought my way back to the breach; and no
sooner had I put my feet outside, than my men, who were
there, seized them to assist in extricating me. They dragged
me out with such good-will, that I was shot down to the
bottom of the town trench, where I fell upon the ruined
stones out of the wall, and broke my lame arm in two other
places. Then, when I recovered from my swoon, and saw
my men about me, I reproached them; and my lieutenant
said he would go through the breach, or die. Ladders
were got and tied together. My men formed two parties.
Both breaches were assailed; and when one was taken, I
bade my lieutenant, La Bastide, take good heed to prevent,
as much as possible, the girls and women from being violated; because I had made a vow to our Lady of Loretto,
that I would spare them on the first occasion; for which
reason I expected Divine aid. Fifteen or twenty were
brought to me, but all the rest were lost. My men could
not be restrained; and out of love to me, and for the pain
I suffered, they left not even a child alive. They then
set fire to the town; and although the bishop of the district pleaded to M. de Lautrec, they would not rest till
it was all reduced to ashes.

"Then M. de Lautrec sent two surgeons, Master
Alême and Master George, to see to me. They said my
arm must be cut off. But there was a young surgeon, who
had served M. de Bourbon, who was my prisoner, and

whom I had about me. He advised me by no means to let that be done. M. de Lautrec commanded me to have my arm cut off, and promised to care for my fortunes. The surgeons came with their tools, and I would have submitted, but the young surgeon, standing behind my bed, continually urged me to refuse. So I refused. The surgeons went and told M. de Lautrec, who said he had just been thinking that it was best such matters should be left to God; and bade them examine my prisoner, to see whether he was versed in surgery, and if so, to commit me to his care. He bore examination well, and thereafter I lay on my back for two months and a half, in a house at Termes di Bressi, where, to ensure my being cared for, two chief citizens and the brother of my host were taken as hostages, with a promise that they should be hung if I was not made comfortable. Certainly it was not their fault that, from lying on my back so long, the flesh all rotted from my backbone.

" Nevertheless, for my comfort, Count Pedro de Navarre assigned to me a handsome portion of the enemy's land, which had been confiscated. I had the Tower de la Nuncide, the first barony of Naples, with twelve hundred ducats of income. A notable prize that would have been, if we had held our ground in Italy. They were endeavouring to subdue Naples by famine, but our galleys failed us, and the sea was open to the Neapolitans. Then came the Prince of Navarre, and from the time of his landing all good-luck deserted us. By that time, I was able to get

about with my arm in a sling, and do some service with
my men. By chance I saw a body of Italians stealing
from the town-gate, to surprise the prince when he was
disembarking. I succeeded in conveying warning, and a
vessel coasted on to overlook the road and act on my intelligence; but the men in the vessel no sooner caught
sight of my troop of harquebuss men, than they took for
granted we were enemies, and opened fire upon us with
their cannon. Two men were shot down close beside me.
Of one man whose head was split open, the brains were
dashed into my face.

" To save ourselves from our friends, we took shelter in
a trench, and presently the enemy defiled along the road
before us. We fired upon them, and effected a diversion.
The Prince of Navarre, having landed, scampered for his
life to reach the camp, whither I and my men retreated,
and, entrenched behind the wall on each side of the camp-
gate, we defended the position for a terrible half-hour.
At last the enemy retired; and I, who had been able only
to instruct my men, too weak for fighting, was leaning
exhausted against a bank, when I heard the high officers
talking as they pointed to me, and saying that they owed
much to the young man with the crippled arm, and those
who had come newly to the camp inquired about me.
That was my reward.

" But the Prince de Navarre brought us bad luck. Misfortune followed on misfortune. We lost our best men,
M. de Lautrec among others; and I travelled home from

Gascony, for the most part of the way on foot; so did the other soldiers who escaped, but they were very few. The journey was a weary one. I had about me more than thirty ells of taffeta, by way of bandage to my arm, which was supported in a sling, and bound fast to my side. All my companions and friends were dead, except M. de Monpezat and poor Don Pedro, our colonel, who was taken prisoner; and he, I learn, has lately been beheaded. So I am come home to my father's house in Gascony, which in these days is poor enough; and when my arm is healed, as I fear it will not be for the next three years, I shall set out for the camp, and so begin the world again."

So might Montluc have spoken in the year 1528; that was the complexion of a soldier's tale, when Palissy came out into the striving world. And to such tales must have been added testimony to the vices of the camp. A war for liberty, or the defence of human rights against aggression, may invoke high thoughts and virtuous emotion; but the wars were base of which we now speak, and they fearfully debased the men who were engaged in them. From King Francis, who after a triumph insolently consented to ordain thanksgiving to God, " because he had proved himself a proper Frenchman," down to the meanest soldier, blasphemy was common. Gambling ruined many officers and men. Drunkenness begetting insolence, caused captains to cut and hack the bodies of their men not rarely, and their cruelty made the assassination of an officer by his own men to be no strange

event. Montluc, in the course of his experience, had
with his own eyes seen four commanders cut down from
behind by their own troops.

Shocked by such narratives, young Bernard would
proceed, out of the simplicity of his own mind, to make
himself contemptible to his companion, by commenting
upon them unreservedly as they walked on, and testing
them, according to the humour born with him, by principles of reason. Soft fledgling he would seem to the
bold man of war, who little knew what battles were to
be fought, what heroism infinitely higher than his own
was to be hereafter manifested by the quiet youth, whose
company delayed him on the way. For the young
Palissy found many stones to crack, and many weeds to
fish out of the ditches; and whatever unaccustomed thing
arrested his attention, he was obstinate in stopping to
examine.

CHAPTER III.

MORE KNOWLEDGE OF THE WORLD.

IT was well for Bernard that he had not to depend on glass-painting alone for a subsistence. Work at a church-window was not to be found in every town; and although there were few noble houses at that time in France which were not decorated with a rather free display of coloured glass, yet, unluckily, the noble tenants were beginning to discover that their painted windows were domestic miseries. They had been, of late years, greatly in fashion. The works of Jean de Bruges, Michael Angelo, Raphael, and Giulio Romano, had been assiduously translated into glass, for satisfaction to the luxury of wealthy men. Even in our own days, any mania for painted windows in a dwelling-house would have within itself the elements of speedy cure; what it implied, however, in the sixteenth century will soon be seen. Palissy, therefore, setting out into the world as glass-painter in a year that was on the wrong side of the climax in the public taste, found it not very easy to exchange his painted glass for bread.

The young wanderer parted from a battered soldier at a hovel-door,* and sped away from the wife's cry of pleasure which arose in his companion's home. Bernard had not a home, and wanted none. He would pause wherever he found work; and when work was exhausted in one spot, would wander on much freer than a bird, whose freedom is a fiction altogether. So the youth parted from his companion, and leapt a ditch, to find the shortest road across the fields to a large country-mansion which he had perceived among the distant trees.

By a brook-side, sheltered among nut-boughs from the mid-day sun, there was a peasant resting from the plough, eating dried chestnuts for his dinner, and drinking water from the stream. Bernard was tempted by the shade, and sat beside the labourer, to talk with him on equal terms. Probably, not even a herald would have thought that he had caste to lose by doing so. It was the abbot, said the countryman, who lived in yonder house—a courtier from Paris, who belonged to the army, and raised troops among them sometimes; and as he was their abbot also,

---

* Of the wanderings of Palissy, which occupied the ten or twelve years before his settlement in Xaintes, our knowledge is only general. We know that he travelled over France, and how he earned his living on the road. We know, also, his tastes and habits. These are correctly represented in the text. The minute details chosen to illustrate what Bernard must certainly have seen and heard during his travels, when they take the form of incidents, are not to be received as true in the letter, but in the spirit.

he raised tithes. He was abbot of other places; and he seemed, moreover, to be concerned, on that domain, with the collection of taxes for the government. "A great deal of our harvest and our money goes to the great house: they are rich people there," the labourer said, in no tone of complaint, as he finished his last mouthful of dried chestnuts. Palissy then, thoughtful of his business, ascertained that there were painted windows in the great house, some of which his friend, when he took tithes, had seen. There was painted on one window a man upon a tower, looking at the crucifixion through a telescope;* another was made up of patterns only; and the great window in the hall, where tithes and taxes were received, was painted with Saint Martin's charity.

With a cheerful farewell, Bernard hastened on; but there was a shell by the wayside which, through all his haste, arrested his attention. Stopping to look at that, he became interested in the movements of its tenant, and spent, accordingly, ten minutes by the side of a green ditch, to see how daintily a snail could eat its dinner. Then the wood, through which the road passed, was so full of sights and sounds, that Bernard was tempted to sit down upon the stump of a felled tree, and listen to the birds, as well as woodcutters would let him. Incessant striking, and the frequent crash of fallen trees, soon

---

* The man being St. Denis. Mrs. Jameson, in her "Sacred and Legendary Art," tells us that she saw this subject for a window-picture in an old French print.

aroused in the young lover of the woods a sense of pain. That closed his reverie, and set his eyes again loose on the outer world. There was a traveller who led his horse over the rugged path and round the fallen timber—a man in grave attire, with a sedate face and abundant grey hair in his beard. The stranger had passed without seeing the quiet Bernard, and was proceeding on the road to the great house. The impulse of good-fellowship belonging naturally to a lively peasant race, brought the youth quickly to the stranger's side, and youth and age found little difficulty in establishing a proper road-acquaintance.

The young Bernard had soon frankly told his little tale, and found in return that his new companion was a man of business, wealthy in his trade, a draper,* and that now, in the course of a long journey, he was about to call at the great house, as Palissy himself proposed to call, in his own humble way, in search of patronage. Those people should have patronage to give, the Draper thought, for they had taken plenty; and they should have money to spend out of the proceeds of their wood-cutting. Bernard thought men could not prosper on the price of blood—of trees:

---

* This Draper comes out of the *Livre des Marchands*, by Regnier de la Planche, one of the most delightful books dust ever covered. Chronicles like that of Montluc are much too prolix to be quoted verbally, but there is vigour with terseness in the *Livre des Marchands*, of which I have been glad to take advantage. Every speech here made by the Draper is an extract picked out of the Draper's chapter in the *Livre des Marchands*. The Draper, therefore, in these pages, speaks really what was put into a draper's mouth by one who wrote while Palissy was living.

fair wood-cutting was just and honest, but to sweep away a forest for the lust of gain! "Wait till you see more of France," the Draper said; "this Gascony is lightly burdened. Monseigneur the Cardinal de Guise—you cannot walk far without stumbling on a benefice of his. He sets a bright example to the Church. There was no need of it. Round Paris, where I live, the woods are swept away so thoroughly that the increased cost of firewood is a tax upon the poor of one-sixth of their income. My Lord Cardinal de Guise sits like an owl upon his perch, to watch for the leanest mouse of benefice. Is a living vacant, though its value be a footman's pay, it is solicited for my lord-cardinal. The rich incumbents are watched greedily, or hurried out of their possessions prematurely, forced to share their livings, or bought out of them if there be wood enough to fell for payment of the purchase-money. So Monseigneur the Cardinal has gathered livings; and when he has despoiled them of their woods they have been thrown to the first comer of his varlets or his protonotaries, as we fling bones to dogs when we have eaten all the meat from them, and sucked the marrow."

"Are not the treasures of the Church in heaven?" inquired Palissy, with simple earnestness. "If what you say be true, can men look every day upon the scandal, and not seek to bring back those offenders to a sense of justice?"

"Men do not see their souls," the Draper answered. "Oh, if the cloak worn by my lord the cardinal had in it

as many pieces of different colours as he has benefices and
different orders and institutions, how ugly and disgraceful
he would think his garments! The cardinal loves better
that the ugliness and infamy should be his own, and be
unseen, than that his cloak should be accused of it in
public. Do you know, my friend, how many beggars ask
for alms now in the country, who used formerly to live in
peace, and pay rents? The poor man, who used to keep two
or three cows, pigs, or sheep, feeding them in the public
woods, and feeding his own household with their increase, has his pasture-ground robbed from him. The poor
among us have no more fat cattle, no more wool to sell,
no more manure to put upon their plots of ground. The
woods are felled by peers and abbots, and the ground of
the poor man is rented to the plough at a high rate, and
with a cruel claim for entrance-money.

" I ask," said the Draper, warming into indignation,
" to whom do these waste lands belong?—to the people or
to the king? If they belong to the people, then it was
cruelty (I say no worse) to rob them of their heritage.
But if they were the king's, they were part of the domain
pertaining to his crown ; to other rights of his they could
not appertain. If they belong, then, to the crown domain, alas·! gentlemen-peers of France, where is the oath
you made, and swore so solemnly on the altar at the conse-
cration and the crowning of the king, to preserve and
maintain his domains?—where is that which you swore
should not be alienated? If you do not fear God by

whom you swore, nor love the king to whom your vow was pledged, at least say why you have abandoned fear of shame, and the reproach of men. It will descend upon your tombs!"*

" You have seen much of France, and know these things?" asked Bernard, in a timid voice, though he looked frankly into the trader's sunburnt face. If these things were so, he thought, the peace of nature is not in the hearts of men. They walked on through a wide clearance in the wood; and to the mind of Palissy, the fallen bodies of the trees which strewed the ground were a sight far more pitiful than to Montluc's eyes would have been the human bodies on a field of battle. " You have seen much of France, and know these things?"

" I have seen much of France and know these men," the trader said. " My business has carried me abroad, especially to Germany. I was long in Lorraine; I have seen France; and as for the affairs of my own town, I have studied them. Our state of trade gives us a great intercourse with people of all classes. No others have equal means of residence and traffic among foreigners; can win so well the attachment of foreign kings and princes; know

* Jean de Guise, Cardinal of Lorraine from the age of twenty, who made a thousand beggars by his lust of wealth, was ostentatious in his charitable use of riches. There is an anecdote of this :—A blind beggar having sued to him, in the streets of Rome, on one occasion, and received a handsome sum, exclaimed, "You are Christ, or the Cardinal of Lorraine !"

the news of foreign courts, their enterprises and their
tempers. Our experience causes us to be sought even by
statesmen, and our traffic is a noble occupation, for we
succour our own land with the blessings which were given
to another. That way our gold and silver comes, we make
none poor for the increase of our houses. What man is
there who acquires wealth better or more honourably
than we traders do, whose profit comes through the convenience of all, by our own industry and labour? The
soldier risks his life; we trade through war and peril,
risking not only life but also wealth. You are a noble
glass-worker." Palissy laughed. "Yes, they call yours a
noble trade, but trade is noble in itself."

The Draper, by the quiet company of a submissive
listener, had been beguiled into that stage of loquacity
which brings a man to dwell upon himself. The simple
faith with which Bernard appeared to use his eyes and
ears, had destroyed for the present in his grave companion
the dread of ridicule, and that is one of the chief penalties
by which men are deterred from revelations of their own
affairs.

"Trade in itself is noble," said the Draper. "The
wisest men, and the men most celebrated for their virtue,
have been traders. Thales, the first of the Seven Sages,
was a trader; Solon, second founder of Athens, was a
trader; Hyperates, the mathematician, was a trader. The
renowned Plato, called, for the excellence of his wisdom,
the Divine, paid the cost of his travelling to Egypt

by the oil he sold there.   In our own day, we have a Kerver, a Merlin, a De Pleurs, honourable traders—there are my excellent friends, Nicolas Bourgeois, Jean Messié, Henry l'Avocat, Jean Aubery, Nicolas Hac, ——."

"I do not understand you now," said Bernard.   "I never heard of Nicolas Hac or Plato."

"Ah!" said the Draper, "you are a wild bird from the forest, and can only pipe as you were taught by nature. Never shrink before a bit of Latin.   Look more at the man than at his habit; substance rather than words. Moreover, I am not a lettered man to make you a harangue; I was not formed for it in my youth.   At ten years old I was sent to college by my father.   All the science of that time lay in making what we used to call *carmens* and Latin verses.   I made good ones, so my master said; and Heaven knows what poets my masters were.   Even my father was pleased with my verses, though he understood them no more than I suppose you can understand high Dutch. At fifteen, the poet was brought home to the shop; for the good man always had intended that I should pursue his way of life.   Then all that I had learnt with pains and trouble in five years, I forgot over diversion in one month. My verses returned into the earth out of which they sprang; for they were not current in business.   So I spent five years in learning what I was not to remember.

"But since then, the goodness of God has been displayed by the hand of our King Francis, the first of his name, who draws, as from a tomb, sciences, arts, letters, and good-discipline; and by the aid of an Amiot, a Jacques Colin,* and many others, the tools of wisdom are made sharp in our own mother-tongue; so that there is no artisan who may not in a few hours become wise, if he will use his leisure. Our shops may be our schools."

"Then," exclaimed Bernard, "I should wish the world to be my shop. I do not know how long it may require to learn all that men know, and how much more time it may need to unlearn their mistakes in knowledge. I feel that earth and air are full of mysteries and wonders of the sublime wisdom of God."

"My dear young friend," said the Draper, "you will find all these things written in books. With a book, we travel for nothing throughout all the regions of the world; we mount with faith to heaven, and descend with security into the abysses; we drive into the whirlpools of the sea, plunge into the midst of battles, capture towns, engage with brigands; and do anything, in short, without lifting a foot. That which long age, hard toil, and heavy experience, formerly brought to a man only at the hour of death, our children (so to speak) may suck from the teats of their mothers and their nurses."

"Explain this rock to me," said Palissy; "what is it, and how came it here?"

The Draper thought that was a foolish question. He

---

* Amiot translated Plutarch. Colin, secretary to Francis I., translated parts of Homer and Ovid. King Francis was styled "Father of Letters."

saw it was stone, and it was there because it was placed there in the beginning. But if he desired to hear nature reasoned upon, he would find in the books a high philosophy.

"I will inquire," said Bernard. "Before I set out on my travels, I had planned to gain admission, where I could, into the workshops of the chemists, and to be taught by conversation with the students."

Conversation with the Draper was here stopped by the arrival of the travellers before the stagnant moat, which coiled like a green snake about the mansion. Chamber-windows opened over it, and sleepers breathed its exhalations. Within the circle of the moat rose an unwieldy mass of scattered towers, round and square, connected, without any reference to symmetry, by massive walls. The thickness of the walls was visible in the deep setting of their eyes, their little windows and large windows, nearly all of which wanted the brightness proper to clear glass, and had that dull fishy look peculiar to painted windows seen from the outside.

Both applicants for favour were admitted to the lady of the house, and were led into her presence over cheerless floors, through thick walls and massive doorways, along passages but dimly lighted. Men were not then distant from the day when right hands—weapon-hands—were grasped ungauntleted, in sign of friendship and assurance that the friendship was sincere; we have degenerated, as the phrase runs, into a punctilious pulling-off of gloves.

Architecture, also, had not yet escaped the influence of monkish tutelage; and a nobleman's mansion, whether his town-house, or his country-house, was some such building as the one through which Palissy was groping with his friend the Draper. They consisted of strong towers, with high-roofed halls connecting them, never symmetrical in town, and in the country, interspersed with stables and such rustic offices, including also a walled garden. Where the country-houses were erected on comparatively level ground, it was thought prudent usually to surround them with a moat; but many were erected upon rocks, or in positions naturally fortified.

The effect of painted glass upon the halls and chambers of homes so constructed, was to fill them with an aggravated gloom. The loss of sunlight was unwholesome, but that was not by any means the only evil which experience discovered. Light sashes, and well-fitting window-frames, were not, in the days of which we speak, a source of household comfort. Household discomfort, on the contrary, was caused by the flapping, in any high wind, of the windows that had hinges, and the destruction of their panes of glass. Breakage of painted glass being expensive, painted windows were in most cases fixed into the wall—not made to open, and excluded, therefore, air as well as light. When Bernard and his friend appeared before the lady of the house, the Draper was received with honour, and rewarded with commissions; the glass-painter was welcomed with a cold politeness, and desired to put a new cheek in Saint

Martin's face, which her son Raoulin had damaged with an arrow, but to do it cheaply, for the windows ate the meat out of her cupboard.

Then Bernard went into the large hall where the window was, and found there nothing needed but a small pane, lozenge-shaped, suffused with colour. While he was preparing this, young Raoulin, who broke the window, busily overlooked the mystery of mending, and blew with good-will at the fire which was to burn the pigment on the piece of glass. Palissy had a proper sense of business, and enough knowledge of the maternal mystery in nature to suggest to him that it would be wise quietly to sketch the child, and suffer it to show the picture to its mother.

The result of this experiment was very satisfactory. So Bernard left the massive country-house, and took with him the good proof of metallic testimonials that he was competent to earn his living.

CHAPTER IV.

PALISSY STUDIES THE PHILOSOPHERS.

RADIANT in the sunny atmosphere which glows about our southern mountain-chain, the young Bernard rested on the summit of a small spur of the Pyrenees. Very few snow-peaks were in sight, for under that warm sky the mountain snows are held more than a thousand feet above their Alpine limits. Brushwood—not lichen—tinted the rocks, which Palissy had climbed by aid of the luxuriant box that grew out of their crevices. Vast forests of oak, and beech, and fir, rose high upon the mountain-steeps; a brawling river, with the tint of beryl, hurried down by an adjoining cliff, and glittered far below, among the fresh green of the watered meadows in the valley. There were forests here to make the palms of all the abbots itch, mountain-peaks cut their outline out against the deep blue of the sky, and here and there sparkled a tiny cap of so much snow as gave variety and point to the rich colours of the landscape. Palissy was reading in a book:

. . . " Before the mountains were brought forth, or

ever Thou hadst formed the earth and the world, even from everlasting to everlasting, thou art God."

The simple-hearted youth felt the divine when he looked out on Nature. The outlook over a grand space had wakened aspirations in his heart: every young heart, that is warm and true, throbs with an instinct of expansion, when the blood is quickened with a sense of space. But Bernard had no consciousness of greatness in himself. He was great; " born," as a famous pupil in his own school* said of him long afterwards—" born to the greatest things;" or in the language of a yet more famous student† in that school, uttered when Palissy survived but as a name to few, he lived to prove himself " so great a naturalist as Nature only can produce."

But his greatness was for time to prove, for others to acknowledge. To his own heart, the youth who sat among the Pyrenees, with his dark hair falling free in forest fashion, clipped for the convenience of no steel cap, was conscious only of an intense love of Nature, and of earnest curiosity for truth. Perplexed among the quarrels of the world upon religious doctrines, his philosophy had taught him to apply his own mind simply to the object of dispute. Therefore he studied in the Bible.‡ Free from all mists of passion, a strong instinctive sense of the unjust or the

---

* Haller.　　　　　† Buffon.

‡ The first translation of the Scriptures into French was made by Guiars des Moulins, a canon, in 1294, and printed in 1498. Raoul de Prèsles, and also some anonymous scholars, had published other versions.

unlikely, led him to put to a strict test all his experience
in human morals and philosophy. He heard strange
closet-doctrines about Nature, which he thought un-
founded; therefore he grew, yearly, more assiduous in
studying the rocks, and woods, and fields. Scripture and
Nature made a harmony together, as delightful as the
harmony of colours between heaven and earth, which had
brought tears up to the eyes of the young painter as he
looked abroad over the valleys of the Pyrenees.

Want of the necessary knowledge renders it impossible for us to follow with exact steps the path of Palissy,
during the nine or ten years of wandering which followed
his first departure out of home into the world. It was to
him a time of education. He traversed France from the
Pyrenees to the sea of Flanders and the Netherlands; he
gathered experience in Brittany and by the Rhine. He
visited Lower Germany, the Ardennes, Luxembourg, the
duchy of Cleves, and the Brisgau. He spent time in his
native district of the Agenois and in the Bourdelois. At
Tarbes, the capital of Bigorre, he dwelt some years, and
remained long in sundry other towns.* During these
wanderings, he lived by his painting chiefly. His skill in
glass-painting probably caused him to dwell, now and then,
for a long period in some town where a church window,
or an abbey window, was in progress; and his skill in

* This is the summary of the travels of Palissy, given by M. Faujas
de St. Fond in the 4to. edition of the works of Palissy, 1777. All
passages from the works bearing on the subject will be found collected
at the end of this biography.

portrait-painting may have brought him, in some towns, an amount of patronage which made it prudent for him to remain, while there was anything to reap, upon the harvest-ground. Another means of livelihood consisted in his knowledge of geometry, and manual skill in the employment of a rule and compass. These instruments had come first to his hand as necessary in copying or inventing patterns for the painted windows; but Palissy never stood still in any branch of knowledge; his eagerness to push attainments constantly to higher ground, compelled him forward with the despotism of a passion. He became, then, as well acquainted as his means allowed with the geometry of his own day, and sought aid therein, as he could, from books. This knowledge made him capable of measuring and planning sites for houses and gardens, of making for its owners maps of landed property. These talents yielded no return to Palissy of more cash than sufficed for his subsistence ; but they, doubtless, did enable him to travel without any sense of suffering from want, and they enabled him to spend such little sums of money as occasionally might procure for him the means of adding to his knowledge.

For his bread-earning talents, at that time, Palissy had not a great respect. " They thought me," he said afterwards in his unaffected way, " a better painter than I was."* He painted and planned that he might live, but

* "They thought me, in our country, a better painter than I was, which caused me to be often summoned to draw plans for use in courts of law. Then, when I had such commissions, I was very well paid."—

he lived only to learn. His quick and indefatigable spirit of inquiry never rested during those ten or twelve years of wandering. He questioned men and Nature, both incessantly; but Nature only gave him answers that could satisfy his shrewd and lively understanding. Much of the knowledge which he applied afterwards to his reasonings in natural history, was gathered during these years from all parts of France. He investigated arts of life, he studied monuments of antiquity, he visited the laboratories of Touraine, Poitou, and Anjou; his curiosity for truth was universal.

The track of Palissy, during the journeys which occupied the first years of his manhood, cannot be followed literally, and if we could discover it, we should be little profited. We know, generally, what every man must have seen during the next years which followed 1528; specially, we know also, by the artless revelation of his whole mind in his works, what most arrested Palissy's attention. His study of Nature must be dwelt upon hereafter, when we count its fruits; but there are external influences in society which act upon a character, as sun, and soil, and wind act on a tree, determining on which side there shall be most growth, and what shall be the prevalent direction of its branches. Since Bernard Palissy was one of those unwearied, nimble-minded men who have thoughts of their own, and thoughts of value, scattered about more fields

The Artist in Earth. And in a prefatory epistle, also included in the selection from the works of Palissy with which these volumes close, he speaks of " tracing and lines of geometry, of which things it is well known that, thanks be to God, I am not altogether ignorant."

than one of human intellect, in following his course we have to keep our own eyes busy. We cannot, therefore, pass over his first years of observation in the world, without connecting fragments of experience notably diverse, and yet all important to the study of his character.

Philosophers, of course, were to be questioned. Palissy aspired to know what could be taught by the men wise in his own day, about the rocks and woods; his early familiarity with chemical substances used in the art of glass-painting, and the changes which they underwent when subjected to fire, had excited in his mind especial curiosity for knowledge that might be communicated by the chemists.

In the suburbs of a town, a little wearied by a morning's travel, Bernard sought admission at the door of a sordid house, belonging, as he had been told, to a great alchemist, who even claimed to be an adept in his art—that is to say, he claimed to have discovered its recondite secret. A small piece of his master's gold—if his pretension to the dignity of gold-maker were true—might have been applied humanely, Bernard thought, to the clothing and feeding of the servant who admitted him into a dusty and neglected chamber. His master, the man said, with a witless look of mystery, was engaged at that moment in his laboratory, marrying gold, in the name of God, to the quintessence of mercury; but when the wedding was over he would attend upon him. Having communicated this fact with a curious admixture of confusing words, the lean

attendant slipped out like a ghost, and went into the
laboratory to play out his part of sexton at the marriage
ceremony.

Bernard waited long, and had little to look at but a
clumsy chair or two, and a table upon which were strewn
some hard crumbs left after the adept's very frugal dinner;
while through the broken lozenges of green glass in the
window, there was to be seen a dusty and dilapidated road.
He fell back, therefore, on his own reflections, and allowed
his thoughts to wander freely through the tedious minutes.
We may do well to follow his example. Philosophy, in
France, was represented ill in that day. But during the
same years which Bernard Palissy was spending as a traveller over the face of France, another wanderer was
shifting restlessly from town to town among the German
states. That wanderer was Paracelsus, a man wiser in
science than his generation. By dwelling briefly on the
memory of this teacher's career, we shall recal sufficiently
well to our own minds the position of philosophy in
Europe at the time when Palissy was seeking information
in the workshop of the alchemist. We shall, at the same
time, make acquaintance with a teacher of whom Palissy
heard much, and whom afterwards he only mentioned
with respect.

The Greeks and Latins supplied knowledge to that age,
and even from the teaching of the Greeks and Latins
many sound doctrines had been lost. In the beginning of
the sixteenth century, Aristotle was to the learned in

Europe, what he is now only to the learned in Oxford—all
in all. Pliny was then the leading naturalist, with a knowledge in advance of his successors; Celsus was a text-book
to physicians. Bombast von Hohenheim disdaining, somewhat angrily, the imperfect knowledge of the past, and
really competent to forward science on the road up to a
higher future, assumed, according to the learned fashion
of his time, a name that indicated his ambition. He
would advance beyond the wisdom of the ancients : he
was—Paracelsus.

High in intellect and bold in innovation, much deficient
in the philosophic calm and the simplicity of mind which
we have noted in the character of Palissy, while Palissy,
aged about twenty-one, was journeying through France,
Paracelsus, at the age of thirty-seven, wandered often
ragged about Germany; a man beardless and feminine
as to the fleshing of his features, yet with a power in the
strange large fashion of the skull over his brain, that
removed from his aspect all expression of a woman's weakness.* Man's weakness, too—man's privilege would be a
truer phrase—was never to be betrayed upon his countenance; fate had removed out of his heart the tinder which
is lighted by the sparkle of a woman's eyes. Inflammable
enough he was upon less gentle provocation. The want

---

* There is a striking portrait of Paracelsus, from an old picture, pre-
fixed to the *Paracelsus, sein Leben und Denken*, by Michael Lessing. I
owe many facts to Lessing's book, but cannot praise it much. How
differently would *the* Lessing—Gotthold Ephraim—have written such
a Life!

of self-command destroyed his chances of prosperity.   He
had travelled much in his youth, and had been educated
carefully.   He had studied alchemy under Johannes
Trithemius, Abbot of Sponheim; and chemistry—for the
two studies were distinct, and even mutually hostile—at
Schwatz, in the Tyrol, under Siegmund von Fugger, one
of the chief chemists of a day when chemistry was little
better than a rudely-shaped desire for knowledge of a
certain class of mysteries in Nature.   In the year before
that which we have assumed to be the date of Palissy's
first independent march into the world, Paracelsus had
been made professor in his University of Basle.   In a prospectus, more remarkable for truth than modesty, he had
declared, that having been invited by a salary, he would
daily, for two hours, discuss and demonstrate publicly
the contents of books of medicine, physics, and surgery,
whereof he was the author, to the great profit of his
hearers.*   He had held his professorship only until the succeeding year.   The value of his teaching men acknowledge now, who look back to him as the first introducer of
mineral drugs into pharmacy, and the first propounder of
two medicines on which enormous reliance is to this day
placed by the physicians—calomel and opium.

But there was, at Basle, a certain canon named Cornelius von Lichtenfels, who was afflicted with the stomach-

---

* The words of the prospectus run: " Dominorum Basiliensium
stipendio invitatus, duabus quotidiè horis tum active, tum inspective
Medicinæ et Physices et Chirugiæ Libros, quorum et ipse Auctor,
summâ diligentiâ, magnoque auditorum fructu, publicè interpretor."

ache; and the stomach-ache of Cornelius von Lichtenfels ruined the worldly prospects of a great philosopher. For the afflicted canon, who no longer dined canonically, had sought ease of the physicians of the town, and swallowed, as good patients ever ought to swallow, many quarts of potion. Then he applied to Paracelsus, who bargained to afford ease for the price of a hundred florins. The canon, having agreed to this, received three little pills containing opium. His pain departed; but since he was a man devoted to the ancient customs of the world, and had expected (as to this day patients often still expect) to get the value of his hundred florins, in six hundred draughts and many mixtures—the canon, who desired to be elaborately, orthodoxly cured, refused to pay for three small pills—not even boluses—so large a sum of money as had been agreed. Paracelsus then sued for his fee before the arbiters of law, and was informed by them that he could not lawfully claim payment of the canon, except according to the custom of the town, by charging for his medicine; and it was well known that one florin would have been a high price for three pills. Thereupon Paracelsus, moved—as he was too often moved—to wrath, informed the judges so emphatically of his opinion of their sense, that, to avoid the consequences of his great contempt of court, he was obliged to quit the town. This was in July, 1528; the wanderings of Paracelsus then began in the same year to which we have referred the commencement of the wanderings of Palissy.

Everywhere testifying his great skill and genius, everywhere at war with men of science, who were too blind to perceive his truths, and too proud to endure his temper, fulminating manifestoes of incompetence against the followers he left at Basle, and his disciples elsewhere—right enough, no doubt, in fact, though wrong in feeling— Paracelsus buffeted his way through Germany from town to town. "Have no heed," he writes, truthfully, bitterly, —"have no heed of my wretchedness, thou reader, let me bear my ills myself. I have two sins upon me—my poverty and my piety. Poverty was reproached against me by a burgomaster, who, no doubt, had seen at Innspruck the doctors in silk-clothes at the prince's courts, not in torn rags, a-baking in the sun. Therefore, the sentence was pronounced that I was not a doctor. For piety's sake the preacher and the parson judge me, for I am not a votary of Venus, and have no love at all for those who teach what they never themselves do."

Paracelsus, thinking on before the world, laboured impatiently to beat into the slow understanding of his generation that which he vividly perceived as truth. Instead of using all the arts of generalship to act on the dull mass, he was as one man labouring to kick into activity a heavy army of dragoons. They turned upon him; and in nearly the same year when Palissy brought to a close the ten or twelve years of his wandering, and felt that the real labours of his life would presently begin, in about that year, Paracelsus closed his wanderings in death, upon the pallet of a miserable inn, not fifty years of age, the victim

of a violence which his own anger had excited. It is said
by some, that he had been severely beaten at the instiga-
tion of offended doctors, and thrown from a rock; so that
the injuries he suffered caused his death to follow shortly,
in the inn to which he had been carried. His skull became a curiosity; and a great physiologist* observed in it,
some years ago, a crack, which he believed was the result
of injuries inflicted before death, because after death
bones do not part as those had parted. We may believe,
however, that the skulls of men, like their reputations,
when they suffer handling by posterity, are liable to
many tumbles, many pickings-up; and skull or reputation may at last receive a crack, of which, after lapse of
time, it will be very difficult for us to say whether we
get it cracked from its possessor, or whether it has been
injured, in some stage of its transmission to us, by im-
proper handling.

Yet although Paracelsus, with his own impetuous philosophy, had made bold strides in medicine, and pushed
his science far beyond the science of his day, it needed
calmness more than he possessed, to separate the philosophic mind from gross and fanciful delusions common
to his age. Instead of subjecting astrology and all its
wonders to the test of a close reasoning faculty, and calling
for witnesses to its truth, according to the simple-minded
way of the untutored Palissy, the great physician was
content to amplify its base, to lessen its absurdity by

* Soemmering.

mending its proportions, and to adorn it with suggestions out of his own ample mind. Accordingly, while Bernard Palissy, a youth, was visiting the alchemists, and penetrating their delusions with the clear light of his own home-bred reason, Paracelsus was at Augsburg, publishing an astrological prediction—a prophecy for the years 1530 to 1534, entitled "Practica* D. Theophrasti Paracelsi." The hieroglyphic on the title-page represented a military man, with a drawn sword in one hand, and a large buckler in the other, who stands on his head in a blaze of fireworks. He balances himself upon clouds, a great star blazes on his body, and light streams out of his mouth, irradiating a group of warriors of all nations, who stand below. A dead king, stretched upon a bier, is master of the foreground. The prophecy of Paracelsus boded a stuggle between two mighty lords, with profit to neither—no very bold thing to foretel, considering the movements caused by the struggle between Charles and Francis, who were quarrelling and fighting like two

---

* "Practica" was, in that age, the common title of an astrological prediction. "Practice," in German at any rate, was a word at first used as applied only to special pursuits, and did not become a general term for many years. Our physicians at this day apply the word specially to the business of medicine, our barristers to the business of law, &c. The first application of the word, in German, was to the business of astrology; and "Practice," in 1530, meant, to a German, only an astrologer's prediction. I do not see any mention of the "Practica" among the works of Paracelsus, in Michael Lessing's Life ; but it is included among other "Practica" of the sixteenth century, in a German black-letter volume which is in the library of the British Museum. It may, or may not, be well known ; it is, certainly, authentic.

naughty boys—the misfortune added, that they happened
to be kings, with nations to be torn instead of pinafores.
"Trade," prophesied Paracelsus, "will suffer ruin; no
man will regard other than his own gain, and honour will
be held in small esteem." One might question whether
Paracelsus went the whole way to the stars for that discovery; but if he did, it is unhappily most certain that
he might have spared himself so far a journey. Deaths of
potentates, and other matters prophesied, did not take
place. On the foundation of a false science, it mattered
not how great might be the genius of a builder; in the
world of shadows, as we were told, long ago, by Mycilus,
the cobbler, "there is no distinguishing the brown from
the fair, for all is of one colour; and who can see a difference between these rags and those robes worn by a
monarch?" The cobbler would paint quite as well as
Zeuxis on a cloud, or raise as fine a work as Phidias upon
a quicksand. There are, however, phrases in the "Practica" of Paracelsus, which one might gladly wrest into the
service of a modern meaning. Forgetting macrocosm and
microcosm, one might apply to a new thought the sentence of Paracelsus, that "those who would understand the
courses of the heaven above, must not omit to recognise
the heaven in man." We may take also a disjointed
sentence from the Augsburg prophecy, and fix it as a
motto to the scientific spirit of its age: "In the concealed
lies that which it is requisite to know." Men had not, at
that time, learned that it was requisite to master thoroughly

the known, and by a slow enlargement of its limits from within, to encroach upon the limits of the unknown. Philosophers spent labour on mysterious assumptions, and spent toil upon astrology and alchemy, as, in our day, philanthropists spent sympathy on Timbuctoo; despising common information as too mean to dignify their calling, they bestowed their labour on a shadow with a name, and were very deeply imbued with a belief that it was only requisite to know that which was not known, and that what little happened to be already known was hardly worth acquiring. The extent, therefore, of the practical acquirements of a work-a-day philosopher in the year 1530, exception being granted for the men of genius—for Paracelsus and his like—a gnat might measure without shifting his position.

Here is the adept, with an eye dulled by his furnace-heat, and an extremely famished countenance, who comes at length to break young Bernard's reverie. A white-haired man, bent possibly with age, and yet his bending looks more like the stoop of a man listening. There is, at times, a quick nervous movement of his eyes from side to side, and an unconscious falling of his features into a vague expression of anxiety, which very soon attract the observation of his watchful visitor.

"You did not hear me enter," said the Alchemist, after a frigid greeting.

"Did you not enter very softly? Or perhaps I was not attentive. I was thinking about Paracelsus."

" Yes, I saw him," said the Alchemist, " in France, before he went to Basle; he is a great rogue. He misuses our divine science. He should be a chemist altogether, if what I am told is true. He is no less a rogue. The greatest man of our time is Cornelius Agrippa."

" I have heard chemists abuse masters in your art," said Bernard, " but I have not joined with them. I desire more knowledge of the truth; and because I heard you were an adept, out of my great boldness I have come to you. Will you disdain to assist one so young?"

" If you have wealth," said the old man passionately, " do not consume it in the furnace. Come with me."

They went into a chamber furnished lavishly with furnaces, with sand-baths, with stills, crucibles, alembics, retorts, and receivers, and pervaded with a suffocating fume, through which the lean assistant might be dimly seen, and more distinctly heard in the convulsions of a cough. Palissy coughed too, but the dry old Alchemist seemed easy as a shepherd in the mist of his own mountain. " I was rich enough once," he said, " but I lost all at the very moment when I was upon the trace of the universal elixir and alcahest." What more the old man said, for many minutes Bernard could not comprehend; for he talked phrases of alchemy, and mingled his speech very plentifully with words like those which Geber, in the seventh century, had given as a model of alchemic elocution, at the same time that he, perhaps, gave his own name to the future uses of the world, as the exponent of a style of speech called, in his honour, gibberish. But Palissy could make out that, in a certain condition of the sal sapientum, the sun and flying dragon were so circumstanced, that a peer of France was induced to speculate in their extrication out of difficulty. " Many nobles," said the old man, " share with alchemists, or practise the divine art—the chemistry of chemistry, distinguished above vulgar miscellaneous experimenting, as al-chemie. The resources of a great peer only," said the old man, " had enabled him to complete the great work." Then the Alchemist, who would almost have cut the throat of Bernard, if he had believed him capable of profiting by the instruction, proceeded, through ten minutes of gibberish, to confound and bewilder the attentive youth, concluding with the quiet statement, that *—" Thus, friend, you have a description of the universal medicine, not only for curing diseases and prolonging life, but also for transmuting all metals into gold. Give, therefore, thanks to Almighty God, who, taking pity on human calamities, has at last revealed this inestimable treasure, and made it known for the common benefit of all."

" Can you show me any token of success ? " asked Bernard.

The Alchemist took from a shelf a silver coin, one half of which appeared, by dipping in some liquor, to have been converted into gold; he showed to the youth, also, a

---

* The words in the text are those of Arnold, of Villeneuve, a famous alchemist.

nail, of which the point was gold, and the head iron. Bernard fancied that he detected in the nail a clever specimen of soldering; the coin he could not understand ;* but he believed deception to exist, because the gold-maker was obviously unable to supply his purse out of his crucible.

"Why are you poor?" asked Palissy.

"I am not poor," replied the Alchemist; "but were I to display wealth, and make known my power, I should be a victim to the avarice of men."

"The chemists say that you are victims to avarice already, of your own."

"No doubt," the old man piped, "for they are envious. Have you talked with chemists? What else do they say?"

"I have found but few," said Bernard, "and those laughed at you alchemists for seeing the perfection of science in the solution of a single problem."

"And what problem!" cried the Alchemist—"wealth and long life, and health, secured to man, by the imperishable property of gold communicated to his living body."

"They say, that since gold came to represent all needs and luxuries of life, it became an object of lust; for the last seven hundred years at least, men, who should have been advancing sciences, have been incited by avarice to labour that they might transmute less precious metals into gold. Had you succeeded, they say, you would be not

---

* The coins so used were of gold, and partly dipped in quicksilver.

philosophers, but only artisans, mere gold-makers; but as
it is, while you do not succeed, you are mere ghosts—me-
chanics in a trade which has not an existence—men from
whom nothing solid is received, and nothing spiritual
learnt. I thought the judgment of the chemists harsh,
and humbly seek your laboratory for instruction."

" You are a good youth, and my instruction is, that
when you see a chemist, you should spit upon him. He
does not know what he desires; he bakes and boils at
random, hoping to alight on something, and he knows
not what. We know the divine object that we have in
view. Never believe that alchemy has no success to
boast. Our science has been studied, not for seven hundred years, but from the beginning; Adam studied it.*
The Egyptians discovered its most secret mysteries, and
wrote them on their walls. The wealth and glory of
Egypt were caused by its wisdom, and its wisdom had
acquired the art of transmuting baser metals into gold.
How else could have been acquired the vast masses of
gold, the statues and platings, of which ancient writers
speak: we never see gold in such masses now. When the
armies of Sesostris, the great King of Egypt, spread over
Asia, some remained in Colchis; and among these were

---

* All that the Alchemist says, is to be found in the writings of his
fraternity; but I am obliged to outrage probability, by making him talk
in an intelligible fashion. Moses and Queen Cleopatra were reputed
authors of two books on Alchemy. Moses was not an adept; Cleopatra
was. Among other names in the list of students are Caligula and the
Apostle John!

priests, adepts in alchemy, who taught the Colchians how
to make gold. You may have heard the story of the
Golden Fleece which Jason fetched from Colchis. No?
I will tell it you. The secret of transmutation was un-
wisely written by the Colchians on the skin of a beast,
skins being used for writing upon in those days; and
from the nature of the secret it was able to reveal, that
skin was called the ' Golden Fleece.' When the Greeks
heard of its existence, they sent out an expedition to
fetch home the prize——"

The loud explosion of a retort caused the Alchemist to
hurry to the furnace which had caused the mischief. Bernard was turning away to escape absolute suffocation,
when the restless eye of the old man detected his attempt
at a retreat, and he followed to present to Palissy his yellow
palm. The miserable creature seemed to have succeeded
in the transmutation of himself, so far as colour was concerned, and to have roasted out his succulence so far as to
assimilate his flesh to a metallic toughness. Palissy put
what coin he could afford into the adept's hand, which
clutched it with strange eagerness. As he continued his
path, thoughtfully and slowly, towards the centre of the
town, Palissy was overtaken by the gold-maker's assistant,
who passed him with an eager run, and disappeared, at a
short distance up the narrow street, within a butcher's
shambles. Poor fellows! thought Bernard; their work
certainly appears to make them very hungry.

CHAPTER V.

COMMOTIONS IN THE CHURCH.

THE great German Reformers of the Church were in
the heat of their zealous labour, far away, when Palissy
came out into the world. Luther, Melancthon, Zuinglius,
and hundreds more, were active workers on the European
mind. Their labour had, however, little influence in
France; the struggle for spiritual emancipation in that
country was a struggle by itself. To the religious strife
in Germany we need scarcely do more than allude. We
assumed 1528 to be the year in which Palissy quitted his
native roof. It was in the next year, 1529, that, in
another part of Europe, the protest of fourteen imperial
cities against the intolerant decisions of the second diet of
Spires, first gave to the reformed section of the Church
abroad the name of Protestant.* These familiar facts we
recal with a word or two to memory. It may help us,

* The cities deserve naming frequently; they were—Strasburg, Nuremberg, Ulm, Constance, Reutlingen, Windsheim, Meiningen, Lindau,
Kempton, Heilbronn, Isna, Weissemburg, Nordlingen, and St. Gall.

also, to connect more easily together, in their due proportions, all the parts of the rough picture which the world
must have presented to the mind of Palissy, if we do not
omit to note how the mists of astrology, in which we have
seen even Paracelsus wandering, could penetrate also into
the discussions of the Church.

The number of the beast in Revelations was a stone
which disputants on either side endeavoured to claim as
their own missile. An orthodox scholiast on three sermons
of St. Vincent, with another sermon of St. Hippolytus—
what Vincent, what Hippolytus, I give myself no trouble
to inquire—informs us that " the learned Staphilus calls
the beast—

Λ	o	υ	θ	ϵ	ρ	a	ν	a
30	70	400	9	5	100	1	50	1

666

not a bad invention. To me," he says, "it is more
frightful to consider, that the whole name of Martin
Luther fulfils the exact number. For if any one knows
the alphabet according to Pythagoras, as it is commonly
employed in the calculation of nativities, let him apportion
to each letter its number, and then add them up, he will
find the sum to be exactly 666, thus:

M	a	r	t	i	n	L	a	u	t	e	r
30	1	80	100	9	40	20	1	200	100	5	80

666"

The good scholiast must have troubled himself much

in the manufacture of this frightful coincidence, before he found that he could make the sum correct by writing " Luther" down as " Lauter." He goes on to say, that many heretics have tried to fit the number to a Pope, but they have always failed; now, here they have it fitted to a nicety on their own apostate leader!

In Germany, the Reformation prospered because princes saw no risk to their possessions when they followed their own choice in countenancing or discountenancing the movement. England had so far advanced in constitutional government, that the mind of the country could not be restrained. France stood entirely in a different position. The tendency of events, during its early history, had been to throw great wealth and power among ecclesiastics. The checks opposed to this had been comparatively slight; so that the Pope had grown to be a stronger man in France than even in his own dominions. In 1649, Louis XI. had been the first who received from the Pope the hereditary title of " Most Christian King;" the great power of the Church had been of value to the throne of France, and the French throne had been, in turn, a valuable buttress of the Church. In the mean time, the French people had found themselves, for many past years, ground among the millstones of Church property, which played into each other over the whole land. Tithes, and fines, and Church dues, for which but little spiritual value was given, made, especially, the peasants in the rural districts, on the provocation of their emptied pockets, very much

disposed to doubt the goodness of their spiritual guides.
Where the population was high-spirited, the disaffection
had been marked. The longing for a Reformation in
France had preceded the Waldensian and Albigensian
Crusades.

Up to the time of Palissy, this feeling had been growing, and in his time it existed throughout France in
many bosoms, as the harvest naturally sprung of manifest
oppression. In the year 1515, Leo X. and Francis V.
had met at Bologna, where they had drawn up an agree-
ment between themselves called the Concordat. By this
the king conceded to the Pope what he desired in France—
an absolute supremacy, and independence of all councils of
the Church. Leo paid the king for his complaisance by
despoiling the ecclesiastical corporations of the power of
nomination to bishoprics and abbeys, transferring that
power to the king. Against this concordat, the clergy,
the university, the parliament, in vain protested. " There
is a king in France," said Francis, and he had his way.
The result may be told in the words of a Venetian ambassador to Paris at the time: " The king gave away
bishoprics at the solicitation of the ladies of his court, and
employed his patronage of abbey lands to reward his soldiers, so that the bishoprics and abbeys of France were
reckoned as much merchandise by the court, as the trade
in pepper and cinnamon is among the Venetians."

Church appointments were thus distinctly perverted
into money speculations, and the money was that of the

working men spread over the fields of France. The rest-
lessness under a Church that cost them much, and gave
them little—often absolutely nothing—in the way of
spiritual equivalent, taught parishioners to grumble and
inquire. They began to question doctrines that had too
often a suspicious bearing on the increase of a Church
revenue, and they began to inquire into prayers, of
which the Amen was always Pay Us. They felt disposed
to ask that those whom they paid for teaching them
should come and teach. That would have imposed pas-
toral duty in French provinces upon polite little children
in Paris very often, or upon grisly men at arms fighting
in the wars of Italy. It was, unhappily, the fate of the
French people, that they could not claim religious liberty
without claiming the overthrow of so large a part of an
unjust political system, as would affect deeply the incomes
of ecclesiastics, peers, and nobles, and cut off a large slice
of the power of the king. Self-interest banded all the
rank and riches of the country into a strong party, against
which the struggle for reform was vain.*

* " Oh, poor Christians, and what place is yours? You thought to
abase idolatry, and to have gained friends to your cause; I know now
that you were not on the road to that ; for if I may believe this counsellor, you have all the courts of parliament against you; and if it be
as he has told me, you have also many great lords who take profit of
the revenue of benefices; and while they are intoxicate with such a
potion, you must fain know that they will always be your capital and
mortal enemies. Therefore I am of opinion that you should return
to your old simplicity, assuring yourselves that you will have enemies
and be persecuted all the time of your life, if by direct paths you will
follow and sustain the cause of God." This, and many other passages

The struggle was made, however, and had already begun. Images of saints, almost the first error against which reason openly rebelled, prompted to vengeance by the recollection that these images had been sharp instruments of Church extortion. They were destroyed in many towns by a tumultuous rising of the people, and the severest punishments had followed to avenge each outbreak. Meanwhile the spirit grew that was to struggle for the right.

The temper of the king towards reformers, during the time when Palissy was travelling through France, cannot however be correctly understood without attention to some other points. We must call to mind the title of King Francis as " Father of Letters." He was, in fact, clever for a king—that is to say, he had wit enough to desire the company of clever people. Some of their opponents tell us that the heretics being commonly deficient in rank and wealth, were driven to depend upon their talents, and became, therefore, exceedingly accomplished. They hoped thus to win converts to their cause. This is not false; but it is also true, that men of sound judgment and quick fancy, men with the largest minds, would be the men most likely to climb boldly up above the prejudices of their day. Such men carry the stamp of high ability about with them, and in his kingly-clever way Francis enjoyed their company, liked them to think

to the same purpose, will be found in the selection from the works of Palissy with which these volumes end.

that he was able to appreciate their talent. For their opinions he did not care a sol. When not under the influence of policy he laughed at doctrinal complaints against his courtiers.

Then there was the king's mother, Louisa of Savoy, and there was his clever sister Margaret, Duchess of Alençon,—Margaret of Valois. They were both clever people. The somewhat recent practice of admitting ladies to the court, had introduced much light frolicking. Boccaccio was a darling author, and to imitate him had become a fashion. Before the reign of Francis, royal brains had been beaten for the production of novelettes; royalty sets a fashion well afloat. In the time of Francis, therefore, it was an established custom at court, in Paris, and in the chief towns of France, for people to give story-parties, as we now give parties for quadrilles, at which they met to sup, and tell each other stories, after the manner of the gentlemen and ladies in the pages of Boccaccio. In this game, mother and daughter, Louisa and Margaret, had tried their skill. Louisa owned that Margaret had beaten her. The novelettes of Margaret of Valois live in print; and though she may have been one of the most cultivated women of that time and country, women of this time and country could not read her compositions without a whole rose-garden of blushes.

Louisa of Savoy was a rigid Catholic; Margaret favoured and protected the reformers. Louisa was not an ascetic, but she persecuted upon policy, for she was shrewd.

Margaret was not a religious woman, but she did not care for policy, and she did care to be surrounded by people of good sense and taste. Persecuted heretics, if they were clever men, had a sure refuge in her circle; and they might preach, if they pleased, as they travelled with her. Louisa was shrewd. When Francis was carried prisoner to Madrid, having sent his mother the bombastic message that he had lost all save honour, Louisa became regent, and displayed her tact for state-craft in sundry ways. One of these ways was the institution of severe measures against the dissentient members of the Church. When Francis was released by his rival on parole, and broke his parole to recover his kingdom, he did not send word to Charles that all was gained by loss of honour. Francis then, resuming the reins of his government, found that the reform horse had been severely punished by the temporary driver; should he relax in that severity? Policy hinted that he should not; so thought also the Pope, to whose power he now had a new cause of attachment:—the Pope had absolved him from all consequences that might follow after death upon the perjury committed at Madrid.

Francis had more to prompt him than his mother. The Pope was already powerfully represented at Paris by the astute and unflinching doctors of the Sorbonne.*

* The chapel, house, and schools of the Sorbonne, a hundred years afterwards magnificently rebuilt by Cardinal Richelieu,—then consisted of the original structure raised in 1253. The priest Robert, native of Sorbonne, a poor village in Champagne, who struggled hard

In the mind of Francis it is not possible to detect the influence of any fixed religious principle; he was essentially a selfish man, and, as selfish men go, not of the best. I may have given some confusion to the idea of court feelings and court motives as they affected the interests of a Reformed Church in France, and I have left it complicated with a mention of extraneous frivolity. This confusion certainly existed in the king's mind, and prompted many inconsistencies; once, for example, he supported Church reform in Switzerland at the same time that he was overthrowing it in France. Let us turn now from kinghood to manhood, and quit Francis I. for Bernard Palissy.

Picture-making, glass-painting, and occasional employment of his skill with rule and compass as a land-surveyor, sustained Palissy upon his travels well enough. Closely observing nature, carefully inquiring into all he saw, acquiring yearly new stores of experience, Palissy ripened, as the years went by, into a practical and earnest man. The outward covering of Frenchmen whom he met in those days, was to him, and is to us, a matter of no great concern. They were the days of knights who rode in armour, and swept down upon the enemy in battle, or on a rival at a tournament with lance in rest.

through poverty to the degree of doctor, and thereafter became chaplain to "St. Louis," little foresaw the curious position in the country which was to be attained by a college founded only for the aid of strugglers such as he had been. It began with sixteen needy pupils and three teachers.

Such men riding along the road in their own portable fortresses, must have been to Bernard every-day sights. If we look at those pictures, on tombs and elsewhere, in which the occurrences thought most worthy of illustration were reproduced by contemporary fingers, we find in the years corresponding to this period of the life of Palissy, mailed knights and crossbow-men in closely fitting dresses; men on foot commonly in dresses fitting closely to the limbs, suggestive of a period of war, and the necessity of putting no encumbrance upon bodies made for animal contention. Even the hair seems to have been rather closely cropped, except upon the heads of men pursuing peaceful occupations. Horsemen, when not in armour, wore a short tunic ; and the same garment over the closely-fitting dress was worn by countrymen and townsmen, who worked on their farms or in their shops. High state had, of course, some robes; and the long robes of scholars and ecclesiastics indicated, by enveloping the body and serving as impediments to action, that they were men of peace as to the flesh, whose business it was to wrestle with the spirit only.

The dwellings of the poor and of the middle class were wretched or uncomfortable, the palaces and mansions of the rich were fortresses. We see them in pictures as dull masses of rock, with windows bored irregularly here and there upon the surface, most of them miserably small, as if too large an opening would be too great a breach by which an enemy might enter.

But we may remark here, to forestal the necessity of again reverting to the subject, that the period occupied by Palissy in travel was the period in which these grim old homes died out. Francis, with his patronage of talent, brought into France new tastes; and it was at the time in which we are just now concerned, that Italian models were about to influence the architects of France. The palace of Chambord had been begun by Francis I. in 1523, and he had then no better idea than to build it in the rude and sombre fortress style. The palace of the Louvre itself was a building of the same description. The rebuilding of the Louvre, under the eye of Francis I., by Serlio, who was protected at his court, and the erection of the present structure from the plans (which Serlio candidly preferred to his own) of Pierre Lescot, indicate how great a change had in a few years come over the architecture of the country, since King Francis built the palace of Chambord.

Examples of religious persecution, cruel punishments of heretics in market-places, and expressions of much discontent on matters of religious doctrine, must have formed no inconsiderable portion of the experience upon which Bernard Palissy looked back at the conclusion of his years of travel.

Palissy was more than once in Paris during early manhood; at what dates we do not know. Let us suppose that he was a day's journey from Paris on the 11th of February, 1535, being then about twenty-five years old. Many people had set out from distant towns and villages, and were a-foot on the same road, for there was a great spectacle impending. A grave man, a member of the University of Paris, had found in the young painter a pleasant road-acquaintance; and through the frosty air, unconscious of the light snow that was falling, they were walking briskly on, earnest in converse. Their feet kept pace with the quick current of their thoughts, as they stepped rapidly together, and passed, forgetful of the customary greeting, many a more dilatory traveller.

" No doubt," said the scholar, " it was a wild act, to incense the king; but the punishment is not upon the act, but on the opinions that prompted it. I do not ask whether you share their heresy" . . . . .

" The real presence in the Sacrament I doubt," * said Palissy.

" Doubt !" replied the scholar. " They say that all sacrament receives the name of sacrament because it is the symbol of a sacred thing; so that it is necessary to com-

* I feel it difficult to mark the time when Palissy began to adopt the opinions of " those of the new religion;" but as he acted upon them certainly soon after he acquired a fixed abode, and was of a temper that would lead him to inquire from the beginning, I feel no doubt that he became a heretic during his early travels. The statement and defence made by the scholar of Reformed opinions—in fact, the whole of the scholar's part in this chapter—is made up of translated fragments from a most able and temperate little book, published during the lifetime of Palissy, for the purpose of stating to the French briefly the reasonableness of the Reformed doctrine. The book is entitled "Apologie ou Défense pour les Chrestiens de France qui sont de la Religion Evangélique ou Réformée, satisfaisant à ceux qui ne veuillent vivre en paix et concorde avec eux." *Geneva*, 1578.

prehend the outward sign by the eye, and by the spirit
the thing signified, which is inward and spiritual. When
we divide these parts in the Holy Supper, the bread and
wine are then the sign which we see with our eyes, and
receive by the mouth; but the body and blood of our Lord
Jesus Christ, they are the thing signified, which we comprehend and receive by the spirit, as a true spiritual viand,
destined to nourish spirit and not flesh. Now, to receive
and eat this spiritual viand, and to cause it to digest in our
souls (which are spirits), to nourish them and make them
live eternally, it is necessary that there be a spiritual man-
ducation, since both food and soul are spiritual" . . . . .

  " But these men," said Bernard — " these *Sacramentaires* as they are called, who too boldly have denounced the notion that the real body of our Lord comes
down from heaven daily—in countless morsels—to be
chewed between the foul teeth of priests, and digested with
the garlic in their belly,—these are the men whom the
Pope has moved King Francis to destroy. In truth, I
doubt the wisdom of the Pope."

  " The Pope," answered the scholar, " is a prince in
defiance of the canons of the Church. St. Gregory,
Bishop of Rome, whom they all call the greatest of the
Popes, wrote thus: ' If any one attributes to himself the
name of Universal Bishop in the Church, what will be
the judgment of all good people?' The universal Church
would fall from its estate when he who was the universal
bishop fell. Far be then from the heart of Christians, says

St. Gregory, this blasphemous name, by which the honour of all priests is taken, being unjustly usurped by one."

" And you have other differences yet," said the young painter, thoughtfully.

" The difference between us, touching the commandments of God, is not small. For we accuse the Church, or rather the Pope, of having effaced from the Decalogue the second commandment, which forbids images, and of having split the last one into two, in order to maintain the number ten. Truly it is a great sacrilege, and a temerity quite insupportable, to have dared to erase a whole commandment of the law of the living God. For if you observe the commandments which the curates are accustomed to pronounce at the parochial mass, you will find, that immediately after the first commandment, ' Thou shalt have none other Gods but me,' they have put the third, ' Thou shalt not take the name of the Lord thy God in vain,' and have effaced the second, which forbids the bowing before graven images, or the likeness of anything that is in heaven and earth. This has been done by the Pope and his supporters, that they might be more easily able, without attracting notice, to fill the temples of Christ with idols, and male saints and female saints, and then draw to them all offerings, obventions, and other profits, as has indeed been the result."

" I have doubt, also," said Bernard, " of the efficacy of masses, except as aids to the coffers of the priests. What have you to say to me of them?"

"If by means of them," the scholar answered, "and of other pretended good works, one can gain paradise, it will follow that paradise must be without comparison more easy to gain by the rich than by the poor. For the rich have much better means than the poor of causing masses to be said, of making gifts to priests, of going on long pilgrimages, of buying good fish that they may abstain on a fast day from eating meat,—they have better means of doing these, and other like things. So for the rich the gate of paradise would have its hinges greased, while for the poor it would be difficult to open; those who have the wherewithal to be happy in this world would be happy in the next, while to the poor both worlds would be miserable. This would be an unseemly thing. But, on the contrary, it is certain that paradise opens its gates more readily to the poor than to the rich, and that it is hard for the rich to enter."

"Truly the poor receive but little in this world," Bernard said.

"Less than their dues," the scholar answered, as he shook away the snow which had collected on his bonnet. "By the ancient canons of the Church, the tithes are called the tributes of the poor: and for this reason they who do not duly pay the tithes are reputed guilty of the death of men who perish in their district through necessity and indigence."

"I have seen two men dead by the roadside since this month began," said Palissy.

" And who will estimate the guilt of those who well know how to exact these tithes, and who keep them for themselves, and who retain the portion of the poor ! What do the canons say of those who retain the portion of the poor? ' The tithes,' says one, ' are the tributes of the indigent souls, so that if you pay well the tithe, not only will you receive abundance of fruits, but also health of soul and body. He who does not pay, is an usurper of the goods of others; and as many poor as die of hunger in the place where he dwells, so many will be the homicides of which he will be held guilty before the seat of the Eternal Judge, because he has converted to his own use that which was destined for the poor.' It is said in a canon taken from St. Ambrose, that ' the Church has gold not to keep it, but to distribute it to the necessitous.' The canon taken from St. Jerome says, that ' to appropriate goods of the poor, is a crime which surpasses the cruelty of the greatest brigands in the world.' There, you have a definitive sentence which the good doctor, St. Jerome, has pronounced against those who retain the goods of the poor, and apply them to their own use. O Eternal God ! how many brigands have we at this day in the world who are condemned by the sentence of St. Jerome."

" Perhaps," said Palissy, " since you are well read in the canons of the Church, you can find it written there that they who clothe themselves with the wool of the flocks ought also to provide them pasturage. Is preaching not ordained to priests?"

" By a canon of the Tolitan Council, 'Ignorance, mother of all errors, should be greatly avoided by the priests,
whose charge it is to preach God's word to the people.
The priests are admonished to read the sacred Scripture
by St. Paul to Timothy: 'Preach the word; be instant in
season, out of season; reprove, rebuke, exhort with all
long-suffering and doctrine.   Let the priests know the
Holy Scriptures and the canons, and all their work be
preaching and doctrine; and let them edify each other as
well by knowledge of faith as by works of discipline.'
But where are now the pastors who undertake to preach ?
Will you find one in a hundred?   There are none but
some monks* who undertake the task, and by them it is
done against the professions of monasticism.   For by the
canons it is not allowed that monks should preach."

* " The bishop, or his counsellors, resolved in those times on a trick
and stratagem extremely subtle; for having obtained some order from
the king for the cutting down of a great number of forests which
were around this town, nevertheless, because many found their recreation in the woods and pastures of the said forests, they would not
permit that they should be levelled; but those following the Mahometan artifices resolved to gain the heart of the people by preachings,
and presents made to the king's party; and sent into this town of
Xaintes, and other towns of the diocese, certain monks of the Sorbonne,
who foamed, slavered, twisted, and twirled themselves, making strange
gestures and grimaces, and all their discourses were nothing but outcry
against these new Christians ; and sometimes they exalted their bishop,
saying that he was descended from the precious blood of Monseigneur
St. Louis; and in this way the poor people patiently allowed their woods
to be cut down; and the woods having been thus cut, there were no
more preachers."—*Bernard Palissy*, in the History of the Troubles of
Xaintonge. This history will be found in the selection from the works
of Palissy at the conclusion of these volumes.

A stout thump on the back took from the scholar his remaining breath, and a ruddy youth, who had lost some of his own wind in the chase after a companion, thrust himself with little ceremony into the conversation.

"Hammering at the canons, Master Alain. You must leave off. Teach whom you will the road to the stake, but for old acquaintance sake, spare me. Pooh, pooh, you look too serious by far. I dare not be seen walking with grave faces, lest I be accused of thinking. If you wish to die in your bed, Alain,—don't think."

CHAPTER VI.

THE FRENCH REFORMER.

FURTHER to divert the attention of his neighbours from a sober train of thought, the ruddy young gentleman proceeded to perform a feat of jugglery with snowballs, and thereafter volunteered a story to beguile the way.

" You know, Alain," he said, " I am a good Catholic, and you are a wicked Sacramentaire. You have talked too much with Pierre Robert, Jean Cauvin, and that set; I go to mass, and faithfully attend the ministries of Jean du Pontalais."

" Is he a preacher?" inquired Bernard.

" Certainly he is. The monk comes badly off who undertakes to preach against him, as I'll tell you presently. But since you seem to be a little ignorant of Paris—not to know Jean is to be ignorant of Paris—I had better tell you more explicitly that Jean du Pontalais fixes his pulpit in the market-places. Ah! you shall go and hear him thunder with a great sword in his hand—O no, not the

sword of the Church; he has no more ill-will to heretics
than to the orthodox, if only they pay their pence; and,
wonderful to tell, *he* is paid always without grumbling."

" He is a mummer," explained the student.

" Mummer! He is the Thespis of our nation. After-
time shall hear of Jean du Pontalais. See him at the head
of his troop, all gay with spangles, marching to the sound
of music through the street, mounting his platform,
speaking his prologue, marshalling his heroes up the steps
which they are to descend each as his turn comes to strut
upon the stage. Let me tell you, Master Alain, that the
Comedy of the Acts of the Apostles* is good preachment.
Now, Alain, it becomes you ill to frown at our thea-
tricals. There is not so much pleasure in the world that
we can spare one harmless source of laughter. If the
preacher makes the church too dark, the people will prefer
to stay out in the sunshine. Well, there was a preacher who
believed himself a fountain of enlightenment. ' Others,'

---

* Jean du Pontalais was at this period the representative of the
drama in France, though his contemporary, Pierre Gringoire, wrote
plays of a more cultivated nature. "The Comedy of the Acts of the
Apostles" was not represented by Pontalais until 1541; the quaintness
of the title tempted me to name it here. The story which follows is
taken from " Les Contes, ou les Nouvelles Récréations et Joyeux Devis
de Bonaventure des Periers," valet de chambre to Margaret of Navarre;
first published in 1548. These jests, if jests they can be always
called, are generally founded on some fact ; but whether true or not,
they help to illustrate the temper of the time. The Margaret of
Valois, Angoulême, or Navarre, sister to King Francis I., mentioned in
this note and in a preceding chapter, will of course not be confounded
with the next Margaret of Valois, sister to King Francis II., who was
contemporary with a later portion of the life of Palissy.

said he to himself, ' may have the doctrine, but I have the
manner. I have the real turn of the wrist—the exact
modulation which insinuates all that I teach infallibly into
the hearer's mind.' He was a man who seldom looked at
his own feet, or saw more of the houses than their chimney-
tops. Now, Master Jean, having to play one Sunday
afternoon, marched his procession straight towards the
church in which the preacher was at work, drew up his
troop in a cross-way under the church-windows, and
ordered his tambourine to be sounded upon strongly, for
the express purpose of stopping the preacher, whose congregation he designed to bear off to the market-place.
But it was not likely to obtain release; for the more noise
the tambourine made, the more the preacher shouted to
be heard in spite of it. So Pontalais and he contested
who should leave off last. Presently the preacher gets
into a rage, and says quite loudly, and full of clerical authority, ' Let somebody go out and stop that tambourine.'
But for all that nobody went, except that if any one went
out, it was to go and see Master Jean du Pontalais, who
caused the beating to proceed louder and louder on his
tambourine. When the preacher saw that, since he was
resolved not to be silenced, ' Truly,' said he, ' I will go
myself; let nobody stir; I shall be back immediately.'
So when he came into the cross-way, furious with rage,
he said to Pontalais, ' Heigh! what has made you so bold
as to play your tambourine while I am preaching ?'
Pontalais looks at him, and says, ' Heigh! what has made
you so bold as to preach while I am playing on my tam-

bourine?' Then the preacher, more vexed than he was before, took the knife of his famulus, and made a great gash in the tambourine with this knife, and returned into the church to end his sermon. Pontalais took his tambourine and ran after the preacher, and dressed his head with it, fitting it to him slily by the hole like an Albanian hat; and then the preacher, ignorant of his condition, remounted his chair, to urge the wrong that had been done to him, and how the word of God had been vilipended. But everybody laughed so much to see the tambourine upon his head——"

" Do you call this a jest?" said Bernard, mournfully.

" Surely," said the scholar, " when worldly dealings have abased the Church, till it is matter for such tales as this among the people, it is fully time for us to think——"

" Then, Master Alain," said the youth, "I wish you a good day. I have a kind mother in Paris, and a sweetheart on the Loire. I love you well, but I cannot afford your company. If there were nothing in the world, and I were wrinkled, I might then consider about getting myself burnt; but I am young, and love the fire of youth much better than the fires they are preparing now in Paris."

The fires preparing then in Paris, and which were to be fed on the succeeding day with human fuel, had a history attached to them, of course. One morning in October, 1534, when the king was at his Castle of Blois, a placard was shown to him which had been affixed to the castle-gates by certain rash Sacramentaires, insulting the thrice holy and blessed sacrament. King Francis, in a fury, quitted Blois for Paris. The next morning there was a similar placard affixed to one of the pillars of the Louvre. King Francis breathed vengeance against the blasphemers of the real presence in the sacrament; the vengeance he desired, however, was against the insulters of the royal presence in the castle and the palace. To his worldly, knightly pride the placard was as a glove of defiance. So he took counsel with the Pope and the Sorbonne; and the result was a determination to affright the heretics, and to support the cause of order with a ceremony. For the 12th of February, 1535, a solemn day of humiliation was appointed; the king and all the high and mighty of the kingdom were to implore pardon from heaven, and avert from France the evils that might follow from the impiety of the Sacramentaires. At the same time an example of severe punishment was to be set, for the edification of the country.

To this spectacle crowds were now travelling, and at this it is not unlikely that Palissy was present; certainly, he witnessed many atrocities like it, even in those early days of the Church trouble in France. We will not, however, follow his steps into the town, nor suffer ourselves to warm into excitement over the horrors and contrasts of the scene he would have witnessed there. We must relate it, because it occupies a determined place in the history of opinion at that time; and for a comprehension of the events and opinions which will belong to the mature life of Bernard Palissy, it is absolutely necessary to have a fair idea of the position of the French Reformers.

The spirit of this day—this 12th of February, 1535 —will be most properly conveyed by telling its tale in the language of an ecclesiastical annalist* who was born at the close of the same century, and wrote as a faithful disciple of the Roman Church. To begin with the procession. Jean Bellay, Bishop of Paris, walked with the most sacred eucharist under a canopy, which was uplifted by the Dauphin, the Dukes of Orleans and Angoulême, sons of the king, and the Duke de Vendôme, first prince of the royal blood; there were also carried through the town, by robed priests, many relics of the saints. But the king himself bearing a lighted torch, his head bare, his eyes downcast, followed with the queen, and with a great pomp of people of all ranks, the sacred eucharist was carried from the Church of St. Germain to the Temple of the most Happy Virgin. Then the king, in a most grave and holy speech which he made, bore witness that he would oppose himself against all guilty heretics,

* Odoric Rinaldi, born 1595. A priest of the Oratory of St. Philip Neri. The " Annales Ecclesiastici " of Cardinal Baronius, member of the Institute of the Oratory, had been broken off by the cardinal's death at the 12th volume, and the year 1198. Rinaldi was appointed by the oratory to complete the great work, and by his hand the series was brought down to the year 1565. The story of the 12th of February, in the text, is simply translated from Rinaldi. It may be worth while to remark that 1535 was the date of the foundation of the order of Jesuits by Ignatius Loyola.

and that he would punish with severity even his children, if they should ever take the pox of heresy, and that he would strike off his own arm, if it ever could commit so great a crime.

On the same day, a most caustic punishment was endured by six offenders, who had published blasphemies against the adorable eucharist, in pamphlets which they had distributed; for they were bound to a huge wheel, which, being made to revolve, dipped them into the fire placed at its foot, and again carried them into the air, and afterwards, as they descended, they again were scorched, until at last, the links being divided, they tumbled headlong into the burning torture, and were consumed by the flames. Other men, guilty of the same impiety, were afterwards arrested in a body, from whom there were exacted cruel penalties. That severity alarmed not only as many French as were infected by the heresy, but also the heretical princes in Germany, who gravely inquired concerning it in letters to King Francis. They were answered, that he had lawfully put in force against them a severity of judgment, because, by the study of new-fangled ideas, they were exciting seditions in the kingdom.

So the tale is told. The grave inquiries of the German princes were not, of course, dictated by terror. Francis, in the network of his policy, had, as allies against the power of the emperor, princes of Germany who had adopted the reform which Luther preached. The violence

of the French king against the heretics, and more especially this public declaration of the 12th of February, suggested to Charles a means of interrupting the political
friendship of his allied adversaries. He caused the German princes to be well informed of the events in France,
and warned of the probable spirit of a friend who acted
thus towards those of his subjects whose crime was only
the being what his allies, the princes, were—Reformers in
the Church. Upon this hint, the allies appealed to
Francis. Francis did not choose to lose a good political
position, and reassured the princes by informing them that
the French heretics against whom the sentence of his
wrath was issued, had no resemblance whatever to the
Lutherans; that they were not mere seekers of Reformed
religion, but men disaffected to the state, enemies to law
and property, firebrands and Anabaptists. The answer
to this slander came from Calvin, when he dedicated
to King Francis his exposition of Reformed opinions, in
a preface dated from Basle, August the 1st, 1536. His
work, translated out of Latin into French, became at once
the text-book of the French Reformers.

Jean Cauvin (Calvin), aged twenty-five, had quitted
Paris and France not many months before that day, in
February, of which we have just been speaking. Calvin
and Palissy were born in the same year, if I have assigned
the right date to the birth of Palissy. The little sketch
of the career of Calvin, which is necessary for the illustration of those troubles in which Palissy was closely in-

terested, we shall chiefly take from the lips of his disciple
and successor in apostleship, Theodore Beza.* The birth
of Calvin, when told in the words of Beza, will recal to
our minds what has been said of the world at that time,
viewed under another aspect.

" I will begin," says his friend, " with speaking of his
nativity, which was the 10th day of July, in the year 1509;
and this I note, not that we may seek in his horoscope the
cause of the events of his life, and much less of the excellent virtues that were in him, but simply with regard
to history. And, in fact, since he himself had in such
horror the deceits which are in astrology, which is called
'judicial,' that he has made a book purposely, in which he
has shown in a lively manner, by good reasons, but principally by the word of God, that it is not a thing to be
supported in a Christian Church, or republic wisely ordered, inasmuch as it is only vanity and lies,—it would be

---

* Theodore Beza, born 1519, was luxuriating on the fat of benefices
until the year 1548, when, after a severe illness, he went to Geneva,
and attached himself with violence to Calvin. He was a man of great
acquirements and refined taste, marred by a turn for polemics surpass-
ing the exigencies even of that age of struggle. In a treatise by Beza,
defending the condemnation of Servetus, the whole doctrine of intolerance is preached as distinctly as it was practised by the ruling
Church. After the death of Calvin, Theodore Beza edited the last
work of his friend, the " Commentaries on Joshua," with a biographic
introduction. From this contemporary record, adding a fact or two,
I have drawn the notice in the text. It was afterwards published
separately, under the title of " L'Histoire de la Vie et Mort de feu
M. Jean Calvin, fidèle serviteur de Jésus Christ. Prinse de la Préface
de Theodore de Bèze aux Commentaires dudit Calvin sur Josué."
Genève, 1656.

doing wrong to give rein to such speculations touching his own person. Only let us content ourselves to know, that God, purposing to employ him at the fitting time, placed him in the world on the abovenamed day. This was at Noyon, an ancient and celebrated town of Picardy."

Cauvin's father, Girard, being known for a shrewd man, of business habits, was much sought in his own neighbourhood, and became a familiar guest at the houses of the surrounding gentry. So it happened that the children of Girard had many well-born children for their playfellows, and Jean was sent to college in company with the sons of a high-born neighbour, though, of course, at his father's cost,—or rather, perhaps, at his own cost; for, by help of his highly-respectable friends, he was endowed with a benefice at the age of twelve. That was an every-day occurrence. Jean Cauvin, while a boy, had pocket-money from his benefice at the Cathedral of Noyon, his native town, and he had also a curacy at Pont l'Evêque, his father's birthplace.

At the College de la Marche, which he first entered, Cauvin had for one teacher M. Maturin Cordier, an earnest, simple-hearted man, who spent the whole of a long life in many places, but always in one work, instructing children; and at last died at Geneva, aged eighty-five, teaching still to within a few days of his death. Then Cauvin entered the College of Montaigu, where a Spaniard was class-teacher; and the youth's private tutor was a Spaniard, who afterwards graduated in medicine. Under these influences, Cauvin advanced much in the study of philosophy.

Now, there was at that time studying in Paris a fellow-townsman, an old companion of Cauvin's, and some years his senior. With this old friend, named Pierre Robert, it was natural for Cauvin to associate. Pierre Robert—known afterwards as Olivetan—had thought himself into Reformed opinions on the subject of religion; and the opinions of Pierre Robert* exercised great influence upon the mind of Jean Cauvin.

At the same time that the youth's mind was swerving from the Church, his father came to the opinion that law would be a more profitable profession for him than divinity. Jean was well pleased with his father's notion, and went to study law at Orleans. There he was a disciple under Pierre l'Etoile, afterwards president in the Court of Parliament of Paris; and he himself profited so well, that he began in a short time to play the tutor, and was employed more frequently to teach than to learn. He was offered a gratuitous degree, but he declined it. Then, because the University of Bourges was in much repute, on account of the excellent jurisconsult, André Alciat, who taught

---

* Many English books follow one another in the statement that Olivetan's was the first translation of the Scriptures into French. It was made for the Swiss, at the instance of the inhabitants of Valais, and printed at Neufchatel, in 1535. There were several prior translations, of which note has already been made at page 43. My authority is a writer in the theologic department of the great French Encyclopédie, under the head "Versions."

there, Cauvin went to Bourges. But everywhere, whatever else he studied, he persevered closely in the pursuit
of sacred letters.

These wanderings of Cauvin, in search of education,
illustrate very well the way in which knowledge was
literally pursued by young men who desired more than a
common-place amount of information. The passage which
I now quote verbally from Beza, pleasantly reminds us of
a time when men and women went to bed at hours appro-
priated now to children. " As to (Cauvin's) apportion-
ment of time to his studies, there still live persons worthy
of faith"—(mark the asseveration needful as a preface to
so wonderful a fact)—" there still live persons worthy of
faith, who knew him familiarly at Orleans, who say that
at that time he very often studied until midnight; and that
he might do this, he ate little at his supper. Then, when
awake in the morning, he remained some time in bed,
remembering and ruminating all that he had studied
overnight." (So, no doubt, he told his landlady; but I
suspect that he was, in fact, not fond of getting up.)
"There can be no doubt," continues Beza, " that such
watches were very hurtful to his health. But he took those
hours for his chief studies, in order to be able to continue
more freely, and without being interrupted."

Among others to whom Cauvin was indebted at Bourges
for intellectual assistance was a German friend, Melchior
Volmar, who, perceiving him to be deficient in a knowledge of Greek, gave him instruction in that language.

At this time, Cauvin preached occasionally in a little town of Berry, named Lignières, and also visited the seigneur of that place. This gentleman afterwards, " having no other apprehension of things, only said in a general way, that it seemed to him that M. Jean Cauvin preached better than the monks, and that he went bluntly to his business."

While Cauvin was at Bourges, his father died. Upon this event, there of course followed family arrangements which recalled him to Noyon; and from Noyon, abandoning his law-studies, he went again to Paris, then first abandoning his benefices also. In Paris, it was not long before he published, in Latin, his Commentary upon Seneca on "Clemency;" they were "Johannis Calvini . . . Commentaria;" and Cauvin the student then first came out into the world as Calvin the scholar. From that time, the Latinized edition of his name began to grow into familiar use.

Among the friends of young Calvin, during this second period of residence in Paris, was Etienne de la Forge, a merchant, diligent and prudent in his business, but a simple-minded man and a good Christian. Calvin retained much love for M. de la Forge, who was eventually burnt for his adherence to the Gospel.

Now, Calvin had resolved to dedicate his life to the Reformed religion, and became intimate with learned men in Paris who were discontented with the existing character of the Church. One of these was Nicolas Cop, rector of the university. Nicolas Cop, in the year 1533, made an oration at. the feast of All-Saints, more advanced in the religious tenets it professed, than suited to the views of the Sorbonne and the parliament. It was determined to arrest him ; and he retired to Basle, of which town his father, Guillaume Cop, physician to the king, was native. The known associates of the heretical rector fell, of course, under suspicion; and among them Calvin, whose chambers at the College Fortret, were entered, a little too late, for the purpose of making him a prisoner. Calvin fled to Saintonge—the very district in which the home of Palissy was afterwards established. There he dwelt in the house of a young man, whose friends were wealthy, and who had a benefice to live upon (Louis du Tillet, canon of Angoulême: his brother, chief notary to the Parliament of Paris, was celebrated for his love of letters). This young man persuaded Calvin, while in his house, to write Christian sermons and remonstrances, which he then caused to be preached by certain curates in the neighbourhood.

While at Saintonge, Calvin, on one occasion, made a voyage to Nérac, to see the good man, Jacques Faber d'Estaples, who was very aged. He had been teacher to the children of the King of France, but being persecuted by the Sorbonne, had retired into those regions. The good old man was much pleased to see Calvin, and to talk to him. After some little time—when the Cop scandal

was probably forgotten—Calvin emerged from his refuge
in Saintonge, and returned to Paris. But very quickly,
he found it advisable to avoid the spirit of persecution, and
quit not Paris only, but also France. He did this in the
year 1534, accompanied by one of his brothers, and by
the young man who had given him shelter in Saintonge.
Calvin himself was, of course, then also a young man,
being twenty-five years old, but full of energy, and
talent, and ambition. Before quitting France, he published, at Orleans, a little book upon the sleep of the soul
after death, called " Plychopanychia." Calvin retired to
Basle, and was at Basle during that month of February,
1535, concerning which I have already spoken, busily at
work upon a digest of Reformed opinions, which he proposed to publish under the title of the " Institutes of
Christianity."

The design of Calvin was not humble; he desired his
book to be received as the declaration of faith and rallying-
point of the Reformed Church in France: but there was
need of such a mouthpiece, and to want ambition, would
be to want manhood, where there exists power to climb
high in any right direction. After the public atrocity of
February 12th, 1535,—after the appeal of the German
princes, and the reply of King Francis, stigmatizing the Reformers as political firebrands and revolutionists,—Calvin
perceived that a good hint was given to him for the framing
of his preface. The preface to his book, in which it was

dedicated to the most Christian king as a confession of faith,* dwelt upon the royal misconception on which persecutions had been founded, and affected to believe that when he had read that confession of the Reformed faith he would be glad to alter his opinions. The Sorbonne called this rank impertinence; so, doubtless, thought the king, since it at least implied that he had made a blunder, though it gave him credit for the candour necessary to a fit acknowledgment thereof. This preface or dedication (which is dated from Basle on the 1st of August, 1536) Calvin tells ·the king is intended † " to mollify your mind aforehand to give audience to the disclosing of our cause; which your mind, though it be now turned away and estranged from us, yea, and enflamed against us, yet we trust that we shall be able to recover the favour thereof, if you shall once have, without displeasure and troublous affection, read over this our confession, which we will to be instead of a defence for us to your majesty." (Here we should pause to remark the decided ambition which prompted Calvin, then but twenty-seven years old, to speak—undeputed—in the name of the French Reformers, and call his Institutes a book " which we will to be instead of a defence for us to your majesty.")

---

* It is called "Præfatio ad Christianissimum regem quâ hic ei liber pro confessione fidei offertur."

† To preserve better the humour of the age, I quote Calvin, not in my own English, but with the spelling modernized, from "The Institution of Christian Religion, written in Latine, by Maister John Caluine, and translated into Englyshe, accordyng to the Author's last Edition, by T. N." London, 1562.

" But if the whisperings of the malicious do so possess
your ears, that there is no place for accused men to speak
for themselves ; and if those outrageous furies do still,
with your winking at them, exercise cruelty in prisoning,
tormenting, cutting, and burning,—we shall, indeed, as
sheep appointed to the slaughter, be brought to all extremities, yet so that in our patience we shall possess our
souls, and wait for the strong hand of the Lord,—which
shall, without doubt, be present in time, and stretch forth
itself armed both to deliver the poor out of affliction, and
to take vengeance on the despisers, which now triumph
with so great assuredness. The Lord, the King of kings,
stablish your throne with righteousness, and your seat
with equity, most noble king." So the dedication closes;
and if Calvin meant it really to be mollifying, it is very
evident that he was no great master in the art of speaking
softly. We are reminded rather of the opinion of the
gentleman at Lignières, that " he went bluntly to his
business."

Of the accusations made against the Reformers, and
which were, in truth, the accusations pleaded by Francis
to the German princes, Calvin tells the king elsewhere in
his dedication : "Herein is violence showed, that without
hearing the cause, bloody sentences are pronounced against
it: herein is fraud, that it is, without deserving, accused of
sedition and cruel doing. And that none may think that
we wrongfully complain of these things, you yourself can
bear us witness, most noble king, with how lying slanders

it is daily accused unto you: as, that it tendeth to no other
end but to writhe from kings their sceptres out of their
hands, to throw down all judges' seats and judgments, to
subvert all orders and civil governments, to trouble the
peace and quiet of the people, to abolish all laws, to undo
all properties and possessions—finally, to turn all things
upside down."

It has already been pointed out that these accusations
against the reformers were not founded upon nothing.
The ecclesiastical abuses had become so completely blended
with the political system in France, that religious became
unavoidably, at the same time, social and political, reform.
In our own country, at the present day, we have our civil
list, our sinecures, and vested interests. We know what
jealous eyes watch over them, and what a revolutionary
thing it would be to destroy or cut down the incomes of
some thousand men—grand falconers, lay impropriators,
pluralists, and others, whose only social title to the income
they derive from their nation, or their parishes, is that
they were born or bred into a habit of regarding it as
theirs. The misuse of Church patronage in France, in
Calvin's time, was so extensive, so inveterate, that the
most elementary principles of Church reform could not
be put in practice, without doing what a warm lover of
existing order in those days might easily declare would
tend " to undo all properties and possessions—finally, to
turn all things upside down."

Of the great mass of rank and wealth, and of the class

of men whose entire little income hung upon a Church-abuse—the benefice-holders, banded by the common tie of interest against reform—Calvin in this dedication speaks as we find all other reformers of the time constantly speaking. They were the great bar to moral progress. " For," says Calvin, " their belly is their God, their kitchen is their religion; which being taken away, they think that they shall not only be no Christians, but no men: for though some of them do plenteously glut themselves, and other some live with gnawing of poor crusts, yet they live all of one pot, which, without these warming helps, should not only wax cold, but also thoroughly freeze."

Calvin, having published his " Institutes of Christianity," left Basle for some months. He went to the court of Queen Renée, a good reformer; travelled in Italy, visited Paris; and was returning to Basle through Geneva, when, at Geneva, his course was stopped. Geneva had freed itself, and for a year past, in that town, the Reformed religion had been legalised. Farel was its expounder, with whom, at first, Viret was associated. Viret had been absent many weeks, and Farel, needing help, had been wanting him back sorely. That was the state of the Genevese Church when Calvin was passing through Geneva on his way to Basle. Calvin immediately was invited, and some say compelled by forcible entreaty, to take Viret's place. He did not need entreating, we may be quite sure. With respect to his book, his ambition had been fulfilled; it had been gratefully adopted by

the French reformers.   Before it was published, they
were banded together by a common sense of Church-abuse,
a common opinion on many leading points of doctrine;
but on minor points, for want of any common spokesman,
each had formed opinions of his own, and there were many
variations in their doctrine.   Calvin, having published a
detailed confession of faith, gave to all weaker minds a
thing to hold by.   A pattern was held up, to which the
mass conformed; and Calvin knew that he was then in a
fair way to become more and more, year by year, what
he desired to be, the head to the great body of the French
reformers.   This was his certain hope when he was
requested to officiate with Farel, in Geneva.   Geneva was
a free town, in which French was spoken, and it was close
to the French frontier; he could be safe there, however
boldly he might speak; he could feel at home among men
speaking his own language, and he could easily and quickly
make, from Geneva, expeditions into France, whenever
he saw opportunity of doing so with safety and with
profit to his cause.   Therefore Calvin settled at Geneva,
and there dwelt and laboured at the time when Bernard
Palissy settled at Saintes.

It is not necessary to dwell more at length on Bernard's
years of wandering.   It was essential to our proper comprehension of his after life, that we should recal to our
minds those points, in the world of which he had experience, by which especially his mind was influenced.   This
has been done; and now we slip over the period of travel,

and find Bernard Palissy settled at Saintes, full of simplicity and full of power. He has the very pattern-mind
of a philosopher, but hitherto he has done nothing, still he
is doing nothing—painting pictures, staining glass, and
drawing plans.

CHAPTER VII.

PALISSY MARRIED AND SETTLED—THE ENAMELLED CUP.

HAVING long hovered over France, Bernard Palissy settled.at length in the small but not quite insignificant town of Saintes. He spelt it Xaintes, and so did his contemporaries. There he probably was fixed ; because he was not proof, like Paracelsus, against woman's charms. I suppose him to have married at the age of about twenty-nine, in the year 1538. This is the last date which it will be requisite to give upon hypothesis. Henceforth, also, it is fortunate that as the biographic details rise in interest, they will become in many parts authentic and minute.

Palissy, having married, was no longer able to wander as he listed, asking questions, studying the rocks and trees, and living as he could, while he was growing in experience, not very careful for the morrow. He therefore fixed himself in an abode at Saintes, and undertook whatever occupation he could get, as a surveyor, as a

painter, or a glass-painter. His engagements as surveyor
usually sprang out of disputes concerning land, formerly a
constant source of litigation in most countries. In such
disputes the quarrel commonly depended on a question
about boundaries, and a plan of the contested property
became essential. When such disputes occurred in his
own district, it was usual to employ Bernard Palissy in
a character similar to that of sworn surveyor; and every
little engagement of this nature was a godsend to the
household purse. But his supplies came slowly, on the
whole; more than he had been used to earn while roving,
it was not easy for Palissy to earn when fixed at Saintes:
and he had now a wife depending on his labour; children,
also, were not tardy of appearance.

In a year or two, if my last date was right, Palissy
already had begun to feel that he was wasting power.
Thirty or thirty-one years old, young, vigorous, and
prompted forward by intense activity of mind, Bernard
began to feel that he was capable of better things than a
long drudge through life, with no aim higher than to get
his bread by meriting the patronage of the nobility,
gentry, and the public in general, of the small town of
Saintes. It abounded in all the jealousies and scandals
which are proper, in all nations, to a district capital. So
Bernard sighed for higher occupation, while he earned a
slender income for the support of his household, in the
first months or years of his establishment at Saintes.

Saintes is the capital of Saintonge, a district which

pretty accurately corresponds to the department of Charente Inferieure. Aunis, Saintonge, and Angoumois, form,
at this day, a province. Saintes and Saintonge are connected intimately with our future story; it is, therefore,
necessary to have some conception of their character.
Saintonge is a district fertile in corn, wine, and fruit; and
its fertility was recognised by Cæsar, who relates how
certain tribes left their more barren soil for that of the
Santones. Saintonge is divided, by the river Charente,
into two unequal parts. Upper Saintonge, on the south
side of the river, is the larger of the two. It is
watered by the Soudre and the Sevigne. Through Lower
Saintonge flows the Boutonne. The wide embouchure
of the Garonne gives a sea-boundary to Saintonge on the
south, in addition to its western coast-line. That portion
of the district beyond the Soudre, which is hemmed in
between the Soudre and the mouth of the Garonne, was
called, in the time of Palissy, the island of Allevert—which
is now written Arvert. About the mouth of the Soudre,
on the side opposite to Allevert, are the salt-marshes of
Marenne; and Marenne also is sometimes called an island.
In the sea—a real island—oppose the mouth of the
Soudre, is Olleron; and others are adjacent. These places
will hereafter frequently be mentioned.* Except that

---

* Thus, it is said of the monks who brought reform into Saintonge:
" Some took to a trade, others kept village-schools; and because the
isles of Olleron, of Marepnes, and of Allevert, are remote from the
public roads, a certain number of the said monks withdrew into those
islands, having found sundry means of living without being known."
Palissy, in the *History of the Troubles of Xaintonge.*

from the famous salt-marshes of Marenne, the salt of Saintonge was produced north of the Charente. Saintonge,
in the time of Palissy, was thought to produce the best salt
in Europe, and was the chief source of salt in France,
until it was obtained more abundantly from Brittany.
The vintage of the district was manufactured usually into
brandy; the town of Saintes is not, indeed, many miles
below Cognac; the same river Charente watering the fields
of both those towns.

Several towns of Saintonge contained, in Palissy's time,
tanneries. The meadows of Saintonge yielded a valuable
pasturage, its horses bore the highest character. Saintonge was able also to send saffron to the markets, and its
wormwood—the Santonic wormwood—found a way even
out of Gaul to Greece and Rome. Dioscorides speaks of
it, and tells us that it comes from Gaul, and that "its
name is taken from the region of the Santones, in which
it grows."* Pliny the Naturalist also speaks of the Santonic wormwood, "so named from a state in Gaul."† The
district of Saintonge contains clay good for bricks and
pottery. It contains also several mineral springs.‡

The town of Saintes, in which Palissy resided, is built
on the banks of the Charente, at the foot of a mountain.
The old town, founded by the Romans, and called Medi-

---

* Book iii., cap. 28.   † Book ii., cap. 37.

‡ It would forestal the narrative, to show, by extracts in a note,
what will, I trust, clearly be seen as we go on, that all these leading
points in the dead world about him were received into the mind of
Palissy, and make part of his life.

olanum, used to stand at some height on the mountain;
that was destroyed by the barbarians, upon their road to
Spain. Many remains were left, however. Over the
new town, built lower down, there looked the ruins of a
Roman capitol. The people of Saintes used, and still use,
a fine Roman bridge over the Charente, built, it is said,
in the reign of Tiberius. A triumphal-arch is raised upon
it, which has an illegible Latin inscription on its frieze.
Roman monuments abounded. There existed, very perfect,
in the time of Palissy (and they are still not indistinct), the
ruins of a Roman amphitheatre, situated in a valley, near a
suburb of Saintes called St. Eutropius. These ruins are
called "The Arches." St. Eutropius is so named from a
church which St. Palais (it does not in the least matter who
he was) caused to be built over the spot where the remains
of St. Eutropius, first Bishop of Saintes, had been discovered. St. Eutropius had been sent out by Pope St.
Clement, in the beginning of the tenth century. The
church had two choirs and a nave; the remains of the
tomb of St. Eutropius were in it years ago—some crum-
bling stones within an iron railing. Of the scrapings from
this tomb, a pinch, taken in white wine for nine successive
mornings, was supposed to cure all kinds of fever. There
are many quarries about Saintes, and near this suburb of
St. Eutropius there is a quarry full of petrifactions; there
is also in the neighbourhood a line of rock, called "The
Rocks," abounding equally in relics of past life.

Saintes itself was a town of narrow, crooked streets,

with low houses, high convent walls, belonging to the Benedictine nuns (ladies of Saintes), abbeys, bad paths, and obstructive gates. There was an old cathedral, dedicated to St. Peter, and said to have been built by Charlemagne. Only the bell-tower now remains, and most of the antiquities in which Saintes used to abound, must be named in the past tense. A great deal of destruction is attributed to the religious struggles, which were carried on in Saintes with an especial fierceness, and of which some records have hereafter to form part of this biography.

Saintes was, in the time of Palissy, an extensive and lucrative bishopric, including more than seven hundred parishes. The episcopal seat of Rochelle was, however, scooped out of it, in the year 1649.

Saintonge yielded to the king much money in taxes. Of the civil government, which was administered by a seneschal and three bailiffs, within the jurisdiction of the parliament of Bourdeaux, it is not requisite to speak at present.

The house of Palissy appears to have been situated in the outskirts of the town of Saintes; for he tells us that at night he heard the dogs barking on one side, and the owls hooting on the other.* Glass-painting required, perhaps, the use of more fire than could prudently be

---

* " I have been for several years, when, without the means of covering my furnaces, I was every night at the mercy of the rains and winds, without receiving any help, aid, or consolation, except from the owls that screeched on one side, and the dogs that howled on the other."—*The Artist in Earth.*

permitted in a town, as towns were then built. It is quite
possible, however, that Palissy inhabited more houses than
one, and did not move towards the outskirts until he commenced experiments in pottery.

Thus labouring for bread among the narrow-minded
people of the narrow-streeted town of Saintes, dissatisfied
with labour that produced food, and only food, Palissy,
conscious of his own strength, hoped that he might yet
live to accomplish something better. He had abundant
spirit and vivacity. In his darkest hours of evil fortune,
he could try like a man to set his friends a-laughing. In
the simplicity of his mind, he was at all times full of hope,
although unconscious that it was the spiritual sense of
power which begot his hopefulness. All that is possible, is
certain to the man who wills, if he has wit enough to use
a little tact or skill, and a great deal of patience. Palissy
had a child upon his arms; land-measuring came only
now and then; glass-painting was not attractive; and the
inhabitants of Saintes were but a limited population to
provide with pictures. The young artist kissed his baby,
and buoyed up his wife with his own hopes. There was
another baby to kiss, but there was no doubt in his mind
about the future.

It was at this time that there was shown to Palissy an
elegant cup of Italian manufacture—" an earthen cup,"
he says, " turned and enamelled with so much beauty,
that from that time I entered into controversy with my
own thoughts, recalling to mind several suggestions that

some people had made to me in fun, when I was painting portraits. Then, seeing that these were falling out of request in the country where I dwelt, and that glass-painting was also little patronized, I began to think that if I should discover how to make enamels, I could make earthen vessels, and other things, very prettily; because God had gifted me with some knowledge of drawing." Palissy then knew nothing whatever of the art of pottery, and there was no man in the nation who could make enamels. That last fact was the attraction to him. Enamels could be made; there he beheld a specimen. What is possible, is sure to him who wills, if he can use a little skill and a great deal of patience. To be the only man in France able to make enamelled vases, would be to provide handsome support for his wife and children; and to work at the solution of so hard a riddle, would be to provide full occupation for his intellect. So Palissy resolved to make himself a prince among the potters; and, "thereafter," he writes, "regardless of the fact that I had no knowledge of clays, I began to seek for the enamels, as a man gropes in the dark."

CHAPTER VIII.

POTTERY THREE CENTURIES AGO.

HERE it becomes requisite to check the progress of this narrative, and spend some minutes in the labour of dismissing from our minds the familiar ideas which the word "pottery" suggests at the present time. In our bedrooms, at our breakfast-tables, and throughout the day, upon our dining-tables, in our drawing-rooms, and on our mantelpieces, pottery and porcelain are rarely absent from the sight or touch. It requires, therefore, some effort to recal to mind the rude state of the art of pottery in England or in France three centuries ago. Cups and saucers, as ideas, we must abandon utterly; remembering that Bernard Palissy began to tempt the muse—if we may suppose a muse—of pottery a century before tea came into Europe. Moreover, in those days, if there had been tea, there could have been few tea-services even of Chinese porcelain. It was only during the boyhood of Palissy, in the year 1518, that the Portuguese had appeared before Canton, and. for their service in destroying the pirates of the Ladrones, obtained leave to establish a settlement at Macao. Thence came, by way of Portugal, the first importations of china-ware into Europe. Porcellana, the Portuguese name given in the East to a cowrie-shell, was thence transferred to Chinese cups, as indicative of their transparent, shell-like texture.*

Porcelain, then, began to be imported as an article of luxury from China, in the times of Palissy. During two centuries afterwards, the Europeans laboured in vain to make it for themselves. It is not likely that by Palissy porcelain had at any time been seen or heard of, up to the day when his mind was prompted into action by the sight of an enamelled cup. That cup, having been made in Italy, of course was composed of an opaque ware, very different from the translucent porcelain.

It is not necessary to dwell here upon the great antiquity of the art of pottery. It arose, early and easily, out of that property of clay which causes it, when in its natural condition, more or less moistened, to be plastic, and when baked, to become more or less hard and co-herent. There are many kinds of clay, differing greatly in the degree of hardness which they acquire when burnt, and differing much, also, in their result, according to the degrees of fire to which they are exposed. When we walk

* But while porcelain was adopted in Europe as a generic name for china-ware, in Portuguese it was, and is, specific, meaning no more than a cup; the name for porcelain-ware generally being, in that language, *loca*.

over a clay soil, in wet weather, we may consider clay to be the worst of earths; but setting aside, for the present, its grand uses in the economy of nature—which we shall find Palissy hereafter fully perceiving—to consider that, without clay, there would have been no pottery, is quite sufficient to establish it in our respect. Of clay, as a plastic material, Palissy himself speaks with a just emphasis, at the same time that he unconsciously supplies us with a catalogue of the chief uses of pottery in his own day. "Consider a little," he says, "how many arts would be useless, if not altogether lost, without the art of treating earth. The refiners of gold and silver must cease from their work, for they could do nothing without furnaces and earthen vessels; inasmuch as no stone, or other matter, could be found, which might serve to contain melting metals, if there were no vessels of earth.

" *Item.*—The glass-workers must cease from their work, for they have no means of melting the ingredients of their glass, if not in vessels of earth. The goldsmiths, founders, all melting, of whatever sort or kind it may be, would be at an end; and there would not one be found who could dispense with clay. Look, also, at the forges of the farriers and locksmiths, and you will see that all the said forges are made of bricks; for if they were of stone, they would be soon consumed. Look at all the furnaces ; you will find they are made of earth; even those who labour upon earths use earthen furnaces, as tilers, brickmakers, and potters: in short, there is no stone, mineral, or other matter, which could serve for the building of a furnace for glass, lime, or any of the beforenamed purposes, which would last for any length of time. You see, also, how useful common earthen vessels are to the community—you see, also, how great is the utility of earth for the covering of houses. You know that, in many regions, they know nothing of slate, and have no other covering than tiles: how great do you suppose to be the utility of earth in making conduits from our fountains? It is well known that the water which flows through earthen pipes, is much better and wholesomer than that which has been brought through leaden channels. How many towns are there built of bricks, inasmuch as there are no means of getting stones to build them with?"

Coarse jars and pipkins, and such humble specimens of pottery as are alluded to by Palissy, when he points out " how useful common earthen vessels are to the community," were the chief products of French art in the year 1540. They were not quite the sole results; for Rabelais, a contemporary of Palissy, in his Panurge, first printed in 1546, speaks of the hard pottery or stoneware of Beauvais—its " Poteries Azurées"—as very celebrated, and fit to be presented to the Kings of France.*

* The only French writer on Pottery in the time of Palissy, was Palissy himself, from whom we shall gather incidentally, hereafter, many details. Most of the facts in this chapter are derived from Mr. Marryat's richly illustrated " Collections towards a History of Pottery and Porcelain in the 15th, 16th, 17th, and 18th centuries," London, 1850. In speaking of the stoneware of Beauvais, Mr. Marryat has

There is a common division of pottery into hard and soft. Hard pottery cannot be scratched with a knife. In the year 1540 there was no hard pottery made in France, except the stoneware of Beauvais, and perhaps a little stoneware in some other places. Soft pottery can be scratched with a knife. It is composed of a clay, sand, and lime. The admixture of sand and other materials with clay, to modify the result of baking, was an obvious contrivance, and is found to have been resorted to even in very rude states of society. The woman among the aborigines of Louisiana mixed with clay pounded shells. Then having shaped her material into a cylinder, of size proportioned to the vessel she proposed to make, she made a hollow in the centre, balanced the clay by this on her wet thumb, and twirled it swiftly round,—shaping its edges with her other hand, and twirling still,—using the principle, without the apparatus, of the potter's-wheel. The well-formed vessels, when a batch was ready, were then rudely baked over a fire. The shells employed by such a labourer supplied the ingredient of lime, which, mixed with clay and sand, is used in the European manufacture of soft pottery.

Pottery covered with glaze, or enamel, is called Fay-

erred in assigning the date of the third book of Rabelais to the year 1500, and of course, therefore, errs in saying that the reputation of the Beauvais ware continued from the time of Rabelais to the time of Francis I. Rabelais wrote in the time of Francis I., and his chief patron was the same Jean du Bellay, Bishop of Paris, whom we lately found heading the procession of the 12th of February. Rabelais died in 1553, aged seventy.

ence.* We have not now to deal with the fame of ancient potters' work, and the Etruscan vases which competed in price with gold and silver vases of their own size, in Rome under Augustus. The dark ages, the transition period of history, shut us out from them. If, therefore, the ancients employed glaze, that fact does not concern us, in the year 1540. The revived use of glaze among the moderns is alike beyond our limits. In the time of Palissy, whatever polish was not proper to the pottery itself, was given by a coating of enamel.

The "earthen cup, turned and enamelled with so much beauty," which had given a new direction to the thoughts of Palissy, must have been of Italian manufacture. Enamelled pottery could, at that time, scarcely have come from any other country. Except that Hirschvögel, an artisan of Nuremberg, had brought from Italy, in 1507, and practised in his native town the art of an enameller, the practice ceasing at his death, there was no enamelled ware produced in Europe out of Italy.

The labours of Palissy and their results were altogether of an independent character. Whatever he introduced into France, he introduced out of his own mind. The first introduction of the manufacture of enamelled pottery into France, by artists from Italy, took place in the Nivernois, in the year 1565. An Italian workman is said to have remarked to the duke (Louis Gonzaga) the fitness

* Perhaps from the little town (now village) of Faience, in the department of the Var, which, so early as the sixth century, is supposed to have been famous for glazed pottery.

of the materials existing naturally in the district, and in
that way to have given a first impulse to the undertaking.
The enamelled cup, therefore, which Palissy admired in
the year 1540, had been imported into France from Italy.

In Italy the modern history of pottery begins. The
men of Pisa, once upon a time, zealous against infidels,—
whom there was need to combat, if not for their religious
errors, yet at any rate for their political aggressions,—the
Pisans undertook to clear all Mussulman corsairs out of the
Tyrrhene sea. There was at that time an infidel King of
Majorca, named Nazaredeck, who busied himself cruelly
about the coasts of France and Italy. Twenty thousand
Christians were said to be confined in the dungeons of
this old King of Minorca: so pure a taste for playing gaoler
was almost without a parallel until we got one in a modern
King of Naples. In the year 1113, on the festival of
Easter, the people of Pisa were exhorted by their arch-
bishop to open the prisons of their Christian brethren, and
to free them from the power of the infidel. The arch-
bishop, in fact, preached a crusade with much success, and
the Crusaders set sail in the month of August, from Pisa
for Majorca. But though, no doubt, they were good
soldiers, they were exceedingly bad sailors, so they did
not get to Iviça till April in the succeeding year. They
took that island, and then passed on to Majorca, where
they besieged Majorca the town, and took it about Easter,
1115, after a fierce struggle of a year's duration. Nazaredeck, the infidel king, was killed: his heir-apparent was

made prisoner, and carried with great spoil and booty into
Pisa. Among the spoil were many plates of Moorish
pottery, which the Pisans stuck into church-walls as ornaments and trophies. Afterwards, it became a custom at
Pisa, with warriors who came home from crusades, and
stopped at Majorca by the way, to bring with them fragments of this painted earthenware. They were tokens of
a triumph over the Philistines. Such Majorca plates are,
therefore, to be seen embedded in the walls of several old
Pisan churches.

For two hundred years this Moorish pottery was regarded only as a thing to be admired for its beauty, and
to be venerated as a religious symbol; it was not till the
beginning of the fourteenth century that the Italians
began to make an imitative ware, named after the old
source of painted pottery, Majolica. The early specimens
of Italian manufacture were painted with arabesque patterns, yellow and green upon a blue ground, simple copies
from the Moorish. Under the house of Sforza the art
was improved, and in 1450 the manufacture of Pesaro
had attained great excellence.

The Italian discoverer of enamel was the Florentine
sculptor, Luca della Robbia, who was born in 1400, and
died in 1481. As Luca della Robbia, in the History of
Pottery, presents many points of curious analogy with
Palissy, it will be well to dwell on some points of his life.
Palissy was much more than a potter; but it is of pottery
that we are speaking now, and the invention of enamel.

A few points in the life of Luca della Robbia, as told in
the words of Vasari, are very interesting in themselves, to
us who study the career of Palissy, and not the less so,
when we remember that Vasari wrote during the same
years occupied by Palissy at Saintes in working out the
hint supplied by the enamelled cup.

Luca della Robbia, Vasari* says, was " carefully reared
and educated until he could not only read and write, but,
according to the custom of most Florentines, had learned
to cast accounts so far as he might require them." Placed
then to learn the art of a goldsmith, and having learned
to draw and model in wax, he aspired to work in bronze
and marble.   " In these also he succeeded tolerably well,
and this caused him altogether to abandon his trade of a
goldsmith, and give himself up entirely to sculpture, in-
somuch that he did nothing but work with his chisel all
day, and by night he practised himself in drawing; and
this he did with so much zeal, that when his feet were
often frozen with cold in the night time, he kept them in
a basket of shavings to warm them, that he might not be
compelled to discontinue his drawings.   Nor am I in the
least astonished at this, since no man ever becomes distinguished in any art whatsoever, who does not early begin
to acquire the power of supporting heat, cold, hunger,
thirst, and other discomforts ; wherefore," Vasari says,
" those persons deceive themselves altogether who suppose

* Where I quote Vasari, it is from the very accessible translation
by Mrs. Foster, in "Bohn's Standard Library."

that while taking their ease, and surrounded by all the enjoyments of the world, they may still attain to honourable distinction—for it is not by sleeping, but by waking, watching, and labouring continually, that proficiency is attained and reputation acquired."

To the labours of Bernard Palissy this preface applies even more emphatically than to the labours of Luca della Robbia. Vasari, then, having detailed Luca's career as a sculptor, and the excellence of his works, goes on to relate how marble and bronze were to Luca very much what we have seen glass-painting and land-measuring to be to Bernard. "When, at the conclusion of these works, the master made up the reckoning of what he had received, and compared this with the time he had expended in their production, he perceived that he had made but small gains, and that the labour had been excessive; he determined, therefore, to abandon marble and bronze, resolving to try whether he could not derive a more profitable return from some other source. Wherefore, reflecting that it cost but little trouble to work in clay, which is easily managed, and that only one thing was required, namely, to find some method by which the work in that material should be rendered durable, he considered and cogitated with so much goodwill on this subject, that he finally discovered the means of defending such productions from the injuries of time. And the matter was on this wise: after having made experiments innumerable, Luca found, that if he covered his figures with a coating of enamel, formed from the mixture of tin, litharge, antimony, and other minerals and mixtures, carefully prepared by the action of fire, in a furnace made for the purpose, the desired effect was produced to perfection, and that an almost eternal durability might thus be secured to works in clay. For this process then, Luca, as being its inventor, received the highest praise; and, indeed, all future ages will be indebted to him for the same."

Vasari, having then told his readers of some works in this enamelled terra cotta, adds that " The master, meanwhile, was not satisfied with his remarkable, useful, and charming invention, which is more particularly valuable for places liable to damp, or unsuited from other causes, for paintings, but still continued seeking something more; and instead of making his terra cotta figures simply white, he added the further invention of giving them colour, to the astonishment and delight of all who beheld them. Among the first who gave Luca della Robbia commissions to execute works of this description, was the magnificent Piero di Cosmo de' Medici, who caused him to decorate a small study, built by his father Cosmo, in his palace, with figures in this coloured earth. * * And it is certainly much to be admired that, although this work was then extremely difficult, numberless precautions and great knowledge being required in the burning of the clay, yet Luca completed the whole with such perfect success, that the ornaments both of the ceiling and pavement appear to be made not of many pieces, but of one only. The fame of these works having spread, not only throughout Italy, but over all Europe, there were so many persons desirous of possessing them, that the Florentine merchants kept Luca della Robbia continually at this labour to his great profit : they then despatched the products all over the world." Luca then took his two brothers, Ottaviano and Agostino, to assist him, and " they sent many specimens of their art into France and Spain." Passing over other notices of the works of Luca, who began to attempt pictures upon level surfaces of enamelled earth, we will conclude with one more extract from Vasari: " For Messer Benozzo Federighi, Bishop of Fiesole, Luca della Robbia erected a sepulchre of marble, on which he placed the recumbent figure of Federigo, taken from Nature, with three half-length figures beside; and between the columns which adorn this work, the master depicted garlands with clusters of fruit and foliage, so lifelike and natural, that the pencil could produce nothing better in oil-painting. This work is, of a truth, most rare and wonderful; the lights and shadows having been managed so admirably, that one can scarcely imagine it possible to produce such effects in works that have to be completed by the action of fire. And if this artist had been accorded longer life" (eighty-one years was a tolerable thread), " many other remarkable works would probably have proceeded from his hands, since, but a short time before his death, he had begun to paint figures and historical representations on a level surface."

Luca della Robbia died about thirty years before the
birth of Palissy, that is to say, in the year 1481. In 1450,
as has before been said, the manufacture of Majolica at
Pesaro had attained high excellence. It was patronised by
the Dukes of Urbino for two hundred years. Raffaelle,
born at Urbino in 1483, and dying in 1520, provided a
new name for the Majolica. It came to be called "Raffaelle
ware," under the idea that many of its rich ornaments were
painted from his designs. The scholars of Raffaelle did,
indeed, furnish designs, and supplied them sometimes
from drawings left by their great master. Compositions
by Raffaelle were also often copied upon vessels of Majolica. This was being done in the year 1540, twenty years
after Raffaelle's death. The year 1540 is the date assigned
to the first specimens of the finest Italian Majolica. It
was in the year 1540, when such things were imported
into France at a high price from Italy, that there was
shown to Palissy "an earthen cup, turned and enamelled
with so much beauty, that from that time," he says, in the
words already quoted, " he entered into controversy with
his own thoughts, and began to think that if he should
discover how to make enamels, he could make earthen
vessels and other things very prettily, because God had
gifted him with some knowledge of drawing." And, thereafter, regardless of the fact that he had no knowledge of
clays, he began to seek for the enamels as a man gropes
in the dark.

CHAPTER IX.

PALISSY RESOLVES TO CONQUER FOR HIMSELF NEW
GROUND—THE FIRST WAR FOR THE DISCOVERY OF
WHITE ENAMEL.

BENT upon intellectual conquest, Bernard Palissy set
forward with energy upon his new career. The man is to
be envied who has intellect enough to strike out boldly,
with a reasonable purpose, through the brushwood, from
the beaten track. With courage to endure all falls and
bruises incidental to a traveller on rough and unseen
ground, not too particular about that ounce of wool which
makes the difference between a whole coat and a ragged
one, not angered by the wise men on the highway who
shrug up their shoulders, or the ignorant who laugh and
hoot at him, the man who makes his own road will enjoy
sharp exercise and have a pleasant journey. No bodily
discomfort can press down as pain upon the buoyant sense
of spiritual freedom.

But men link women to their fortunes. Whoso with

lusty mind desires to fight beyond the common limits of
his time, and stand on ground through which there is to
be no road for the next fifty, hundred, or two hundred
years, should take good heed what partner he selects to
share his scratches and to see him made into a common
jest. She must either have a strength of intellect accorded
to few men and women in a generation, or a strength of
love almost as rare. Palissy married as a glass-painter—
a clever man, able in two or three odd ways to add to his
resources, and maintain a household in a lowly sphere of
life. His wife, joining him out of the same rank in society, was doubtless quite prepared to bear with him,
and to console him under all those seasons of inevitable
poverty which might arise from dearth of occupation.
But could she have imagined that a man so clever would
neglect his occupation, let his earnings become less, and
out of that less would buy pots only to break them?

"Without having heard," says Palissy, "of what materials the said enamels were composed, I pounded, in
those days, all the substances which I could suppose likely
to make anything; and having pounded and ground them,
I bought a quantity of earthen pots, and after having
broken them in pieces, I put some of the materials that I
had ground upon them, and having marked them, I set
apart in writing what drugs I had put upon each, as a me-
morandum; then, having made a furnace to my fancy, I
set the fragments down to bake."

The purchase of the drugs, the buying of the pots, the

building of the furnace, and the loss of time from customary occupation, made, of course, a very serious impression on the household purse. The wife cared naturally
more about her children than about the best of white
enamels, but she doubtless had consented with not much
reluctance to the present sacrifices. It seemed to be quite
true that if Bernard discovered the enamel, he would
make them rich: how difficult the task might be, it was
impossible to foresee: of course it would be difficult, but
then Bernard was clever. Let the old funds fall, therefore, since there really was hope of a new and rich invest-
ment.

So the old funds fell. Ordinary work was to be done
only at the call of strict necessity. The enamel when
discovered—if discovered—would be useless except as a
covering to ornamental pottery, and Palissy would have
to learn how to make that. He set himself to rival the
enamelled cups of Italy, when he would have failed in an
attempt to make the roughest pipkin. He knew nothing
of clay, and he had never even seen the inside of a pottery. He " had never seen earth baked." But what of
that ? Enamelled cups were made in Italy; why should
they not be made also in France ?

Household cares bound Palissy to home. It was requisite to abide by and support his family. Had he been free,
he could have wandered among potters, as he had already
wandered among alchemists. He could have acquired all
that was already known of pottery in France, and started

from that more advanced point on his journey through the undiscovered region. But the discovered was to him unknown. From absolute ignorance, to a point far beyond the knowledge of his time, he was to feel his way on without a teacher.

" I know," says Theory to him in one of his own dialogues,* " that you endured much poverty and pain in searching, but it will not be so with me; for that which gave you so much to endure, was the fact that you were entrusted with a wife and children. Then, while beforehand you possessed no knowledge, and were forced to guess your way, through this you were unable to quit your household to go and learn the art in some shop, and you had no means of engaging servants who might help you somewhat to discover the right way. These drawbacks were the cause of your checks and miseries; but it will not be so with me, because, according to your promise, you will tell me in writing all the means of obviating the losses and hazards of the furnace; also, the materials of which your enamels are made, and their proportions, measures, and composition. You doing so, why shall I not make pretty things without being in danger of any loss, provided that your losses serve as an example to protect and guide me in the exercising of your art?"

The first experiment was the first loss. Palissy had made a furnace in his house, which he thought likely to be suitable; and he had strewed upon many broken bits

* The Artist in Earth.

of pottery many chemical mixtures, which he then proposed to melt at furnace-heat. It was his hope, that of all
the mixtures one or two might run over the pottery,
when melted, in a form which would convey to him some
hint of the composition of the white enamel. He had been
told that white enamel was the basis of all others, and
sought only for that. " I set the fragments down to bake,"
he says, " that I might see whether my drugs were able
to produce some whitish colour: for I sought only after
white enamel, because I had heard it said that white
enamel was the basis of all others." In the selection of his
chemical ingredients, he had more than chance to guide
him. It is to be remembered, that he had been familiar
for many years with such metallic colours as are used in
glass-painting, and to a certain extent with their behaviour
when exposed to fire. Some facts, therefore, he had to
suggest hints to him in the mixing of those chemicals
which he distributed upon the bits of earthenware, and
put into his furnace, each duly marked, and a memo-
randum of the exact contents of each against a corresponding mark set down in writing.

The plan of the experiment was promising. The words
of Palissy himself will best relate and account for its repeated failure. " Then," he says, " because I had never
seen earth baked, nor could I tell by what degree of heat
the said enamel should be melted, it was impossible for me
to get any result in this way, though my chemicals should
have been right; because, at one time, the mass might have

been heated too much—at another time, too little; and when the said materials were baked too little, or burnt, I could not at all tell the reason why I met with no success, but would throw the blame on the materials, which sometimes, perhaps, were the right ones, or at least, could have afforded me some hint for the accomplishment of my intentions, if I had been able to manage the fire in the way that my materials required. But again, in working thus, I committed a fault still grosser than that above named; for in putting my trial-pieces in the furnace, I arranged them without consideration; so that if the materials had been the best in the world, and the fire also the fittest, it was impossible for any good result to follow. Thus, having blundered several times at a great expense, and through much labour, I was every day pounding and grinding new materials, and constructing new furnaces, which cost much money, and consumed my wood and my time."

Through many successive months Palissy persevered in these experiments. The building, destroying, and rebuilding of furnaces, in which the chemicals he bought with household money were always only burned and spoiled, was anxious labour. Wood was then the fuel used throughout the country. It was not too cheap ; and Bernard had to take, not only food out of his kettle, but also wood from under it, when he bought drugs and burnt them in his furnace-fire. "He fooled away," he tells us, in this manner, "several years."—"With sorrow and sighs," he adds—for the bread of his children lessened—he was weighed down by domestic care. This time was not, however, wasted. When men grope in the dark, it is by touching on all sides upon what they do not seek that they at length find what they desire. Palissy knew this well; and though his heart was troubled for the souls that waited on his industry, he steadily continued groping, and employed his old arts only for the earning of a bare subsistence, and to help him in the purchase of his chemicals. Perhaps he had already incurred some debt.

His narrow means were quite unable to support a full continuance of these experiments. If he would not be ruined long before he could attain his purpose, he must work for its attainment with economy. The most expensive part of his system, both as it regarded time and money, had been the building and rebuilding of his furnaces, the watching them, and feeding them with fuel from his kitchen. " Therefore," says Palissy, " when I had fooled away several years thus imprudently, with sorrow and sighs, because I could not at all arrive at my intention, and remembering the money spent, I resolved, in order to avoid such large expenditure, to send the chemicals that I would test to the kiln of some potter ; and having settled this within my mind, I purchased afresh several earthen vessels, and having broken them in pieces, as was my custom, I covered three or four hundred of the fragments with enamel, and sent them to a pottery distant a league and a half from my dwelling, with a request to the potters that they would please to permit those trials to be baked within some of their vessels: this they did willingly." The man who bought and broke so many pots was a good customer to potters. He was a proper man to be obliged. Probably he paid also some money for his privilege.

With how much trepidation Palissy watched the departure of his first batch of three or four hundred potshards, with a little powder sprinkled upon each,—with how much fear lest the powders be all spilt upon the way, he gave his last directions,—we may easily imagine. The arrival of the fragments in the absence of their owner was, no doubt, a great joke at the pottery. The potters, however, baked them with all due solemnity; and before the appointed time Palissy was present with a palpitating heart to wait the drawing of the batch. "But when they had baked their batch," he says, "and came to take out my trial-pieces, I received nothing but shame and loss, because they turned out good for nothing; for the fire used by those potters was not hot enough, and my trials were not put into the furnace in the required manner, and according to my science. And because I had at that time no knowledge of the reason why my experiments had not succeeded, I threw the blame (as I before said) on my materials; and——" And what? There was but one course to pursue—"beginning afresh." The man can achieve nothing who despairs. "And beginning afresh, I made a number of new compounds, and sent them to the same potters, to do with as before ; so I continued to do several

times, always with great cost, loss of time, confusion, and
sorrow."

But the family of Palissy kept pace in increase with his
perplexities. The beginning of his groping was not fortunate; in his war against difficulty he was worsted for
the present, although, of course, quite unsubdued. The
private furnace and the potter's furnace, both had failed,
and had together wasted terribly his home resources, while
the home wants had increased.

When we are foiled repeatedly in an endeavour to
adjust some point exactly to our wish, and our reiterated
attempts, at last, have brought our wits to " confusion and
sorrow," it is a common and wise practice to cease from
effort for a while—to think no more, if possible, upon the
subject which has occupied our thoughts too much. Then
when, after an interval of rest, we come back to the old
knot, it happens now and then that we untie it easily.
Considering this matter, and perceiving well how much
his family required that he should do a little steady work
on their behalf, Bernard resolved to close this his first
struggle for the discovery of white enamel. With his
own charming simplicity, Palissy himself tells us: " When
I saw that I could not at all, in this way, come at my
intention, I took relaxation for a time, occupying myself
in my art of painting and glass-working, and comported
myself as if I were not zealous to dive any more into the
secret of enamels."

CHAPTER X.

A TRUCE : THE GABELLE AND THE SALT-MARSHES OF SAINTONGE.

PROSPERITY soon came to sit in Bernard's chimney-corner. If his wife had grieved over the wasting of their home resources during that hard struggle which appeared so profitless in its result, she had her consolation now. The tide in their affairs turned rapidly. Palissy " comported himself as if he were not zealous to dive any more into the secret of enamels," and prepared heartily to resume those occupations by which he had formerly obtained a living. A bright flood of sunshine suddenly poured in to chase the gloom out of his dwelling. The time of Palissy was soon completely taken up with that which he had considered at all times the most profitable of his occupations. In consequence of an edict given from Saint Germain-en-Laye in May of the year 1543, it became necessary that the islands of Saintonge and the district surrounding the salt-marshes should be surveyed. For

K 2

this task there was no man in the diocese more competent
than Bernard Palissy. Accordingly, as he tells us—having
suspended his war for the discovery of white enamel—
" some days afterwards there arrived certain commissaries,
deputed by the king to establish the gabelle in the district of Xaintonge, who appointed me to map the islands
and the country surrounding all the salt-marshes in our
part of the world."

The Gabelle is a familiar word, connected intimately
with a very well-known story. Nevertheless, it may be
advisable, before we pass on to the illustration of this period
in the life of Palissy, to note six or eight facts concerning
that famous impost in the days when it was young, and
ascertain what aspect a gabelle presented in the year
1543 to the rough people of Saintonge.

Gabelle, meaning a tax, is a word common to many
languages; it is by no means peculiarly French, nor has
its original meaning in France, or any other country, been
confined to taxes levied upon salt.*   Formerly there were

---

* The word is in Italian, gabello; in Spanish, gabela; in German—
used only as a plural, and in certain districts—die Gabellen. In English, it used to exist as gabel. " The gabels of Naples," says Addison,
" are very high on oil, wine, and tobacco."—"This may be done," says
Bishop Taylor (Diss. from Popery, iii., § 3) "if he impose new gabels
or imposts on his subjects." (These authorities I copy from an English
dictionary.) The word is ancient. We derived it from the Anglo-
Saxon gafel, a tribute; which is from gifan, the root of our word " to
give." Gabhail, in Gaelic, means a tenure—a thing taken—being the
noun to the verb gabh, to require or take possession of. Commonly,
the word is traced down to a Hebrew root, gab, which is said by one
to mean any kind of tribute; by another, to mean a present. I greatly

gabelles in France on wine, on draperies, on cattle; six years after the date which we have now reached, and in the time of Palissy, an edict of Henry II , dated September 10, speaks of a gabelle on drugs and spices. There was also, among others, a gabelle on salt; and for the tax on this commodity, by slow degrees, the name gabelle, already in Palissy's time, was beginning to be used in France as a specific term.

It is of course only as a tax on salt that the gabelle concerns this history. There was no salt-tax at all under French kings of the first and second line. Salt-makers, on the contrary, were somewhat favoured. Charlemagne reserved to himself the task of personally settling their disputes. The seigneurs of the ninth century exercised, of course, a little profitable jurisdiction over vessels laden with salt on their domains, as in Lorraine and Franche Comté; but royal rights were not at that time in existence.

A trifling salt-tax began to appear here and there— probably not very long after the establishment, by Hugh

distrust Hebrew roots, because, when any one adduces them and errs, if he be a general authority at all respectable, his error is incessantly repeated, with few chances of detection. My own knowledge of Hebrew stops at the alphabet; but that enables me to look into a lexicon, and find (by Gesenius) that the ordinary Hebrew words for tribute are by no means gab; and that the only thing which answers to the common statement is an unused root of Arabic origin, which means, chiefly, to collect water, and, in a secondary sense, to collect tribute. I find reference also for the origin of gabelle to the Arabic cabala, which is said to mean "receipt" of anything. Perhaps it does. I give these illustrations, careless of any theory, simply to show how very far the word is from being purely French.

Capet, of the third race of kings. Immunity from a
gabelle on salt is found to occur among the privileges
given by Louis IX. (Saint Louis) to the town of Aigue-
mortes,* and he was then confirming privileges granted
in 1079 by Philip the First.

The first decree that has been found having direct reference to a gabelle on salt, speaks of it as a tax already
existing. It belongs to the reign of Philip V., who therefore commonly receives the credit of having been the inventor of one of the most oppressive taxes against which
a civilised nation ever has had reason to rebel. The first
mention of it is already ominous. The royal order bears
date February 25, 1318, and his majesty therein, " since
it had come to his knowledge that the gabelle on salt
gave much displeasure to his people," summoned his pre-
lates, barons, and so forth, to talk over that and other
matters.

The tax at that time—like our modern income-tax—
professed to be only temporary; but the people feared that
it would be permanently fastened on their backs. At the
council which he had convoked, King Philip declared that
he was quite sincere in wishing to remove the salt-tax as
soon as possible, and that he would gladly remove it on

* " Sed neque gabellæ salis, seu alterius marcimonii, possint ibi fieri
contra homines villæ." For the date and nature of any edicts, &c.,
concerning the gabelle mentioned in the text, I am indebted to either
the commercial department of the great Encyclopédie, or to the notes
and illustrations added by MM. Faujas de St. Fond and Gobet to the
quarto edition (1777) of the works of Palissy.

the instant, if better means could be devised by any one for meeting the expenses of his wars. The tax was then a small one, of two deniers upon the pound.

The next king, Philip VI. (of Valois), was compelled, by his struggles with the English, to increase the tax. On the 20th of March, 1342, he established a system for super-vision and storage of the salt, and appointed officers of the gabelle. The tax was doubled, and became four deniers upon the pound; but it was not to be perpetual. In 1350 salt is found to be included among free articles of commerce.

In 1355, the successor of Philip of Valois, John II. of France, imposed a gabelle on salt, and again doubled the tax, so that it then rose to eight deniers upon the pound. The more the people had to pay, the more they grumbled. This tax, therefore, perished ignominiously in three months, a less obnoxious measure being substituted. But John having been soon afterwards captured by the English, it became necessary to make extraordinary levies for his ransom. In 1358, the states met at Compiègne re-esta-blished the gabelle; it was extended in 1359 over some districts previously privileged, and still further extended in 1360. It was decreed that storehouses should be esta-blished in district towns for the more efficient levying of the royal rights, and that in places without storehouses the king should receive one-fifth of the selling price. In 1363, the gabelle was so strict that payment was enforced

from fishermen for salt used in salting the fish they caught,
and from dwellers on the marshes for salt used in their
own families. Preventive officers were on the watch for
all salt which changed hands without paying the king his
share of the purchase-money; such salt was confiscated,
heavy penalties were levied on offenders, and other precautions against fraud were established of a kind not likely
to be popular. He who had salt to sell must take it to
the government storehouse. There it would be sold for
him by the government officials when his turn should
come. Each storehouse was locked with three keys; the
government controller had one, the owner of the salt
another, and a notary kept the third. To avoid any col-
lusion, storekeepers and notaries were forbidden to hold
social intercourse with salt-merchants, or to receive presents or communications from them. Whether it was in
consequence or in spite of these immense precautions I
will not attempt to decide, but certainly the king found
himself defrauded of a very large portion indeed of the
gabelle he claimed.

In the year 1380, Charles VI., being pressed sorely by
his subjects, abolished the salt-tax. In the year 1382,
having quenched the tax-hating Parisians by force of arms,
he restored the gabelle on salt, which thenceforward continued unrepealed for centuries.

In Saintonge, in the year 1388, the seller paid as tax
half the price obtained for his salt on a first sale; the

same salt, whenever it was sold again, paid five sols on the pound. They who conveyed untaxed salt were liable for the offence with goods and body.

We may come now to the century with which we are especially concerned. Royalty having been greatly cheated of the dues it had thought prudent to exact on salt, found it necessary, between the years 1500 and 1508, to issue ordinances forbidding individuals to acquire exclusive right of supplying local storehouses, regulating the order in which sales should take place, and other matters. In June, 1517, the same king who still reigned in the year 1543, and under whom Palissy received his commission to survey the marshes of his neighbourhood— Francis the First—ordered that storekeepers and controllers, having charge of local storehouses for salt, should keep a register of all the people in their district by whom salt was to be bought, arranged according to their parishes. The collectors of the impost—elected by the parishes— were ordered to transmit to the storekeepers and controllers a duplicate list of the names and surnames of all the inhabitants in each parish, the number in each family, and the amount of tax assigned to it. For, whereas it is a common consequence of taxes upon articles of necessary consumption to reduce the quantity consumed, it was resolved that this gabelle should be held free from any inconvenience of that nature. The head of every family was informed how much salt the king wished him to use every year.

The storekeepers and controllers* were ordered by this edict of Francis I. to make domiciliary visits in each of their parishes ; and if they detected any one who did not procure salt from the appointed district storehouse, or did not procure the quantity proportioned to his wealth, or to the number of his family and household, the defaulter so detected was to be condemned to heavy penalties.

Up to the period of this edict, and beyond it to the year 1541, salt in the storehouses was sold for the merchants by government officials, who retained the taxes and paid over the balance to its owners. In 1541, it being found that the most stringent laws remained still powerless to prevent extensive fraud, the plan of tax-gathering was altered. Francis caused an estimate to be made of the quantity of salt yearly producible in the marshes of Languedoc, Guienne, and Bretagne. This, it will be observed, took place two years before Bernard Palissy received his commission to survey the marshes of Saintonge. It was decreed that salt should thenceforward pay tax as it was taken from the marshes. Francis hoped thus, by forestalling the opportunities of fraud, to raise a larger tax at less cost to the people. This edict abolished storehouses and all their officers; but it raised up a new set of conser-

---

* The controller was the " counter of the roll " of duty payers. Since tax-paying was of old, even more than it is now, an acknowledgment of duty over which men growl, we get a word out of the oppressive imposts of the good old times, when we say that a person is controlled, and mean that he is brought unwillingly into subjection.

vators, controllers, guards, measurers, &c., and it set a band
of spies about the salt-marshes. The merchant having
paid his tax, and obtained a permit in which his name was
written with the quantity and price of salt and receipt for
the gabelle, might go into the market when he pleased.
In the marshes of Saintonge, the right of gabelle was
equal to the market price of the salt itself; the market
price being fixed for the traders every month by the conservator, the attorney for the king, guards, and controllers.
The price of salt, therefore, was doubled to the public as
it issued from the marshes. Having once escaped into the
country, it had of course to be sold and resold in the towns
and villages. Every time it was sold it paid a tax. This
tax was no less than a quarter of the price obtained on each
occasion. Upon each fresh sale, therefore, by which the
original mass of salt brought from the marshes was dispersed among retailers, its price augmented terribly; and
when it got into the lanes and villages, it was precisely to
the poorest people in the land that the salt had to be sold
at its highest artificial price. No sales were allowed in any
place where there were not officers provided to enforce
the payment of " the king's quarter."

But with all this reckless energy of taxation, difficulties
and diversities and frauds still perplexed the tax-receiver.
In the very next year, 1542, Francis was altering his
plans; and in April, lowering the home tax, in consideration that he meant thenceforward to levy also upon
foreigners. He ordered, in fact, one uniform tax to be

levied on all salt sold or bartered at the *salines* and marshes of Bretagne, Poitou, Saintonge, the town and government of Rochelle, Guienne, Picardy, Normandy, Languedoc, Provence, Dauphiné, and other provinces and places of the kingdom, " with whatever persons it might be, his subjects or others, excepting none."

The taxation was then obviously mad. The salt merchants and proprietors of marshes humbly represented that if salt for exportation was to pay gabelle, there would be no salt exported, so the king would gain nothing, while their commerce would be lost; the same law, if not repealed, put a complete stop to the fisheries. This having been made clear to the royal comprehension, there was a new decree made on the 29th of May, 1543. A small tax was imposed, instead of the gabelle, on salt taken by foreigners. The fishers of Saintonge, &c., were freed from the gabelle for salt taken from the marsh for use in their own trade. The proprietors of marshes residing on the spot, or within ten leagues of it, were honoured with permission to retain a fixed quantity of their own salt untaxed for domestic use. The inhabitants of Bretagne were exempted from gabelle on salt used for their own consumption. The gabelle, which had been reduced with the design of making foreigners enjoy a share of it, had again to be raised at home; and leave was given, when the whole amount of salt-tax payable by any one person was high, that it should be paid in four equal instalments. It was in this decree that for the securing of the rights of

gabelle in Saintonge a survey of that district was commanded. The conservator of Saintonge, governor of Rochelle, with his notary, were established for the first time
at Saintes, and Bernard Palissy received then his commission to prepare a map.

I may add, that in the same year, 1543, the old system
of district storehouses was re-established, and officers appointed in the old way to conduct the sales. How the
people of Saintonge—who were not of the civillest—liked
these arrangements, will be seen as we pursue the narrative; to which we now return.

While we are contemplating the first struggles of Bernard Palissy towards the discovery of white enamel, and
noting some of the embarrassments occasioned by his poverty, we must not omit to consider that his energetic
efforts to dive into one secret of art did not suffice to fill
or satisfy his mind. Bernard was too good an economist
to spend a life on any one idea. His quick eye and shrewd
wit were ever busy on the mysteries of Nature. Ignorant
man as he was—happily ignorant—in all the learning of
the schools, he had observed the chemists and the schoolmen quite enough to see that, as naturalists, they were all
lost in a wilderness of theory. Palissy being gifted with
the perfect temper of a naturalist—being, in the words of
Buffon before quoted, " so great a naturalist as Nature
only can produce"—with wonderful simplicity and strength
of mind (qualities essentially allied) devoted himself
wholly to experiment and observation. With a mind of

the finest philosophic quality, unprejudiced by any theory,
Palissy observed minutely all the ways of Nature, reasoned
upon them with natural vigour, and in those matters upon
which he reasoned thus, he in the end outstripped by a
century or two the knowledge of his contemporaries. At
this stage of our narrative we must not lose sight of the
fact that Palissy, while he was searching for the white
enamel, and while he was measuring the marshes of Saintonge, was at the same time watching assiduously the ways
of Nature, and reasoning upon her mysteries with patient
care.

Of the profitable task assigned to him by the commissioners of the gabelle, Palissy has left us some memorial in
an account of the salt-marshes of Saintonge. The subject
of salt seems to have been one of the first which had arrested
his attention as a naturalist; and as, in stating his opinions
about it, he draws frequent illustration from experience
acquired during his early travels, there is good reason to
suppose that in the year 1543, at which our narrative now
stands, Palissy had already arrived at some of those con-
clusions which he afterwards developed in his writings.
Since he himself takes care to place before his account of
the salt-marshes* his theory concerning salts,† it may be

---

* In an article, *Du Sel Commun*. None of the treatises by Palissy
ever exceed the length of an article in one of our quarterly reviews, or
volumes of philosophical transactions. When he had written six or
eight, he published them.

† *Des Sels Divers*. This and the treatise upon common salt are not
contained in the selection from his writings added to the present
volumes.

advisable, before we pass to his survey of the salt-marshes,
to indicate, by a few sentences, how far his unassisted wit
was taking him beyond the knowledge of his day. Remembering that he lived when there were said to be four
elements, and two hundred and fifty years before there
was any philosophic chemistry, let us see what sort of
self-taught science could be talked by the illiterate glass-
painter.

Using the form of dialogue and the name of " Practice," by which he commonly distinguishes his views from
those of the schoolmen, he astonishes " Theory" by speaking of plurality of salts, and says: " I tell you that there
is so great a number of them, that it is impossible for any
man to name them all; and tell you further, that there is
nothing in this world which has no salt in it, whether it
be in man, the beast, the trees, plants, or other vegetative
things, or even in the very metals; and tell you yet more,
that no vegetative things could grow without the action
of salt, which is in seeds; what is more, if salt were taken
from the body of a man, he would fall to powder in less
than the winking of an eye. If the salt were separated
from the stones that are in buildings, they would fall suddenly to powder." . . . . " Copperas is a salt, nitre is a
salt, vitriol is a salt, alum is a salt, borax is a salt, sugar
is a salt,* sublimate, saltpetre, &c. . . . . all those are

---

* The Malagasy call sugar " sweet salt." The word "salt," as used
by Palissy, does not of course correspond exactly with its use by chemists in our own day. In each case it is an arbitrary term, applied to

different salts; were I to name them all, I never should have done." . . . . "You must not suppose that the ashes of plants have power to blanch linen except by virtue of their salts; otherwise they would admit of being used several times. But inasmuch as the salt in the said ashes comes to dissolve in the water that is put into the copper, it passes through the linen," &c., &c. " Salt bleaches everything: salt hardens everything: it preserves everything: it gives savour to everything: it is a mastic which binds everything: it collects and unites mineral matters, and of many thousand pieces makes one mass. Salt gives sound to everything: without salt no metal would yield a voice. Salt rejoices human beings: it whitens the flesh, giving beauty to reasonable creatures: it preserves friendship between the male and female, by the vigour given to the sexes: it gives voice to creatures as to metals. Salt causes many flints, when finely powdered, to combine into a mass, forming glass and all kinds of vessels: by salt, all things can be converted into a translucent body. Salt causes all seeds to vegetate and grow.

" And though there be few people enough who know the reason why manure is of service to the seeds, and they are induced to bring it only by habit, not by philosophy,

a class of things. A comparison between the knowledge of Palissy and that of his own time and ours respectively, belongs to a later por-tion of this book. The extracts in the text serve only to indicate the progress of his mind, and the direction it was taking.

yet so it is, that the manure carried to the fields would be quite useless, if it were not for the salt which the straw and the hay deposited in rotting : wherefore they who leave manure-heaps at the mercy of the rains are very bad managers, and have neither acquired nor innate philosophy. For the rains which fall upon the heaps, running off down any declivity, carry with them the salts of the said manure, which will have been dissolved by the moisture, and on this account it will no longer be useful when it is taken to the fields. The thing is easy enough to believe; and if you will not believe it, watch when the labourer shall have carried manure into his field; he will put it, when unloading, into little piles, and he will come after a few days to scatter it about the field, and will leave none on the spots where the said piles have been; and for all that, when such a field shall have been sown with grain, you will find that the grain will be finer, greener, thicker, on the places where those piles had rested, than in any other part; and that happens, because the rains which fell upon the said hillocks, took with them the salt in passing through and descending to the earth; by that you may know that it is not the straw which is the cause of generation, but the salt which the seeds obtained out of the ground." . . . . " By that, too, you will understand the reason why all excrements can aid in the generation of seeds." . . . . " When God formed the earth, he filled it with all kinds of seeds: but if any one sows a field for

many years without manuring it, the seeds will draw the
salt from the earth for their increase, and the earth, by
this means, will find itself deprived of salt, and will be
able to produce no more; wherefore it must be manured,
or left at rest some years, in order that it may regain some
salsitude proceeding from the rains or snows. For all
earths are earths, but some abound much more in salts
than others. I do not here speak only of a common salt,
but of salts that are vegetative."

Professor Liebig comes to our mind in reading passages
like this. But Liebig is a chemist highly trained in the
knowledge of our own day. Palissy was an illiterate man
of genius, born of humble parents, in a miserable state of
human society, three centuries ago.

We may now take part with "Theory," and say to
Palissy: "Describe to us the way of making common
salt, as it is practised in the Islands of Xaintonge, and
show us a plan of the form after which the salt-marshes
are made: for you know it very well; since we have
heard it said that formerly you were upon the spot, with
commission to make a plan of the said marshes."

"That is quite true," Palissy answers;* "it was at the

* I translate the account literally from Palissy's article, "*Du Sel
Commun*," omitting only a few passages for want of space. I preserve,
also, the method of punctuation employed by Palissy in what he calls
his "rustic style." The punctuation employed by an untaught writer
depends a good deal upon his cast of mind. When I call the style of
Palissy untaught, I ought to add, that the reader will, in the course of
these volumes, have full opportunity of judging whether its fresh
vigour, liveliness, and grace, have any need of artificial polish.

time when they resolved to establish the gabelle in the said country. Now since you desire to understand these things, let me have audience, and I will cheerfully give you an account of them, and then I will let you see a plan.

" In the first place you must understand that inasmuch as the sea is almost entirely bounded by great rocks, or lands higher than the sea, for making the salt-marshes, it has been necessary to find some plain lower than the sea: for otherwise it would have been impossible to find means of making salt by the heat of the sun: and it must be believed that if there had been found in any other part of France bordering on the sea, a spot proper for forming marshes, there would be such things in many places. Now it is not sufficient to have found a plain or country lower than the sea: but it is also requisite that the earths on which one proposes to establish marshes be tenacious, clammy or viscid like those of which are made pots, bricks, and tiles.

" There is a seigneur of Antwerp who has spent a great deal upon the endeavour to make marshes in the Netherlands, according to the form and semblance of those in the islands of Saintonge: but though he has found plenty of low ground upon which he can bring the water of the sea, notwithstanding this, since the earth was not clammy or tenacious like that of Saintonge, he could not succeed in his intention, and his expenses have been lost: because the earths which he caused to be dug for the forming of

L 2

the said marshes being dry and sandy, were unable to contain the water.*

" Although our predecessors of the Saintonic islands have found certain flat or low grounds on the margin of the sea, and the earths at their foundation have been found naturally clammy or argillaceous, yet that has not sufficed for the attainment of their design: for it has been necessary to invent a way of beating the said earth in the manner which I will explain to you hereafter.

" If our said predecessors had not used great judgment and consideration in forming the salt-marshes, they would have done nothing that would have been of value: having then considered upon the grounds lower than the sea, they found that it was necessary to cut a channel which might bring readily the sea-water to the desired spots, for the making of the salt. Having thus dug certain channels they caused the sea-water to come into a great receptacle which they named the IARD:† and having made a

---

* The seigneur of Antwerp was a Marquis de Rhien; and how much it was worth his while to make an effort for the establishment of a salt-marsh on his own domain, is illustrated by the statistics that occur in a *Description des Pays Bas*, by Guichardin, printed in French, at Antwerp, in 1582. The town of Antwerp then paid to France 198,000 dollars annually for salt from Brouage. The price was at the rate of about three dollars for an English ton.

† The editors of the quarto edition of 1777, rightly considering that the words of the provincial salt-makers would convey no meaning by themselves to ordinary Frenchmen, and still less to foreigners, have illustrated the terms used among the marshes of Saintonge, by an extract from a book which I should have been very glad to have used frequently in illustration of this narrative, if it had been procurable. It is a description, in Latin, of Saintonge, by Nicolas Alain, a physician

sluice to the said IARD, they made at the end of the same
other great receptacles which they named CONCHS*, into
which they allow the water of the Iard to run in limited
quantity, and from these conchs they cause the water to
pass" through sieves of pierced planks, and by very tor-
tuous passages descending slowly by a series of steps, that
it may finally arrive, after much evaporation, in the great
square of the salt-marsh.

" These things have not been made without great labour
and expense of time, it has been necessary to excavate the
square of the marsh-field at a level lower than the canal
coming from the sea, lower also than the Iards and Conchs,
in order to give slope or inclination to the steps and parts
above named in order to convey the water into the great
square of the marsh.   And it must be noted that in hol-
lowing this great square, it has been requisite to heap the
earth and rubbish all about the border of the said square,
which being put about the border makes there a great
platform which they call BOSSIS,† upon which they are

at Saintes, while Palissy resided there. The book was written by
Nicolas "during the first troubles," and published by his son Jean, a
lawyer, in 1598. Its style and title is " De Santonum Regione et Illus-
trioribus Familiis,—in 4to. form. min. Santonibus apud Franciscum
Audebertum. From the pages of this work, reprinted in the Quarto
Palissy, I append such illustrations as I find of the terms used in salt-
making. The great receptacle, which Palissy calls Iard, Alain calls
Jacos, perhaps for the sake of adding a classical derivation—" fortassè
quod illîc immota aqua *jaceat.*"
     * " Quas à concharum cavitate similitudineque, *Conchas* appellant."
—*Nicolas Alain.*
     † "Quod quia extuberascit et intumescit, Galli ut id genus alia
Bossiam, quasi tumorem indicantes, vocant."—*Nicolas Alain.*

able to put great mounds of salt, called cows of salt* (VACHES DE SEL); and when it happens in winter that the season for making salt is passed they cover the said mounds of salt with rushes, which have a good sale on account of their utility. The said Bossis serve also in going from marsh to marsh for the passage of men and horses at all times: and it is requisite that they should be of a great size, because when any one has sold a cow or two of salt, according to the distance at which the salt lies for carrying into the ship, it is necessary for those in distant places to use a great number of beasts to carry the salt on board, and that is done with a marvellous diligence, so that one might say, who had never seen it done before, that they were squadrons bent upon fighting one another. There are people on board the vessel who do nothing but empty the sacks, and another marks, and each beast carries but one sack at a time ; and those who drive the horses are commonly little boys, who directly the horse is unloaded and the salt discharged, throw themselves with speed upon the horse, and do not cease to gallop posthaste to the cow of salt, where there are other men who fill the sacks and load them upon the horses, and being reloaded the said boys lead them back promptly to the vessel. And inasmuch as from one side and the other all go and come busily, it is requisite that the said Bossis or platforms should be tolerably large, or else the horses would impede each other.

* Are they related to the pigs of lead ?

" Understand now the industry which it has been requisite to use in making the marshes fit, so that the earth shall not absorb the water put there to deposit salt. When the great square has been scooped and the rubbish cleared from it, before the steps and ways are made by which it is connected with the Iard, they have a number of horses and mares, which they fasten to one another so that they may be led, then they put them into the said great square where they wish to form the marshes. There is a person who holds the first horse by one hand, and has in the other hand a whip, who busily leads about the said horses and mares, until the earth underfoot has been well stamped and is able to hold water as if it were of brass . . . . After the earth has been thus stamped they form their" (connecting channels, &c., from the Iard), " as if they moulded them in potter's earth: you see now why I before told you that though one could find places lower than the sea, it would be impossible to prepare salt-marshes if the earth were not naturally argillaceous or viscid, like that of the potters.

" There is another great labour which our predecessors have found it proper to undertake in preparing the marshes ; there can be no doubt that the first who formed them chose places as close as possible to some natural channel: for if there were no channel it would be difficult to bring the salt made on the marshes to the ship in the great sea, because great ships cannot approach the coast by reason of their size ; wherefore they who sell salt, take little barks which penetrate the flat country and come as near as they can to the salt which has been sold ; they cast anchor, and so the said salt is brought first into the bark, then the said bark is taken to discharge into the ship: and it is to be noted that most frequently, by certain channels, entrance can be made only at high water: and to pass out, if the sea has retired, it becomes necessary to wait for the tide.

" And though some natural channels have been found, notwithstanding this it has been necessary to aid nature: in order that the barks and little vessels may approach the places where the salt is made: and it is not to be doubted that our predecessors have also been constrained to form channels in places where they did not exist by nature: for otherwise they could not get the salt out of the said marshes. Therefore it all looks like a labyrinth, and one could not pass to the distance of a league without travelling six, because of the deviations one would have to make: and if any stranger were enclosed there, he would scarcely find a way out without a guide: because he would have to find a great number of bridges, which he must seek one to the left another to the right, sometimes in a direction exactly opposite to that in which he is going: for it must be understood that all the plain of the marshes is hollowed into canals, jards, conchs, or marsh-fields ; some of the said fields are square, and others long and narrow, others run aslant: in order that all the ground may be employed in the formation of marshes: just as in

a town the first builders have commonly taken a place
squared according to their own convenience, and the last
have occupied the nooks and vacancies left by the others,
as they were to be found. The like has happened in the
marshes ; for the first have occupied a place at their convenience as near as possible to the great channels and to
the sea, and the last comers have taken places not exactly
such as they desired, but they have formed their ground
sometimes on spots vèry distant from the channels and
the sea-coast, for which reason they find fewer purchasers:
inasmuch as the cost of carrying their salt becomes too
great.

" Others have constructed marshes of little value, because very often the water fails them at the time of
greatest need, inasmuch as the channels, jards, and conchs
are not low enough in their level to receive sea-water
always when they want it ; and a singular point has here
to be noted, which is that in each marsh there is a canal
made by labour of men, to bring the sea-water into the
Iard, and other channels like small rivers, which serve for
the passage of barks between the several marshes, in which
they carry the salt to the great ship as I said before.

" By such means all the earth of the valley of the
marshes is laboured, dug and trenched for the use and
service of the said salt, and for these causes I have said
already that if a stranger were in the midst of the marshes,
though he could see the spot which he desired to reach,
he scarcely could arrive at it: inasmuch as very often

he must travel back to look for the bridges: also because
he has no road or way except upon the Bossis, which are
built in oblique lines, and it is not possible to find road or
way in the said marshes other than the Bossis, which
have been built high because the soil dug from all the
marsh-fields has been heaped there ; and if one were there
in winter one would see all the said fields covered with
water like great lakes, without any appearance of their
form.   On this account some painters, when they had
been sent into these isles to know the reason why it is
impossible for an army to march over the said salt-marshes,
have been deceived: inasmuch as they visited them in the
season when the water was spread over the said marshes,
and took back with them inaccurate plans."

Palissy proceeds to relate how this happened to a certain
Master Charles, whom he calls an excellent painter. It is
very probable that inaccuracies and inconsistencies prevailing in the maps formerly supplied to government, had
partly caused the order for that fresh survey upon which
Bernard had been occupied. The marshes were flooded
every winter, in order that the dikes and passages formed
in the clay, being protected under water, might not suffer
from the destructive bite of frost. The custom of flooding
thus saved to the proprietors, yearly, a very large sum for
repairs.

The salt was (and is) made by evaporation during the
hot months, the season extending from the middle of May
to the middle of September. Upon the details given by

Palissy on the subject of salt-making we must not dwell.
They are not less distinctly set forth in his treatise than
the view of the marshes, which he has painted for us in
his own methodical and lively way. It must suffice for us
to note, that the jards were replenished twice in the season,
during the high tides of March and July; so that if an
unusually hot summer chanced to dissipate the store,
there was a loss of time and money. In a wet summer no
salt could be made. If, during a whole day or night, rain
fell upon salt drying in the marsh-field, Palissy informs
us, "even if the rain lasted two hours, no salt could be
made for fifteen days afterwards,—because it would be
necessary to cleanse the marshes and to take all the water
from them, as well the salted as the fresh,—so that if it
were to rain once in every fifteen days, salt could never
be made by the heat of the sun: wherefore we must
believe that in rainy and cold countries salt could not be
made as it is made in the islands of Xaintonge, even
though they possessed all the conveniences already mentioned."

Palissy also takes some pains to point out the vast
quantity of wood dispersed between the embankments and
among the labyrinth of marshes, in the form of gigantic
sluices, bridges, beam-partitions, and sieves; much of it
consisting of the very largest timbers. "I tell you this,"
he adds, "that you may understand that the wood in the
marshes being rotted or burnt, the forests of Guienne
would not suffice to replace it. And there is no man

having seen the labour of all the marshes of Xaintonge,
who would not judge that it has cost more expense to
form them, than would be necessary for the building of a
second town of Paris." This last fact will appear less
startling, when we remember that, three centuries ago,
Paris was not by any means a capital which we should
now call large. But at that time the labyrinth of marshes
in Saintonge formed the most important source of salt in
Europe. During three centuries the salt-marshes of
Saintonge have decayed in fame and substance; they
were long since distanced in competition by the salt-
marshes of Brittany. In the mean time, Paris has become
a place which all the world is learning to regard with
wonder. So that, in truth, we could afford anything
rather than the building of a second town of Paris.

From the account which Palissy has given of the marsh-
district, we may perceive that it involved no slight labour
to survey it accurately. Hard at work during the dry
season of 1543, and mapping the adjacent towns and
villages during the winter, when the marshes were all
flooded,—Palissy brought his work to a conclusion certainly before Midsummer in the succeeding year. An
edict of St. Maur des Fosses, dated in July, 1544, is
subsequent to the completion of the survey.

" Then," says Palissy, " when the said commission was
ended, and I found myself paid with a little money, I
resumed my affection for pursuing in the track of the
enamels."

CHAPTER XI.

SECOND PALISSIAN WAR FOR THE DISCOVERY OF
WHITE ENAMEL.

UNDAUNTED by the failure of his early efforts, and relieved for a while from care about his household bread, Palissy no longer " comported himself as if he were not zealous to dive into the secret of enamels." If the thrifty wife had calculated upon long possession of a hoard of money, retained from the profits of the marsh-surveying, to which she could have recourse at any season of unusual pressure, she was quickly undeceived. Let us not spend all our admiration on the inflexible energy with which we shall find Bernard Palissy battling his way on through adversity; sympathy is due to her who, as his wife, stood by him in the contest, sharing all the blows he suffered, unable to comprehend the battle that he waged. If she repined a little when she looked down on her ragged dress, during the years of struggle, and knew that her husband could have earned her bravery and ribbons ; if she complained much when she saw her children hungry, can we say that she was weak. The first act which Bernard chronicles, as opening the second war for the discovery of white enamel, was of a kind likely to terrify the most placid of wives,—" I broke about three dozen earthen pots—all of them new."

His home-made furnaces had failed, and potters' furnaces had failed, because they were not hot enough. The next step was to try the furnaces used by glass-workers, resuming his old method of experiment, now that he could again buy earthenware to break and chemicals to burn. " Seeing," Bernard says, " that I had been able to do nothing, whether in my own furnaces or in those of the before-mentioned potters, I broke about three dozen earthen pots, all of them new; and having ground a large quantity of different materials, I covered all the bits of the said pots with my chemicals, laid on with a brush; but you should understand that in two or three hundred of those pieces, there were only three covered with each kind of compound. Having done this, I took all these pieces and carried them to a glass-house, in order to see whether my chemicals and compounds might not prove good when tried in a glass-furnace." By covering three separate fragments with each compound that he thought likely to melt into a white enamel, Palissy hoped that— these being in different positions in the furnace, and subject to such variations as there might be in the heat—he was securing to himself a fair chance of success with one

fragment in every three. But at the same time, groping as he
was in the dark, he knew that there was little promise of a
satisfactory result unless he felt his way abundantly, sub-
mitting to the test about a hundred guesses at a time.
One of the hundred, he might reasonably hope, would
direct him on the road to what he sought. Up to this
point his experiments had failed in the first necessary
stage of getting his drugs properly melted; but the glass-
furnace on which Bernard now depended for assistance,
cheered him on immediately with a ray of hope. He had
sent his first batch of trial-pieces to the glass-house.
"Then," he tells us, "since these furnaces are much
hotter than those of potters, the next day when I had
them drawn out, I observed that some of my compounds
had begun to melt ; and for this cause I was still more
encouraged to search for the white enamel, upon which I
had spent so much labour."

No more encouragement was needed. "This little
symptom, which I then perceived," says Palissy, " caused
me to work for the discovery of the said white enamel for
two years beyond the time already mentioned, during
which two years I did nothing but go and come between
my house and the adjacent glass-houses, aiming to succeed
in my intentions:" two years of zealous labour without
visible result ; two years of idleness, as the world reckons
industry: for Palissy, labouring rarely in his former calling, consumed the profits of his labour on the marshes,
and saw his home falling again into decay. Still children

were being born to him, and one or two he had seen buried. Yet through anxiety and mourning he worked on, upon no higher encouragement than the discovery that he could now sometimes get his chemicals to melt. So during two years he bought pots and broke them, he bought drugs and burnt them, and did nothing but go and come between his own house and the adjacent glass-houses. To force a path into the unknown is toilsome labour; but when the intellect is active with an innate sense of strength, it feels in its own way as a man feels who is vigorous in muscle, and prefers a tour on foot among the mountains to a morning's ride in the old family coach.

But Palissy was poor. He had a wife and children, for whose well-being he had made himself responsible. His domestic argument was of an obvious character:—Dear wife, I vex you now; but you know well that glass-painting is little patronised, and that our living would be scanty to the last if I adhered to my old callings. Stand by me now through a year or two of poverty; let us submit to privation, and get through the dark days as we can; for when I have discovered the enamel, as I surely shall if I still persevere in seeking for it, you can be the best-dressed woman in the town of Saintes, and we can put our sons into good trades or into farms, and we can give dowries to our daughters. With such arguments the wife's ear could be satisfied for a few months; but when the months multiplied and grew to years, and still the present facts were poverty and hope,—when Bernard's hope was daily made to appear inconsistent with his daily crosses, how could her satisfaction last? Bernard had a sanguine temperament, which was not to be trusted, modern wives would say; and it would be their duty to fight against it, and, if possible, to check him on the road to ruin. Thoughts of this kind clouded about the temper of the wife of Palissy. She could not understand the energy of will which converts hope into foreknowledge, and the bold instinct of power which hangs that hope so high above the common estimate of human reach, in the true man of genius.

During two years, then, after the discovery that he could sometimes get his chemicals to melt when they were put into a glass-furnace, he pursued his experiments without success, and equally without fatigue. And then again, the urgent cares of home bade him desist. He determined, therefore, to send one last batch of trial-pieces to the furnace, and if that should, as usual, lead to no good practical result, he would pause while he devoted himself wholly to his early trades, and to the present small, rather than the future great well-being of his family. But since this trial was to be his last, he was resolved that he would not give up his search easily, but close with an unusual effort. He broke more pots than ever, purchased a still greater variety of drugs and chemicals, and made no less than three hundred different mixtures, each of which might possibly contain the substances used in the cover-

ing of the enamelled cup. Having placed these, each on
its own piece of broken pottery, duly marked and regis-
tered, he walked beside the man who carried them to the
glass-furnace. He had no longer courage to support the
sight of that domestic poverty which his experiments had
caused: yet it was grievous to give up the struggle—not
the less grievous because it had cost so much—before he
had justified his efforts by success. The trial-pieces were
all put into the furnace; and by the furnace-mouth sat
Palissy, determined to watch through all stages the
success of this, his last attempt.

On such moments in a life the mind dwells as upon the
recollection of a picture. We see the glow of the furnace,
through the two mouths by which it is fed, upon the walls
of the surrounding hovel. We have a glimpse of some rich
foliage, with broken bits of sunbeam scattered over it, as a
glass-worker enters by the hovel-door, bringing in billets
from the wood to feed the fire. Three or four men of Saintonge are occupied about the place, rough, coarsely-featured
men, whose flesh is in strong contrast with the spirit that
looks out of the face of Bernard, anxious and very still.
Bernard Palissy, a man in the full strength of life, aged
about thirty-seven, with a vigorous frame, paled and thin-
ned by care, sits on a heap of fagots, sometimes laughing
with the men, to cover his anxiety, at other times reverting with a fixed gaze to the furnace-mouth. During four
hours he has waited there. The furnace is opened, and
his whole form is shining with a bright glow from the

molten glass, as his eyes run over his regiment of pot-shards. The material on one of them is melted, and that piece being taken out, is set aside to cool. The furnace is closed, and Palissy has now to watch the cooling of that compound which had been so quickly melted ; not with great hope at first; but as it hardens—it grows white! All that was black in the thoughts of Palissy begins to whiten with it. It is cold. It is "white and polished;"—a white enamel, "singularly beautiful."

A crowd of cares were nesting in the mind of Palissy when he went with his trial-pieces to the furnace; they all fly away—perhaps like pigeons, only to settle again—at any rate, they fly away, and Palissy goes back to his poor home over the meadows, carrying the white enamelled potshard in his hand, to tell good tidings to his wife, and bid her share his triumph as she had shared too often his defeats. In what way he told the story to his wife, we do not know; to us he tells it thus: "God willed that when I had begun to lose my courage, and was gone for the last time to a glass-furnace, having a man with me carrying more than three hundred kinds of trial-pieces, there was one among those pieces which was melted within four hours after it had been placed in the furnace, which trial turned out white and polished, in a way that caused me such joy as made me think I was become a new creature."

This took place in the year 1546, Palissy then being, as I before said, about thirty-seven years old. "I thought," he says, "that from that time I had the full perfection of

M 2

the white enamel, but I was very far from having what
I thought. This trial was a very happy one in one
sense, but very unhappy in another: happy, because it
gave me entrance upon the ground which I have since
gained ; but unhappy, because it was not made with substances in the right measure or proportion."

His wife found reason to consider it unhappy in another
sense. The pressure of extreme poverty had forced him
to resolve that he would confine his investigations to one
other trial. The success of that trial urged him onward,
set aside his design to return to his old business, encouraged
him (and perhaps in the first instance, his wife also) to increased endurance, while he laboured with more zeal than
ever,—for he sought now to turn the knowledge, earned
with so much pain, to practical advantage. He still had
all to learn; experience had yet to teach him that his past
labours were light, compared with the difficulties which
were yet to be surmounted before he should have learnt
to rival the enamelled cups of Italy.

Henceforth his work was to be private, and he was to
produce very soon, he believed, illustrious results. A
furnace like that of the glass-workers sufficed, as it was
proved, for the melting of his enamel. He must have
such a furnace in his house, or rather in a shed appended
to his house, which at that time certainly was situated in
the suburbs of the town. But they were miserably poor.
Bernard having found means to obtain bricks, perhaps
upon the credit of his future earnings, could not afford to

hire a cart for their delivery upon his premises; he was
compelled to journey to the brickfield, and to bring them
home on his own back. He could pay no man for the building of the furnace; he collected the materials for his mortar,
drawing for himself the water at the well; he was brick-
layer's boy and mason to himself; and so with incessant
toil he built his furnace, having reason to be familiar with
all its bricks. The furnace having been at length constructed, the cups that were to be enamelled were immediately ready. Between the discovery of the white enamel
and the commencement of the furnace there had elapsed a
period of seven or eight months, which he had occupied
in experiments upon clay, and in the elaborate shaping of
clay vessels that were to be in due time baked and enamelled, and thereafter, on the surface of the enamel, ele-
gantly painted. The preliminary baking of these vessels
in the furnace was quite prosperous.

Then the successful mixture for the white enamel had
to be tried on a large scale—such a mixture as that which
Luca della Robbia had found " after experiments innumerable." Its proportions we do not know; but the materials
used include, Palissy tells us, preparations of tin, lead,
iron, antimony, manganese, and copper,* each of which
must exist in a fixed proportion. The materials for his

---

* " The enamels which I use are made of tin, lead, iron, steel, antimony, sapphire (sulphate) of copper, sand, ashes of tartar, litharge,
stone of Perigord (manganese). These are the materials proper for the
making of my enamels."

enamel Palissy had now to grind, and this work occupied
him longer than a month without remission, beginning
the days very early, ending them very late. Poverty
pressed him to be quick; intellectual anxiety to witness a
result was not less instant in compelling him to labour.
The labour of the grinding did not consist only in the
reduction of each ingredient to the finest powder. When
ground, they were to be weighed and put together in the
just proportions, and then, by a fresh series of poundings
and grindings, they were to be very accurately mixed. The
mixture was made, the vessels were coated with it. To
heat the furnace was the next task ; it had to be far hotter
than it was when it had baked his clays—as hot, if possible, as the never-extinguished fires used by the glass-
workers. But Bernard's fire had been extinct during
the days of grinding: poverty could not spare a month's
apparent waste of fuel.

Bernard lighted then his furnace-fire, by two mouths,
as he had seen to be the custom at the glass-houses. He
put his vessels in, that the enamel might melt over them.
He did not spare his wood. If his composition really did
melt—if it did run over his vessels in a coat of that same
white and singularly beautiful enamel which he had
brought home in triumph from the glass-house—then
there would be no more disappointments, no more hungry
looks to fear; the prize would then be won. Palissy did
not spare his wood ; he diligently fed his fire all day. he
diligently fed his fire all night. The enamel did not melt.

The sun broke in upon his labour, his children brought him portions of the scanty household meals, the scantiness impelled him to heap on more wood, the sun set, and through the dark night, by the blaze and crackle of the furnace, Palissy worked on. The enamel did not melt. Another day broke over him: pale, haggard, half-stripped, bathed in perspiration, he still fed the furnace-fire, but the enamel had not melted. For the third night his wife went to bed alone, with terrible misgivings. A fourth day and a fourth night, and a fifth and sixth—six days and nights were spent about the glowing furnace, each day more desperately indefatigable in its labour than the last; but the enamel had not melted.

It had not melted; that did not imply that it was not the white enamel. A little more of the flux used to aid the melting of a metal, might have made the difference, thought Palissy. "Although," he says, "quite stupefied with labour, I counselled to myself that in my enamel there might be too little of the substance which should make the others melt; and seeing this——" What then? not, "I regretted greatly the omission;" but, "I began, once more, to pound and grind the beforenamed materials, all the time without letting my furnace cool; in this way I had double labour, to pound, grind, and maintain the fire." He could hire no man to feed the fire while he was sleeping, and so, after six days and nights of unremitting toil, which had succeeded to a month of severe labour, for two or three weeks more Palissy still devoted himself

to the all-important task. The labour of years might be
now crowned with success, if he could persevere. Stupefied, therefore, with a labour under which many a weaker
body would have yielded, though the spirit had maintained
its unconquerable temper, Palissy did not hesitate, without an hour's delay, to begin his entire work afresh.
Sleeping by minutes at a time, that he might not allow
the supply to fail of fresh wood heaped into the furnace,
Palissy ground and pounded, and corrected what he
thought was his mistake in the proportions of the flux.
There was great hope in the next trial; for the furnace,
having been so long alight, would be much hotter than it
was before, while at the same time the enamel would be in
itself more prompt to melt. All his own vessels having
been spoiled—the result of seven months' labour in the
moulding,—Palissy went out into the town, when his fresh
enamel was made ready, and purchased pots on which to
make proof of the corrected compound.

For more than three weeks Palissy had been imprisoned
in the outhouse with his furnace, haggard, weary, unsuccessful, but not conquered yet, his position really justifying hope. But the vessels which his wife had seen him
spend seven months in making, lay before her spoilt; the
enamel had not melted; appearances were wholly against
hope to her as an observer from without. Bernard had
borrowed money for his last experiments: they were worse
than moneyless, they were in debt. The wood was going,
the hope of food was almost gone. Bernard was working

at the furnace, desperately pouring in fresh wood; his wife sat in the house, overwhelmed with despair. Could it lessen her despair that there was no result when all the stock of wood was gone, and, wanting money to buy more, she vainly strove to hinder Palissy from tearing up the palings of their garden, that he might go on with a work which had already ruined them.

Bernard knew well how much depended on his perseverance then. There was distinct and fair hope that the melting of his present mixture would produce enamelled vessels. If it should do this, he was safe. Though in themselves, since he now had mere jugs and pipkins to enamel, they might not repay his labour, yet it sufficed that they would prove his case—justify all his zeal before the world, and make it clear to all men that he had a secret which would earn for him an ample livelihood. Upon the credit of his great discovery from that day forward he could easily sustain his family, until he should have time to produce its next results. The furnace, at a large expense of fuel, was then fully heated; his new vessels had been long subjected to its fire: in ten minutes— twenty minutes—the enamel might melt. If it required a longer time, still it was certain that a billet in that hour was of more value than a stack of wood could be after the furnace had grown cold again.

So Bernard felt; but any words of his, to his wife's ear, would only sound like the old phrases of fruitless hope. The labour and the money perilled for the last nine months, were represented by the spoiled vessels in the outhouse; they were utterly lost. The palings were burnt in vain; the enamel had not melted. There was a crashing in the house; the children were in dismay, the wife, assisted doubtless by such female friends as had dropped in to comfort her, now became loud in her reproach. Bernard was breaking up the tables, and carrying them off, legs and bodies, to the all-consuming fire. Still the enamel did not melt. There was more crashing and hammering in the house; Palissy was tearing up the floors, to use the planks as firewood. Frantic with despair, the wife rushed out into the town; and the household of Palissy traversed the town of Saintes, making loud publication of the scandal.

Very touchingly does Palissy himself relate the position to which he had now been brought. " Having," he says, " covered the new pieces with the said enamel, I put them into the furnace, keeping the fire still at its height; but thereupon occurred to me a new misfortune, which caused great mortification, namely, that the wood having failed me, I was forced to burn the palings which maintained the boundaries of my garden; which being burnt also, I was forced to burn the tables and the flooring of my house, to cause the melting of the second composition. I suffered an anguish that I cannot speak, for I was quite exhausted and dried up by the heat of the furnace; it was more than a month since my shirt had been dry upon me. Further to console me, I was the object of mockery; and

even those from whom solace was due ran crying through
the town that I was burning my floors! And in this
way my credit was taken from me, and I was regarded as
a madman.

"Others said that I was labouring to make false money,
which was a scandal under which I pined away, and
slipped with bowed head through the streets, like a man
put to shame. I was in debt in several places, and had
two children at nurse, unable to pay the nurses ; no one
gave me consolation, but, on the contrary, men jested at
me, saying, ' It was right for him to die of hunger, seeing
that he had left off following his trade.' All these things
assailed my ears when I passed through the street; but
for all that there still remained some hope which encouraged and sustained me, inasmuch as the last trials had
turned out tolerably well; and thereafter I thought that I
knew enough to get my own living, although I was far
enough from that (as you shall hear afterwards).

"When I had dwelt with my regrets a little, because
there was no one who had pity upon me, I said to my
soul, ' Wherefore art thou saddened, since thou hast found
the object of thy search? Labour now, and the defamers
will live to be ashamed.' But my spirit said again, ' You
have no means wherewith to continue this affair; how will
you feed your family, and buy whatever things are requisite
to pass over the four or five months which must elapse before you can enjoy the produce of your labour?' "

CHAPTER XII.

A HERETIC IS BURNT AT SAINTES : NEW TROUBLES
AFFLICT BERNARD PALISSY.

WE have now arrived at the beginning of the year
1547. The greater part of the year 1546 had been employed by Palissy, as we have seen, in the examination of
clays, and the modelling of those vessels upon which he was
to make the first trial of his white enamel. But although
Bernard bestowed upon such labour enough energy to
justify us in assuming that it was the sole thought of his
mind, we shall err greatly if we content ourselves with
any such assumption. In the month of August, 1546,
not long before they were taught to regard Palissy as a
madman, the people of Saintes had been enlightened by
the fire in which a heretic was burnt alive. It was " the
brother at Gimosac, who kept a school, and preached on
Sunday, being much beloved by the inhabitants."

This was nearly the beginning of the horrors perpetrated in Saintonge for the benefit of Christianity. From

the beginning, Palissy paid to such events eager attention, and he was soon led to throw the whole force of his energy upon the side of the reformers. The persecutions were not new to France, though new to Saintonge, in the year 1546: they must have been familiar to Palissy, as we have seen, during his years of wandering. Every year had supplied its list of martyrs. Beyond the limits of Saintonge, in that year 1546, there had been destroyed Pierre le Clerc, Etienne Mangin, Michel Caillon, Jaques Bouchebec, Jean Brisebarre, Henri Hutinot, François le Clerc, Thomas Honoré, Jean Baudouin, Jean Flêche, Jean Pigneri, Jean Mateflon, and Philippes Petit. Also a peasant who, in the forest of Lyori, questioned prisoners upon the way to execution, and having learned the reason of their sentence, claimed a place upon the cart and went to execution with them. " In this year," says a contemporary historian, " France began to redouble persecution by the death of Pierre Chappot, executed at Paris with five others, of which the names have escaped; Etienne Pouliot burned with Bibles, and a François d'Angi, at Nonnay, in Vivarets."

The interest taken by Palissy in the religious struggles of his time was manifested in his life and writings, not less vividly than his strong interest as a philosopher in nature, or his almost unexampled patience in the prosecution of researches as an artisan. In one of his treatises there is contained a History of the Troubles of Saintonge, in which he relates much that he himself saw and knew

of the events connected with the religious history of
Saintes. The events which occurred in the year 1546 left
a deep impression on the mind of Palissy, and are related
by him, many years afterwards, from memory, in great
detail. It becomes necessary, therefore, that we interrupt
the story of his struggle to produce enamelled vases, while
we dwell upon some other facts on which the mind of
Palissy was also at the same time dwelling.

Historians will recognise the philosophic motive which
induced Palissy to interpolate among his works a history
of his experiences in Saintonge. Their labour would be
light, if all men who have power, had the will to act on
Palissy's suggestion. " I should think it well," he says,
" that in each town there should be persons deputed to
write faithfully the deeds that have been done during
these troubles; and from such materials the truth might
be reduced into a volume." For this cause, Palissy informs us, he has written his short narrative.* " You
must understand," he continues, " that just as the Primi-
tive Church was built upon a very small beginning, and
with many perils, dangers, and great tribulations, so, in
these last days, the difficulty and dangers, pains, labour,
and afflictions, have been great in this region of Xaintonge. I say of Xaintonge, because I will leave the
inhabitants of any other diocese to write of it themselves

---

* It will be found exactly as he wrote it, in the selection from his
works at the conclusion of this volume, where it is entitled the *History
of the Troubles of Xaintonge.*

that which they truly know." This preface is the language of a naturalist, who has acquired a close habit of observation, and who understands how many small experiences must be put together for the forming, with anything like accuracy, of one great general conclusion.

Palissy begins his narrative in the year 1546, when "certain monks, having spent some days in parts of Germany,* or, it may be, having read some books of their doctrine, and finding themselves deceived, they had the boldness, secretly enough, to disclose certain abuses ; but as soon as the priests and holders of benefices understood that these people depreciated their trade, they incited the judges to descend upon them: this the judges did, with an exceedingly good will, because several of them possessed some morsel of benefice which helped to boil the pot. By this means, some of the said monks were constrained to take flight, to exile and unfrock themselves, fearing lest they might die in too hot a bed. Some took to a trade, others kept village schools ; and because the isles of Olleron, of Marepnes, and of Allevert, are remote from the public roads, a certain number of the said monks withdrew into those islands, having found sundry means of living without being known."

---

* It has already been observed that the French reformers were by no means copies from the German. Palissy, however, knew and honoured the name of the great German reformer whose sound was then filling the world, and identified him naturally with the entire movement. Subsequent facts will abundantly suffice to connect the reform movement in Saintonge with the teachings of Geneva.

We have already seen that many heretics, and among
them Calvin himself, had fled for refuge to Saintonge
before the year 1546. When Palissy assigns that date to
the commencement of his tale, he does so, probably, from
two reasons, one very much dependent on the other. The
first reason is, that in the year 1546 persecution was re-
doubled,* and the number of refugees would consequently
be multiplied ; the second reason is, that the increased
number of refugees, and their exemplary way of life,
probably in that year arrested more strongly than usual
Palissy's attention. If he had, before that date, only
advanced to a state of vague dissent from the inconsistencies and worldly dealings of the orthodox Church, it is
to the year 1546 that we must assign his own distinct
enrolment in the body of reformers. If this be so,
the reference must be considered personal, as well as
general, in the succeeding portion of the statement concerning the reformed monks of Olleron, Marepnes, and
Allevert: "And as they visited people, they ventured to
speak only with hidden meaning, until they were well
assured that they were not to be betrayed. And after
that, by this means, they had reformed some number of

---

* This fact was stated a few pages back, in a quotation from a history written by one of Palissy's contemporaries, *L'Histoire Universelle
du Sieur d'Aubigné*, &c.: its title might be fairly modernised into
D'Aubigné's History of his own Time, between the years 1550-80.
As it contains many minute details of the doings of the French reformers, I shall be frequently indebted to it in the later portions of
this narrative.

persons, they found means to obtain the pulpit, because in those days there was a grand-vicar who tacitly favoured them: thence it followed that by little and little, in these districts and islands of Xaintonge, many had their eyes opened, and knew many errors of which they had before been ignorant; for which cause many held in great estimation the said preachers, inasmuch as but for them they would view their errors poorly enough."

The favour of the grand-vicar, by which the reformers of Saintonge were encouraged, was not a matter of unusual good fortune. The secret growth of the Reformed doctrines had been most decided among educated or intellectual men; and for this reason we are told that there was scarcely a set of officials in the country which did not include one or two men willing to assist reformers.*

The Bishop of Saintes did not, of course, often reside at Saintes; Saintes was no more to him than one bone in his mess of potage. His fit place was at court, for he was no less magnificent a person than Charles, Cardinal of Bourbon, an august personage, then twenty-three years old, " descended from the precious blood of Monseigneur St. Louis."† But " there was in those days," says Pa-

* " This religion being received principally by men of letters, there were very few seats of justice in France which was not attended by some officer favouring this doctrine; by means of such men, they who compiled the great Book of Martyrs authenticated their reports by Acts and entire lawsuits taken from the official records."—*Les Histoires du Sieur D'Aubigné*, bk. ii., ch. vii.

† He was born in 1523, at Ferté-sous-Jouarre, and died at Fontenai-le-Comte, in 1590. He was brother to Antony, King of Navarre, and

lissy, "a man named Collardeau, a fiscal attorney, a man perverse and of evil life, who found means to give notice to the Bishop of Xaintes, who was at the time at court, giving him to understand that the place was full of Lutherans, and that he gave him charge and commission to extirpate them." This busy person wrote more than one letter, and crowned his energetic efforts with a trip to Paris, for the express purpose of speaking to the great man. "He succeeded so well by these means, that he obtained a commission from the bishop and from the parliament of Bourdeaux"—within whose jurisdiction I have already said that the diocese of Saintonge is included—"with a good sum of deniers that were taxed to him by the said court. This he contrived for gain, and not through zeal on behalf of religion."

The natural inclination of educated men towards the reformers was, throughout these troubles, held constantly in check by appeals from within or from without to their self-interest. Income, dependent on some benefice, restrained the larger number from all active sympathy. Collardeau, in the present instance, "tampered with certain judges, as well in the island of Olleron as of Allevert, and likewise at Gimosac; and having corrupted these judges, he caused the arrest of the preacher of St. Denis,

was afterwards called Charles X. by the Leaguers. In 1584, D'Aubigné overstates by fourteen years the age of Cardinal Bourbon; this is worth noting, as I must hereafter show why I believe him to have made a like error in the case of Palissy.

which is at the end of the island of Olleron, named Brother Robin, and by the same means caused him to be
passed into the island of Allevert, where he arrested another preacher named Nicole; and some days afterwards,
he took also the brother of Gimosac, who kept a school
and preached on Sundays, being much beloved of the
inhabitants. And although," says Palissy, "I believe
the story to be written in the Book of Martyrs,* yet,
nevertheless, because I know the truth of certain facts, I
have found it well to write them, namely, that they well
disputed and maintained their religion in the presence of
one Navières, theologian, canon of Xaintes, who had himself formerly begun to detect errors, however much—because he had been conquered by his belly—he maintained
the contrary." Of this they took care, of course, duly to
remind him. However the right may stand, it rarely
happens in a contest that the scolding is monopolised by
either party. "However that might be, these poor folk
were condemned to be degraded and caparisoned in green,
in order that the people might esteem them fools or mad-
men; and what is more, because they maintained manfully the cause of God, they were bridled like horses by
the said Collardeau, before being led upon the scaffold,
which bridles had to each an apple of iron which filled all
the inside of the mouth—a very hideous thing to see."
Hideous indeed! This, then, was one sight which amused

* This is the book referred to in a note upon page 177. Its com-
pilers closed their labour with the year 1562.

the town of Saintonge, and largely occupied the thoughts
of Palissy while his fingers laboured in the moulding of
those earthen vessels which were afterwards destroyed in
his first effort at enamelling. His clay was then within
a few months of destruction, but those pieces of God's
clay—Brother Robin and his friends—were to be broken
sooner. " Being thus degraded, they restored them into
prison to conduct them to Bourdeaux, in order that they
might be condemned to death."

Palissy soon found more subject for discourse and cogi-
tation in connexion with these ministers. Brother Robin
was the best of them, that is to say, the most active; and
him, accordingly, " it was designed to put to death with
the most cruelty." Brother Robin was a tit-bit to be
guarded carefully. He was kept with his companions,
heavily ironed, in a prison attached to the bishop's palace.
A sentry was put outside their cell, to listen for all sounds
that indicated efforts to escape; and a by no means friendly
grand-vicar had contributed a number of large village
dogs, " which were set at large in the bishop's court, in
order that they might bark if any prisoner attempted to
come out." All the precautions were so thoroughly complete, that the watchman saw no reason why he should not
go to sleep during the orthodox hours appointed for that
purpose. He was not a heretic, and so he went to sleep.

The heretical monk, Brother Robin, preternaturally
wakeful, had found means to keep or get possession of a
file. He had already filed his chains asunder, and was

scraping a hole by which his body might pass through the prison-wall, selecting for his purpose an unreasonable hour, consistent with his usual perversity. It is obvious that no Christian watchman of regular habits could have anticipated so indecent a proceeding.

Brother Robin had contrived to remove a good number of stones out of his prison-wall, and would have got to the free air. if a bishop's household had been something less familiar with good liquors. The good service done by all retainers in their master's absence was attested by a pile of empty hogsheads in the court, heaped up against the prison-wall; and Brother Robin tapped his wall, unluckily, into the barricade of them. How many were there piled he could not tell; his obvious duty was to give a lusty push, and so he did, and down they came, making, as empty hogsheads will, a heavy drumming.

The reveille thus beaten roused the watchman, who came out into the night to listen. Brother Robin was too wise to make a noise. The watchman heard that there was nothing to hear, though there had been a noise—one of those unaccountable noises made by that unaccountable tumbling-down of things which will occasionally startle all of us at night. The watchman went in to end his nap, and Brother Robin came out, if possible, to finish his adventure. "And so the said Brother Robin went out into the court, at the mercy of the dogs."

But Brother Robin, by much barking, had long been made aware that he should have dogs to contend with.

He had stored up for them a supper from his bread. It is
the nature of dogs, as of most other creatures who dance
about the doors of great men, to be always hungry. A
dog in the year 1546 would scarcely have been able to
rank as the companion of man, in France, if he had not had
a tender corner in his belly, by the soothing of which he
could be managed easily. Brother Robin filled the mouths
of his antagonists with sturdy lumps of bread, and neither
man nor dog will care to bark while he has anything to
swallow.

So Brother Robin had his own way for a little time.
"Now you must know"—I drop again into the quaint,
terse narrative of Palissy—"now you must know that the
said Robin had never been in this town of Xaintes, for
this cause being in the bishop's court, he was still shut up;
but God willed that he should find an open door which
led into the garden; which he entered; and finding himself again shut up between certain somewhat high walls,
he perceived, by the light of the moon, a certain pear-tree
which was close enough to the said wall, and having
mounted the said pear-tree, he perceived, on the other side
of the said wall, a chimney, to which he could leap easily
enough. Seeing which, he went back to the prison, to
know whether any one of his companions had filed his
irons." He had given them his own file, and if they had
chosen to risk the adventure with him, there would have
been time enough to cut an iron chain or two while
Brother Robin was boring through the wall. Probably,

however, they esteemed it honourable to await their martyrdom.* Brother Robin, though he would not have tampered with his soul, was ready to deny his body to the executioner, if he could carry it by any skill into a place of safety; so, finding his companions with their chains whole, " he consoled and exhorted them to battle manfully, and to take patiently their death; and embracing them, took leave of them, and went again to mount upon the pear-tree, and thence leapt upon the chimneys of the street."

The bishop's wall was only "somewhat high," and as Brother Robin leapt down from it upon the chimneys of the street, the houses in that part of Saintes must have been somewhat low. To find a way down, therefore, from the chimneys to the road was not a difficult proceeding.

The escaped heretic, outside the bishop's walls, traversing on a moonlight night the streets of Saintes, was treading upon unknown ground. He might find his way to the outskirts, but what would the town guards say to a man stealing out into the country at midnight, with a strange face and no very clear account to give of his proceedings? Every house contained a stranger, and almost

---

* Every man murdered in the name of Christ was not then called a martyr. That honour belonged only to those who, to the last, had power to save their lives by a rejection of their faith, and went to their death deliberately refusing the temptation. This, at least, is the definition given in the contemporary Book of Martyrs, previously mentioned.

every house an enemy; but since it was absolutely necessary
to find shelter somewhere, and while wandering about the
street to have some ostensible purpose for so doing, Brother Robin began, in a most reckless manner, to disturb
the slumbers of the orthodox.

Though he did not know of any friend in Saintes, it so
happened that during his imprisonment the clever monk
had been attacked with pleurisy, and been attended
during illness by a physician and apothecary. The
names of these people he remembered. Accordingly, the
wily fellow tucked his dress about his shoulders in such
fashion, that under the moonlight it resembled the cos-
tume of a footman ; to increase the resemblance, he fastened his fetters to his thigh, and then, with that violent
haste which suited his own purpose, and appeared very
well to suit the purpose of a messenger from some family
afflicted with a sudden illness, he proceeded to knock up
the people of Saintonge, " inquiring for the said physician
and apothecary, of whom he had remembered the names.
But in doing this, he went to knock at several doors belonging to his greatest enemies, and among others at the
door of a counsellor who employed all diligence next
morning to get news of him, and promised fifty dollars on
the part of the grand-vicar, named Sellière, to him by
whose means the said Robin should be taken."

Brother Robin, however, had met with the success he
deserved ; he had found " refuge in a house, and was from
thence, in the same hour, conducted out of the town."

Probably, the physician or apothecary had an educated sympathy with the reformers, and answered the trust placed in his generosity by Brother Robin, trotting out with him in his disguise of footman, as with a person by whom he had been summoned to an urgent case. Subsequent suspicion never would be fastened on so commonplace an incident. This escape of Brother Robin, in August, 1546, was an event over which Palissy no doubt rejoiced abundantly ; he styles it "an admirable accident." The companions who remained in prison, and made no endeavour to escape, were burnt during the same month; "one in the town of Xaintes, and the other at Leghorn, because the parliament of Bourdeaux had fled thither by reason of the plague, which was then in the town of Bourdeaux." This incidental mention of a parliament ejected by the plague, reminds us duly of another feature in the sixteenth century. Bodies were plagued nearly as much as souls.

Purses were also plagued, those which were naturally slender in their constitution being always first to suffer. It was at this time, Palissy tells us, that "the bishop, or his counsellors, resolved upon a trick and stratagem extremely subtle ; for having obtained some order from the king, for the cutting down of a great number of forests which were around this town, nevertheless, because many found their recreation in the woods and pastures of the said forests, they would not permit that they should be levelled; but those, following the Mahometan artifices, resolved to gain the heart of the people by preachings, and presents made to the king's party; and sent into this town of Xaintes, and other towns of the diocese, certain monks of the Sorbonne, who foamed, slavered, twisted and twirled themselves, making strange gestures and grimaces, and all their discourses were nothing but outcry against these new Christians; and sometimes they exalted their bishop, saying that he was descended from the precious blood of Monseigneur St. Louis; and in this way the poor people patiently allowed their woods to be cut down; and the woods having been thus cut, there were no more preachers. Thus you see how the possessions of people were practised upon, as well as their souls."

While we speak now of the cutting of the forests round Saintonge, which took place during this portion of the life of Palissy, it becomes fit that we should regard Palissy as lover of the woods and fields, and understand the spirit in which he regarded this wholesale destruction. The avarice which prompted holders of the benefices to attack the forests in almost all provinces of France, has been illustrated in a previous chapter. It concerns us only now to know how Palissy was accustomed to think, speak, and write, about such things. It has to be remembered that in those days wood was synonymous with fuel, and France depended upon forests for that necessary part of civilised existence. After recounting with the fresh breath of a naturalist many of the delights of nature, Palissy says :* " All these things have made me such a lover of the fields, that it seems to me that there are no treasures in the world so precious, or which ought to be held in such great esteem, as the little branches of trees and plants, although they are the most despised. I hold them in more esteem than mines of gold and silver. And when I consider the value of the very smallest branch of tree or thorn, I am filled with wonder at the great ignorance of men, who seem, in our day, to study only how to break through, cut down, and destroy the beautiful forests which their predecessors had been guarding as so precious. I should not find it wrong in them to cut the forests down, if afterwards they planted any portion of the soil ; but they think not at all of times to come, not considering the great harm they are doing to their children in the future.

" *Question.*—And why do you find it so wrong that forests should be cut down in this manner? There are many bishops, cardinals, priories and abbeys, monasteries and chapters, which, in cutting forests down, have obtained treble profit. First, they have had money for the wood, and have given some of it to women, children, and men also. *Item.*—They have leased the soil of the said

---

* In a treatise, of which the chief part will be found at the end of these volumes, there entitled " The Naturalist looking out on Evil Days.".

forests at a rental, out of which they have reaped much money also in entrance-fees. And afterwards, the labourers have sòwn wheat and seeds every year, of which wheat they have had always a good portion. You see, therefore, how much more income lands yield than formerly they yielded. For which reason I cannot think that this ought to be found wrong.

"*Answer.*—I cannot enough detest such a thing, and can call it not a fault, but a curse and a misfortune to all France ; because, when all the woods shall have been levelled, there must be an end of all the arts, and artisans may go and browse on herb like Nebuchadnezzar. I have sometimes attempted to put down in order the arts that would cease, if there came to be an end of wood; but when I had written a great number of them, I could see no way to an end of my writing; and having considered all, I found that there was not a single one to be exercised without wood: that all navigation and all fisheries must cease; and that even the birds, and several kinds of beasts, which nourish themselves upon fruits, must migrate to another kingdom, and that neither oxen, cows, nor any other bovine animals, would be of service in a country where there was no wood. I had studied to give you a thousand reasons; but this is a philosophy which, when the outside waiters shall have thought about it, they will judge that without wood it is impossible to exercise any art ; and it would even be necessary, if we had no wood, for the office of the teeth to become vacant, and where there is no wood, there is no need of wheat, nor any other kind of grain for making bread.

"I think it a very strange thing that many seigneurs do not compel their subjects to sow some part of their land with acorns, and other parts with chestnuts, and other parts with filberts, which would be a public good, and a revenue that would grow while they were sleeping. That would be very fit in many parts where they are constrained to amass the excrement of oxen and cows, to warm themselves; and in other regions they are obliged to warm themselves and boil their pots with straw; is not this a fault and public ignorance? If I were seigneur of such lands so barren of wood, I would compel my tenants to sow trees in at least a part of them. They are much to be pitied; it is a revenue which would come to them while sleeping; and after they had eaten the fruits of the trees, they could be warmed by their branches and their trunks."

Long afterwards, France really had become so much denuded of its forests, that advice like that of Palissy for the encouragement of plantations had to be promulgated by enactments. Upon this, however, it is not our province to dwell. Before we return to a relation of the struggles made by Palissy upon the track of the enamelled cup, we will add one more illustration of his breadth of mind, by following the clear-sighted philosopher into the fields. There we shall see him fretted by a state of things

which has continued over a large part of Europe ever
since his time, and throwing out suggestions which even
in England at the present day stand in the front rank
among thoughts connected with the future progress of
humanity. How few must there have been to sympathise
with this clear sense, among the errors and confusions of
society three centuries ago. In days when ignorance made
much pretension, how inattentive would ears be to the
philosophy of a poor potter, without Latin and Greek,
who spoke clear thoughts in his own clear, delightful way,
but in a way so homely and so unassuming, that even
among the big words of the nineteenth century we almost
need to reassure each other that it is true philosophy, high
manly thought, which has been written with so modest and
so touching a simplicity.

Palissy was struggling against difficulty, and regarded
with contempt by his own townsmen, with just doubts
about his " common sense" by his own wife. If his sense
had indeed been common, let the world judge whether
France might not have been some degrees more happy.
Palissy looked about, with his habitually shrewd attention,
in the fields.

" Many," he says, " devour their income as retainers of
the court in hectorings, superfluous expenses, as well in
accoutrements as in other things ; it would be much more
useful for them to eat onions with their tenants, and teach
them how to live well, set them good example, adjust
their disputes, hinder them from ruining themselves with

lawsuits, plant, build, trench, feed, sustain, and, at the requisite and necessary time, hold themselves ready to do service to their prince for the defending of their country.

" I wonder at the ignorance of men, when I look at their agricultural implements, which ought to be in more request than precious bits of armour; yet for all that, it seems to certain striplings, that if they had handled any implement of agriculture, they would have been dishonoured by it ; and a gentleman, however poor he may be, and up to his ears in debt, would be debased in his own eyes if his hands had been for a short time in contact with a plough.

" I could wish that the king had founded certain offices, estates, and honours, for all those who should invent some good and subtle agricultural tool." (Three centuries ago, the spirit of this suggestion was three centuries and a half in advance of the time when it was uttered.) " If it were so, everybody's mind would have been bent on achieving something. Ingenious men were never in demand at the siege of a town, but there were found a few; and precisely as you see men despise the ancient modes of dress, they would despise also the ancient implements of agriculture, and in good sooth they would invent better ones.

" Armourers often change the fashion of the halberds, swords, and other harness; but the ignorance in agriculture is so great that it abides ever accustomed to one method; and if the tools were clumsy at their first invention, they preserve them ever in their clumsiness; in one

province, one accustomed fashion without any change;
in another province, another also without ever changing.

"It is not long since I was in the province of Bearn
and of Bigorre; but in passing through the fields, I could
not look at the labourers without chafing within myself,
seeing the clumsiness of their implements: and why is it
that we find no well-born youth, who studies as much to
invent tools useful to his labourers as he takes pains over
the cutting of his coat into surprising patterns : I cannot
contain myself to talk over these things, considering the
folly and the ignorance of men."

" The cutting of his coat into surprising patterns" was
a task which Palissy just now was spared the pains of
undertaking for himself ; poverty looked at his garments,
and was hard at work for him on the hole-making part—
in those days not a small part—of a tailor's duty.   From
this short wandering among the wealth of Bernard's mind,
we must return now to the worldly wretchedness that he
endured at home, and to his unrelaxed exertions in that
labour which had yet to find success, and earn its fair re-
quital from the world.

CHAPTER XIII.

PALISSY BECOMES A POTTER.

BERNARD PALISSY, plunged in disaster, nevertheless had reason to be sure that he had discovered the profitable art of which he had been for the last six or seven years in search. High as his faith then was in himself, the faith of other men in him had never been so weak as at that most critical point in his whole struggle. His assault upon the floors and tables, reasonable and judicious as undoubtedly it was, had suffered judgment at the hands of all his neighbours. The result of that act, as it concerned himself, had been, that he had produced some melting of his enamel over the common household jars which he had purchased; they were whitened. Family and friends might cry that he was mad, but he had gained the desired knowledge, and the difficulty now was, overwhelmed with poverty, to make a proper use of it. One question, too, he had to put to himself, as we have already seen,—"How will you feed your family, and buy whatever things are

requisite to pass over the four or five months which must
elapse before you can enjoy the produce of your labour ?
Then," he says, " when I was thus seized with sorrow, and
debating in my spirit, hope gave me a little courage."
The man of genius who hopes and strives will never be
defeated in his efforts to achieve whatever man can do.

Bernard believed firmly that the next batch he baked
would begin, for him and his, the long-postponed repay-
ment for their toil and suffering. Comparatively ignorant
as he then was of clays, it had occupied him on the previous occasion seven months to mould his vessels. It
would be braving death—and not indeed his own, but
that of his children—to prolong so tediously the struggle
while they all lay ground under the heel of want. Therefore, he tells us, " more promptly to cause to appear the
secret which I had discovered of the white enamel, I took
a common potter and gave him certain drawings, in order
that he might make vessels in accordance with my own
designs ; and whilst he made these things, I occupied
myself over some medallions." These medallions, probably, were figures in relief of natural objects which he
proposed to enamel and to paint; they may, however, have
been copies of some of the Roman coins and curiosities
which were continually being dug up in the town of
Saintes, rich, as I have shown already, in antiquities.
" But this," adds Bernard, " was a pitiable thing."

Indeed it was. Hope gave him courage to take a step
which his wife must have pronounced rash, and over which

she must have grieved abundantly. He was unable to feed his children with his own resources, he was falling into debt, and he engaged now an assistant in the labours which seemed destined to work out his ruin. The wages he engaged to pay the potter whom he hired, he expected confidently to draw out of his furnace; he could not maintain him in his house. His wife could not spare food enough; and if she had been able, would have given to the accomplice of her husband, both before and after meat, a grace that would not have assisted his digestion. It is curious that there could be found at that time an innkeeper in Saintes—but such a man was found—who gave the potter all his meals, and lodged him for six months, putting the cost down to the account of Bernard Palissy. Bernard, however, had in him a purity of spirit which must have inspired many men with confidence in his integrity, who had but small faith in his judgment, and mutual goodwill towards the new religion may have formed a bond between himself and the confiding publican.

They laboured for six months, during which time the potter worked from the designs supplied to him by Palissy. Then, when there was no more need of the potter's services, he had to be discharged, and of course waited for his wages. Bernard had an empty pocket, and well-nigh an empty house; there remained little to strip except his person; so when the potter went, says Palissy, "for want of money, I was forced to give part of my clothes for wages."

Being left alone, he had to make an improved furnace. "Then," he tells us, " because I had not any materials for the erection of my furnace, I began to take down that which I had built after the manner of the glass-workers, in order to use the materials again. Then, because the said furnace had been so strongly heated for six days and nights, the mortar and the brick in it were liquefied and vitrified in such a manner, that in loosening the masonry, I had my fingers bruised and cut in so many places, that I was obliged to eat my pottage with my fingers wrapped in rags.*

" When I had pulled down the said furnace, it was requisite to build the other, which was not done without much difficulty; since I had to fetch for myself the water, and the mortar, and the stone, without any aid and without any repose. This done, I submitted the beforenamed work to the first baking, and then, by borrowing, or in other ways, I found means to obtain materials for making the enamel for the covering of the said work, which turned out well from the first baking; but when I had bought the said materials, there followed a labour for me which appeared to baffle all my wits; for, after I had wearied myself through several days in pounding and calcining my chemicals, I had to grind them, without any aid, in a hand-mill which it usually required two strong men to turn: the desire which I had to succeed in my enterprise

* " In France, at the end of the sixteenth century, forks even at court were entirely new."—*Beckman's Hist. of Inventions.*

made me do things which I should have esteemed impossible. When the said colours were ground, I covered
all my vessels and medallions with the said enamel; then,
having put and arranged them all within the furnace, I
began to make the fire, thinking to draw out of my
furnace three or four hundred livres, and continued the
said fire until I had some sign and hope of my enamels
being melted, and of my furnace being in good order."

This time Palissy was right in all his calculations; his
furnace was so much improved, and his enamel so correctly
mixed, that one day was sufficient for the melting. But
a mischance had happened upon which he had not calculated, and thus he tells us that, " the next day, when I
came to draw out my work, having previously removed
the fire, my sorrows and distresses were so abundantly
augmented that I lost all countenance."

The enamel was right, the furnace was right, but the
whole work was spoilt. The elaborate designs, the play
of Bernard's fancy as an artist for six months,—the debt
incurred for maintenance and wages of the potter, who
had wrought his fancy out upon the clay,—the hands
wounded with labour at the furnace,—the money begged
and borrowed to buy chemicals,—the weeks of drudgery
in grinding, the hope and self-denial of eight months,—all
led to " sorrow and distresses so abundantly augmented."
Yet the enamel was right, and the fire was effectual, and
all Bernard's speculations had been perfectly fulfilled.
Why then was all his labour lost?

" It was because the mortar of which I had built my furnace had been full of flints, which, feeling the vehemence of the fire (at the same time that my enamels had begun to liquefy), burst into several pieces, making a variety of cracks and explosions within the said furnace. Then, because the splinters of the flints struck against my work, the enamel, which was already liquefied and converted into a glutinous matter, retained the said flints, and held them attached on all sides of my vessels and medallions, which, except for that, would have been beautiful." Palissy says but a few touching words about his grief: " Then I was more concerned than I can tell you, and not without cause, for my furnace cost me more than twenty-six gold dollars. I had borrowed the wood and the chemicals, and so had borrowed part of my hope of food in making the said work. I had held my creditors in hope that they would be paid out of the money which would proceed from the pieces made in the said furnace; which was the reason why several began to hasten to me after the morning when I was to commence the drawing of the batch."

Palissy had referred all things to this day, which was to have extricated him from his embarrassment and misery. The poor are always promise-breakers. The rich man, if one expectation fails, is able to fall back on his reserves. The poor man, when he is in debt, compelled to pay his expectations out as promises, has fifty broken promises charged at his door for every unforeseen mischance that baulks his foresight. Palissy could not have foreseen the misadventure which made the long-anticipated day of his deliverance, the day of his descent into new depths of sorrow. He had expected three or four hundred livres. " I received," he says, " nothing but shame and confusion; for my pieces were all bestrewn with little morsels of flint, that were attached so firmly to each vessel, and so combined with the enamel, that when one passed the hand over it, the said flints cut like razors. And although the work was in this way lost, there were still some who would buy it at a mean price; but, because that would have been a decrying and abasing of my honour, I broke in pieces the entire batch from the said furnace, and lay down in melancholy—not without cause, for I had no longer any means to feed my family. I had nothing but reproaches in the house; in place of consolation, they gave me maledictions. My neighbours, who had heard of this affair, said that I was nothing but a fool, and that I might have had more than eight francs for the things that I had broken; and all this talk was brought to mingle with my grief."

" And all this talk was brought to mingle with my grief!" If one could sketch a scene like this with the pencil of a master, it would make a goodly picture. The dilapidated outhouse, its breaches rudely filled up with green boughs; Palissy grand in his own grief, tattered in dress, with a litter of beautiful vases, cups, urns, and medallions, the products of his rich taste and fancy, broken at his feet;

the angry creditors ; the village gossips pouring their
much talk over his bowed spirit ; his thin, pale children
crouching, wondering, about ; his lean wife—God forgave
her on the instant—pouring on him maledictions, ignorant
or careless how his heart would open in that hour of anguish to receive one syllable of woman's consolation.

Palissy retired into his chamber, and lay down upon
his bed. He had done well to break his vessels. His
skill as an artist, and his really discovered secret of the
white enamel, placed before him a wide field for ambition.
He meant to produce costly articles of luxury, and he
could not afford, because the flints had speckled them, to
hurt his future reputation by sending his rich creations
into the world at the price of well-side pitchers. Princes
were to be his paymasters. But he had no longer any
means to feed his family. His wife could not forget that;
and he might have had more than eight francs for the
things that he had broken.

If the wife could have seen and understood the spirit
of her husband, she would have followed his melancholy
step when he withdrew to the recesses of his chamber.

Confusion, shame, melancholy, grief, Palissy connects
with this event; but he has never named the word despair.
He retired from the discussions of his neighbours, missing
painfully the consolation of his wife; but he retired to
have his own discussion in himself, to ascertain in peace
what was his present duty. We have already seen enough
of Bernard Palissy to know that he is not likely to bow his

head, and own that he is vanquished by the most imperious of difficulties. After experiencing this last severe rebuff, Palissy withdrew into his chamber; and there, he says, " when I had remained some time upon the bed, and had considered within myself, that if a man should fall into a pit, his duty would be to endeavour to get out again"—a very simple rule, which all men have not strength enough to follow ; they often die while they are waiting to be pulled out—" I," Palissy adds, " being in like case, set myself to make some paintings, and in various ways I took pains to recover a little money."

That is to say, he tranquilly abandoned his experiments, while he devoted himself for a short time wholly to the repair of his household fortunes. People thought him a good painter, and as he had by no means glutted his market lately in that character, he probably found it not difficult to sell the sketches that he made. About their price he was not at all proud or particular. He drew from nature with minute accuracy, and was versed in the common details of a painter's art ; but his genius had dwelt upon the works of masters, and he thought, therefore, but little of his own. People, he said, " thought him a better painter than he was."

Having paid just attention to these things, and with, perhaps, about a year's toil having revived some of the gloss on his establishment, and earned a little money in reserve, Palissy was at leisure to resume his enterprise. " I said within myself, that my losses and hazards were all past, and there was no longer anything to hinder me from making good pieces; and I betook myself (as before) to labour in the same art."

The date at which this narrative now stands is the year 1549. A king of France died by way of portent when Palissy was tearing up his floors, and Francis the First has been succeeded by his son, Henry the Second. In the year 1549, Palissy was about forty years old, and his labour to invent enamelled ware had been spread over a period of some eight years. It cost him eight years more, but the worst portion of his toil was over. Palissy had now only to learn the temper of his clays, and buy with experience a knowledge of those numerous mishaps which practical potters only can appreciate, and against which, in those days of rude appliances, incessant watchfulness was needed. The mishaps, at first, were lamentably frequent. The very next batch of vessels with which Palissy endeavoured to redeem his credit, and for which he built another furnace, carefully eschewing flints, was lost as unexpectedly as its predecessor, "for there occurred an accident of which I had not thought; for the vehemence of the flame of fire had carried a quantity of ashes against my pieces; so that in those parts which had been touched by the ashes, my vessels were rough and ill-polished; because the enamel, being liquefied, had united with the said ashes. In spite of all those losses, I remained in hope of remounting in fortune by the said art; for I caused to be made, by certain potters, a large number of earthen lanterns, to

contain my vessels when I put them in the furnace, in
order that, by means of the said lanterns, my vessels might
be protected by the ash. The invention proved a good
one, and has served me to the present day."

During the next two years Palissy prospered little; he
made, indeed, vessels of different colours, which kept
house tolerably, and enabled him to abide by his furnace,
losing the greater part of his more ambitious work by
various mischances; " as, when I had made a batch, it
might prove too much baked, or another time, too little,
and all would be lost in that way. I was so inexperienced
that I could not discern the too much or too little. One
time my work was baked in front, but not baked properly
behind; another time I tried to obviate that, and burnt
my work behind, but the front was not baked at all;
sometimes it was baked on the right hand, and burnt on
the left; sometimes my enamels were put on too thinly,
sometimes they were too thick, which caused me great
losses; sometimes, when I had in the furnace enamels
different in colour, some were burnt before the others had
melted."

These difficulties belonged to his whole career as a
potter, but, of course, more especially to the first years.
Then there were difficulties in the choice and management
of clays. They differ greatly in their nature. " Some
are sandy, white and very thin, and for these reasons a
great fire is needed before they are baked properly."
" There are other kinds which, when they are baked,

whether in pottery or in bricks, it is needful that the
master of the work take good heed in drawing his affair
from the furnace, lest it take cold; and, what is more,
those who work with it are constrained to stop all the
vent holes of their furnace as soon as their batch is baked,
because if it felt the very slightest wind in cooling, the
pieces would all turn out cracked." Other kinds Palissy
enumerates, and by way of illustration, " once," he says, " I
had collected some of the earth of Poitou, and had laboured
upon this for the full space of six months before I had
my batch complete, because the vessels that I had made
were very elaborate, and of a somewhat high price. Now,
in making the said vessels of the earth of Poitou, I made
some of them of the earth of Xaintonge, on which I had
worked for some years before, and was sufficiently ex-
perienced in the degree of the fire which was needed by
the said earth, and thinking that all earths might bake at
a like degree. I baked my work which was earth of
Poitou, among that of earth of Xaintonge, which caused
me a great loss; inasmuch as the work in earth of Xaintonge being baked sufficiently, I thought that the other
work would be so too; but when I came to enamel my
vessels, those feeling the moisture, it was an unpleasant
joke for me; because as many pieces as were enamelled,
came to dissolve and fall to pieces, as a limestone would
do soaked in water; and at the same time the vessels of
the earth of Xaintonge were baked in the same furnace,
and at the same degree of heat as the above named, and

turned out very well. You see, then, how a man who labours in the art of earth is always an apprentice, because of the unknown nature of the diversities of earth."*

" Then, because my enamels did not work well together on the same thing, I was deceived many times; whence I derived always vexation and sorrow. Nevertheless, the hope that I had caused me to proceed with my work so like a man, that often to amuse people who came to see me, I did my best to laugh, although within me all was very sad."

Great strength of body must have enabled Palissy to endure, in addition to privation and distress, the intense toil to which he subjected himself in the prosecution of his struggles. But his physical frame bore strong marks of the contest. " I was for the space of ten years," he says, " so wasted in my person, that there was no form nor prominence of muscle on my arms or legs ; also, the said legs were throughout of one size, so that the garters with which I tied my stockings, were at once, when I walked, down upon my heels, with the stockings too. I often walked about the fields of Xaintes considering my miseries and weariness, and, above all things, that in my own house I could have no peace, nor do anything that was considered good. I was despised and mocked by all." More than

---

* From the treatise *Des Terres Argiles*, much of which will be found translated at the end of these volumes, under the title of " The Potter's Clay." The other words of Palissy used in this chapter are from *L'Art de Terre*, which, under title of " The Artist in Earth," will be found complete in the Appendix.

once breaks out this yearning for domestic love, so simply,
with so quaint a pathos, that we sometimes half wonder
how a man so loveable could be denied the consolation of
domestic sympathy. But it is nothing strange; it would
have been more strange had he been mated with a wife
as capable as he himself was of endurance.

She was afflicted with more grief than I have named;
her family was large, but death had removed six of her
children. In one of his treatises,* speaking of wormwood,
Palissy says, " before I knew the value of the said herb,
the worms caused me the death of six children, as we
discovered both by having caused their bodies to be
opened, and by their frequently passing from the mouth,
and when they were near death the worms passed also by
the nostrils. The districts of Xaintonge, Gascony, Agen
Quercy, and the parts towards Toulouse are very subject
to the said worms."

It is very characteristic that Palissy should not have
rested satisfied until he had assured himself, by causing a
post mortem inspection, of the reason of his children's
death. These deaths concern us now as representing to
Bernard and his wife an additional large source of pain;
the wife might well be dulled in spirit, might easily be
broken down into a scold, by poverty and sorrow.

Just now I spoke of the dilapidated outhouse in which
the furnaces of Palissy were built. It was, of course, absolutely necessary for the success of his work that his fur-

* *Des Sels Divers.* Not translated in the Appendix.

naces should be protected from the wind and rain; but to get such protection was not by any means an easy matter. Since there could be no space for a furnace in any room of a small suburban house, Palissy had to make not only a furnace but a shed; and the amateur roofing of a man who had no money to buy materials, was of a character extremely trying to the temper of his wife. At first he borrowed laths and tiles—his clumsy work soon fell into decay; the wind and rain spoilt more than half of it; protection was essential, means of getting it in any usual way did not exist, and Palissy was glad to patch his shed in a rude manner with green boughs and sticks, until he could afford a little money upon more effectual contrivances. These shiftings and changes, of course, fell under the judgment of the entire population of judicious neighbours. In a provincial town with about ten thousand inhabitants, every man is plagued with officious neighbours to the number of nine thousand, nine hundred, and ninety-nine. Then,—when the holes in his outhouse, on a rainy, windy night, were letting in such blasts as promised the destruction of some costly work,— Palissy did not comfort his wife greatly by awakening her with the noise he made in wrenching off perhaps her bedroom door; which, for want of other material, he was obliged to use, at one of his critical moments, for the patching of his ruinous outbuilding. The wife had not enough philosophy to feel that doors, and tables, and house-nails, were such accidents of life as could be parted with for the

attainment of an object intellectually high ; an object, even
in a worldly sense, worth many doors, and nails, and tables.
Every day she went out telling new distresses to her
neighbours in the town ; and every night when Palissy
came up to bed, perhaps arousing her long after midnight,
cold, wet through, and stupid with work, she administered
to him the wholesome cordial of a curtain-lecture. We
will let Palissy state his own case in the matter, and then
let women of England judge whether they would not, to
a woman, have resented his behaviour.

"I had another affliction, allied with the before named,
which was that the heat, the cold, the winds, and rains,
and droppings, spoilt the largest portion of my work before I baked it ; so that I was obliged to borrow car-
pentry, laths, tiles, and nails, to make shift with. Then,
very often having nothing wherewith to build, I was
obliged to make shift with green boughs and sticks.
Then again, when my means augmented, I undid what
I had done, and built a little better; which caused some
artisans, as hosiers, shoemakers, sergeants, and notaries, a
knot of old women—all those, without regarding that my
art could not be exercised without much space, said that
I did nothing but boggle, and blamed me for that which
should have touched their pity, since I was forced to use
things necessary for my house to build the conveniences
which my art required; and, what is worse, the incite-
ment to the said mockeries proceeded from those of my
own house, who would have had me work without ap-

pliances—a thing more than unreasonable. Then, the more the matter was unreasonable, the more extreme was my affliction. I have been for several years, when, without the means of covering my furnaces, I was every night at the mercy of the rain and winds, without receiving any help, aid, or consolation, except from the owls that screeched on one side, and the dogs that howled upon the other; sometimes there would arise winds and storms, which blew in such a manner up and down my furnaces, that I was constrained to quit the whole with loss of my labour, and several times have found that, having quitted all, and having nothing dry upon me because of the rains which had fallen, I would go to bed at midnight, or near dawn,* dressed like a man who has been dragged through all the puddles in the town, and turning thus to retire, I would walk rolling, without a candle, falling to one side and the other like a man drunk with wine, filled with great sorrows, inasmuch as, having laboured long, I saw my labour wasted; then, retiring in this manner, soiled and drenched, I have found in my chamber a second persecution worse than the first, which causes me to marvel now that I was not consumed with suffering."

Worse than wind and rain and ruin, was the want of a wife's sympathy in those hours of fatigue and suffering; but I should like to hear of any British matron who is

* The reader will remember Beza's wonder that Calvin should have studied until midnight. The night of work, the retirement at midnight, or "near dawn," contrasted more strongly then than it now does with the habits of the people.

shocked at the behaviour of the wife of Palissy. She had
not her husband's courage for a journey among thorns;
and truly, there are few men who, for any object, would
have courage to go far through such a thicket as that from
which we now discover Palissy at length emerging.

It occupied him for fifteen or sixteen years to teach
himself by his own genius, without aid from without, the
full perfection he attained in the moulding and enamelling
of ornamental pottery. During the last eight of these, however,—more especially during the last six,—he produced
many things in his vocation as a potter which enabled
him to keep his family in tolerable comfort. At the tenth
year he might have stopped and rested comfortably on his
profitable knowledge, but Palissy never did stop, he never
did account himself to have attained an end; to the eye of
his genius there lay always before every range of thought a
long vista of almost infinite improvement. Palissy was at
no time satisfied with his attainments: no man with a
grain of true philosophy within him ever yet has been
self-satisfied. After fifteen or sixteen years, Palissy took
heart to call himself a potter; but he still laboured ever to
advance in his own art, still spent a large part of his earnings in experiments and labours, tending to a point of
excellence not yet attained. The sixteen years formed his
apprenticeship. " I blundered," he says, " for the space
of fifteen or sixteen years. When I had learnt to guard
against one danger, there came another, about which I had
not thought. During this time I made several furnaces,

which caused me great losses before I understood the
way to heat them equally. At last I found means to
make several vessels of different enamels, intermixed in
the manner of jasper. That fed me for several years; but
while feeding upon these things, I sought always to work
onward with expenses and disbursements—as you know
that I am doing still.* When I had discovered how to
make my Rustic Pieces, I was in greater trouble and vexation than before; for having made a certain number of
rustic basins, and having put them to bake, my enamels
turned out, some beautiful and well-melted, others ill-
melted; others were burnt, because they were composed
of different materials, that were fusible in different degrees
—the green of the lizards was burnt before the colour of
the serpents was melted, and the colour of the serpents,
lobsters, tortoises, and crabs, was melted before the white
had attained any beauty. All these defects caused me
such labour and heaviness of spirit, that before I could
render my enamels fusible at the same degree of heat, I
thought I should be at the door of my sepulchre."

A stranger to the kind of ware produced by Palissy
may fairly wonder what he means by his mysterious allusions to the green of the lizards, the colours of the serpents,
the enamelled lobsters, tortoises, and crabs. The pottery
made by Bernard Palissy, of which, under the name of
Palissy ware, exquisite specimens are still existing, was of

* Some twenty years after the expiration of his first sixteen.

a kind extremely characteristic of its maker.   He wished
to make beautiful things, but he was a naturalist, and his
sense of beauty was his sense of nature.   To reproduce
upon his ware the bright colours and elegant forms of
plants and animals over which he had hung so often with
his pencil in the woods and fields,—combining his qualities
of naturalist and potter,—he founded his reputation on
the manufacture of what he called Rustic Pieces.   The
title which he took for himself was that of Worker in
Earth and Inventor of Rustic Figulines (small modellings)
—Ouvrier de Terre et Inventeur des Rustiques Figulines.
These rustic figulines were, in fact, accurate models from
life of wild animals, reptiles, plants, and other works of
nature, tastefully combined as ornaments into the texture
of a vase or plate.   The rich fancy of Palissy covered his
works with most elaborate adornment ; but his leaves and
reptiles, and other " rustic" designs, are so copied in form
and colour with the minute accuracy of a naturalist, that
the species of each can be determined accurately.   There
has been found scarcely a fancy leaf, and not one lizard,
butterfly, or beetle, not one bit of nature transferred to
the works of Palissy, which does not belong to the rocks,
woods, fields, rivers, and seas of France.*

* Mr. Marryat, a connoisseur in porcelain and fancy pottery, says
of the Palissy ware, " The natural objects which are placed upon this
fayence are very true in form and colour; for, with the exception of
certain leaves, all were moulded from nature.   The choice he has made
shows that this potter was a skilful naturalist; for the fossil shells with
which he has ornamented his different pieces, are the tertiary shells of

Enough has now been said concerning the toils of Palissy during his sixteen years' struggle to acquire the art of manufacturing enamelled pottery. The close of that period will bring us to the year 1557, the age of Palissy then being about forty-eight. At this point, therefore, we leave the history of Palissy the Potter, to chronicle the toil of the same active mind on other paths of progress.

the Paris basin, and their species can be clearly recognised. The fish are those of the Seine; the reptiles and plants of the environs of Paris. There is no foreign natural production to be seen on his ware." It is not at all requisite to bind Palissy to Paris for his models, as Saintonge lies also upon tertiary clay. But we shall see hereafter that the neighbourhood of Paris must have furnished him with many subjects.

CHAPTER XIV.

THE REFORMED CHURCH AT SAINTES.

" THERE was in this town a certain artisan, marvellously poor and indigent, who had so great a desire for the advancement of the Gospel, that he demonstrated it every day to another as poor as himself, and with as little learning, for they both scarcely knew anything ; nevertheless, the first urged upon the other that if he would employ himself in making some form of exhortation, that would be productive of great fruit."*

The " certain artisan, marvellously poor and needy," would have been named, had he been any other man than Palissy himself. The mode of expression, and the known character of Bernard, leave us very little room for doubt that it was he who, in the days of his hard struggling, being unable to find consolation in the orthodox services of the town, satisfied the strong devotional im-

---

* Words of Palissy, used in this chapter, are all from a work which will be found entire in the Appendix.

pulses of his character by studying the Scriptures daily
with one poor companion. The writings of Palissy display throughout a close and reverent acquaintance with
the Bible; his quaint cheerfulness of temper, his artless,
simple-minded style, are beautifully mingled in his works
with a solemnity of religious feeling, that would have led
to asceticism any man with a less healthy intellect. The
grave, uncompromising piety of the Huguenot, who knew
that he might be called upon to die for his faith, formed
a large feature in the character of Palissy. Very ear-
nestly he sought after religious truth, and what he thought,
he spoke with perfect fearlessness. We have found out
by this time, that when his way was chosen, it formed no
part of the character of Palissy to flinch from trouble.

Bernard, then, while he toiled and suffered in acquiring
the skill which was to make him immortal in the history
of art—Bernard, at that time " marvellously poor and
indigent," demonstrated the truths of Scripture daily to
another man, poor like himself. Then, distrustful of his
power or his leisure to prepare for a more public exposition, he communicated to his friend the impulse of his
own active spirit, and urged him to " employ himself
in some form of exhortation, that would be productive of
great fruit."

His friend felt himself to be too simple and unlearned,
but the persuasions of Bernard gave him courage; " and
some days afterwards," Palissy tells us, " he assembled,
one Sunday in the morning, nine or ten persons, and be-

cause he was ill versed in letters, he had taken some passage from the Old and New Testament, having them put
down in writing. And when they were assembled, he
read to them the passages and texts, saying : ' That each
man, according to the gifts he had received, should distribute them to others ; and that every tree which bore not
fruit, would be cut down and cast into the fire.' Also,
he read another text taken from Deuteronomy, where it
is written: ' Thou shalt declare my words, when thou
sittest in thine house, and when thou walkest by the way,
when thou liest down, and when thou risest up ; and thou
shall write them on the door-posts of thine house, and on
the gates.' He proposed to them, also, the parable of the
talents, and a great number of such texts ; and this he did,
tending towards two good ends: the first was to show, that
it was the duty of all people to speak of the statutes and
ordinances of God, and that his doctrine might not be
despised on account of his own abject state ; the second
end was to incite certain auditors to do as he was doing ;
for in this same hour they agreed together that six from
among them should make exhortations weekly—that is to
say, each of the six once in six weeks, on Sundays only.
And because they undertook a business in which they had
never been instructed, it was said that they should put
their exhortations down in writing, and read them before
the assembly. * * That was the beginning of the Reformed Church of the town of Xaintes."

Palissy adds, " I am sure there was, at the beginning,

such a congregation, that the number was of five alone."
Each of the six took his turn to be the preacher to five
listeners, and of these Palissy was one ; his name is chronicled in a contemporary list of preachers. Six poor and
unlearned men, among not a few who were infected with
the taint of heresy, were all who had the boldness, with
grave faces and determined minds, to form themselves into
a Church in that town, which had so recently beheld the
burning of a heretic. Poor as they were, perhaps they
were below the wrath of a grand-vicar, and it may be
that M. Collardeau had warmed himself sufficiently at the
first bonfire of his making.

But there was imprisoned in the town of Saintes, and
through the zeal of this fiscal attorney, Collardeau, " one
named Master Philebert Hamelin." Philebert had taught
the Reformed doctrine, and had contributed by his advice
some part of the impulse towards that formation of a little
Church, which took place while he was in prison. By
some dissembling of his faith, for which he afterwards
" had always a remorse of conscience," Philebert obtained
his freedom at that time, and travelled to Geneva. There,
at the head-quarters of the French reformers, he acquired
a great increase of earnestness ; " he enlarged," Palissy tells
us, " at the said Geneva, both his faith and doctrine.
Then," continues Bernard, " because he had dissembled
in his public confession in this town, and wishing to repair his fault, he exerted himself, wherever he went, to
incite men to have ministers, and to erect some kind of

church, and so travelled through the lands of France,
having some servants who sold bibles, and other books
printed in his press. For he had given his mind to it,
and made himself a printer. In doing this, he passed
sometimes through this town, and went also to Allevert.
Now he was so just, and of so great a zeal, that although
he was a man ill capable of walking, he would never accept horses, although many urged him so to do with full
affection. And being slenderly provided as to the wherewith, he took with him no other outfit than only a simple
staff in his hand, and went his way alone, in this manner,
without any fear.

" Now it occurred one day, after he had concluded some
prayers and little exhortations in this town—having at
most seven or eight auditors—he went upon his way to
Allevert, and, before parting, he prayed the little flock
of the assembly to congregate themselves, to pray, and to
exhort one another; and so he went to Allevert, labouring to win the people to God; and there, being received
kindly by the chief part of the people, brought them by
the sound of a bell to certain sermons, and baptized a
child. Seeing which, the magistrates of this town constrained the bishop to produce money for the maintenance
of a pursuit of the said Philebert, with horses, gensd'armes,
cooks, and sutlers."

The quick, painter's fancy of Palissy, and the clearness
of thought which guides him always to the fittest words,
have filled his works with a great deal of picture-writing.

Nothing could be more happily sketched than this repre-
sentation of Philebert, " a man ill capable of walking, who
took with him no other outfit than only a simple staff in
his hand, and went his way alone in this manner, without
fear," to whom Palissy drily appends a pursuit " with
horses, gensd'armes, cooks, and sutlers."

Undoing as they could the mischief that had been done
by the heretic, the bishop and certain magistrates of Saintes
betook themselves to the scene of the calamity, and caused
the child which had been baptized by Philebert to be
re-baptized into orthodoxy. Philebert was taken in the
mansion of a gentleman. " And so," says Palissy, " they
brought him into this town, as a malefactor to the crimi-
nals' prisons, although his works give certain witness that
he was a child of God and truly of His chosen. He was
so perfect in his works that his enemies were compelled to
own that he was of a holy life, always without approval
of his doctrine."

This second imprisonment of Philebert Hamelin took
place in the beginning of the year 1557, the date named
at the end of the preceding chapter, as the last year of
Bernard's first sixteen as a potter. The date concerns us,
because Philebert Hamelin commanded the love and reverence of Bernard Palissy, and there is connected with
this event a circumstance which admirably illustrates
the potter's earnest character. Notwithstanding all the
terrors threatened against heretics, Bernard Palissy spent
his whole energy, when Philebert was cast into prison, in

labour on his friend's behalf. Careless of any danger to his own life (and we shall hereafter see that he incurred no trifling risk), the grand-hearted potter visited six of the chief judges and magistrates, attacking each of them in his own house with a bold remonstrance. Revealing his own heresy to men bound to condemn it, was nothing; he thought only of doing battle against a monstrous wrong, and proclaiming the virtue of Philebert, who had been, since the old time when he was in Saintes, before his previous imprisonment, until now, for eleven years, his venerated friend.

" I am full of wonder," Bernard says, " that men should have dared to sit in judgment of death over him, seeing that they knew well, and had heard, his blameless conversation ; for I am assured, and I can say with truth, that after the time when he was brought into the prisons of Xaintes, I mustered hardihood (although the days were perilous in those times) to go and remonstrate with six of the principal judges and magistrates of this town of Xaintes, that they had imprisoned a prophet or an angel of God, sent to announce his word and judgment of condemnation to men in the last days; assuring them that for eleven years I had known the said Philebert Hamelin to be of so holy a life, that it seemed to me as if the other men were devils when compared to him. It is certain that the judges used humanity towards myself, and heard me kindly : also I spoke to each of them in his own house.

" Finally, they treated with tolerable kindness the said

Master Philebert, although they could not acquit themselves of being guilty of his death. True it is they did
not kill him, as Pilate and Judas did not kill the Lord ;
but they delivered him into the hands of those by whom
they knew well that he would be slain. And the better
to come by a wash for their hands that would acquit their
hearts, they reasoned that he had been priest in the Roman
Church ; therefore they sent him to Bourdeaux, with good
and sure guard, by a provost-marshal.

" Would you know," continues Palissy, revealing much
of his own character while he applauds his friend—" would
you know how holy was the life of the said Philebert ?
Liberty was given to him to live in the apartment of the
gaol-keeper, and to eat and drink at his table, which he
did while he was in this town. But after, for many days,
he had laboured and taken pains to repress the gamblings
and blasphemies which were committed in the chamber
of the gaol-keeper, it was so displeasing, seeing that they
would not check themselves, that to prevent himself from
listening to such evil, as soon as he had dined, he caused
himself to be led into a criminal cell, and remained there
the whole day long in solitude, to avoid the evil company.

" *Item.* Would you know still better how he walked
uprightly ? To him, being in prison, there came an advocate of France, belonging to some region in which he
had founded a little Church, which advocate brought three
hundred livres, which he offered to the gaol-keeper, provided he would, at night, put the said Philebert outside

the prisons. Seeing which, the gaol-keeper was almost
incited to do it; he requested, however, to take counsel
with the said Master Philebert, who answering, told him,
' that it was better worth his while to die at the hands of
the executioner, than to expose another man to evil for
the good of self.' Which learning, the said advocate took
back his money. I ask you, which is he among us who
would do the like, being at the mercy of enemies as he
was ? The judges of this town knew well that his life
was holy ; nevertheless they acted through fear, lest they
should lose their offices: so we must understand it.

" I was well informed," adds Bernard, " that while the
said Philebert was in the prisons of this town, there was a
person who, speaking of the said Philebert, said to a
counsellor of Bourdeaux: ' They will bring you, one of
these days, a prisoner from Xaintes, who will speak to you
well, messieurs.' But the counsellor, blaspheming the
name of God, swore that he should not speak to him at
all, and that he should take care not to be present at this
judgment."

It was not in the temper of the sturdy Potter to see
wrong committed, and to fold his hands in peace; we
readily anticipate, therefore, his comment on the indolent
determination of the counsellor: " I ask you whether this
counsellor called himself a Christian, who would not condemn the just? At any rate, since he was constituted
judge, he will have no excuse; for while he knew that
the other was a good man, he ought with his power to

have opposed the judgment of those, who through ignorance, or through malice, condemned him, delivered him
up, and caused him to be hung like a thief, the 18th of
April, in the abovenamed year."

That is to say, in the year 1557. A contemporary
historian* of the Reform party connects with the death of
Hamelin a quasi miracle. A heretic who was to have
shared his fate, recanted his opinions to save his life.
Hamelin warned him that he would, notwithstanding,
die. This companion was assassinated as he left the
prison, and Philebert was questioned for the purpose of
ascertaining whether his prophecy did not imply complicity. Of course it did not. Indeed, the whole anecdote
may be untrue ; for there were not a few divine inter-
positions current, as arguments, among religious combatants on either side. For example, the historian above
mentioned cites, with full credence, a contemporary book
called " Dan," in which there seems to be collected a most
edifying set of stories, about judgment done on persecutors.
The following is one: " A Piedmontese in Angrongne,
having sworn that he would eat the nose of the pastor, a
wolf in broad noon, and before a great multitude, going to
this man, devoured his nose, and returned without wound-
ing any other person, as if he had no other business to
do." Such tales remind us of the ignorance and super-
stition proper to the world three centuries ago—conditions

* D'Aubigné's *Hist. Univ.*

which we might too easily forget, while we have our minds
intent upon the intellect of Bernard Palissy.

Soon after the commencement of the little Church of
Xaintes, while there was still a congregation of no more
than about half a dozen—during the first imprisonment
of Philebert Hamelin—a minister named De la Place had
been engaged; and De la Place had been succeeded after
a few years by another minister named De la Boissière.
"While the Church was so little," Palissy tells us, "and
the said Master Philebert was in prison, there arrived in
this town a minister named De la Place, who had been
sent to go and preach in Allevert.   But on the same day,
the attorney of the said Allevert happened to be in this
town, who assured him that he would be very unwelcome
there, on account of that baptism which Master Philebert
had performed; because several assistants thereat had been
condemned to very heavy penalties, and it was for this
reason that we prayed the said De la Place to administer
to us the word of God; and he was received for our
minister, and remained until we had Monsieur de la
Boissière, which is he whom we still have at the present
time.   But this was a pitiable thing, for we had the good-
will, but the power to support the ministers we had not;
inasmuch as La Place, during the time that we had him,
was maintained partly at the expense of the gentlemen,
who frequently invited him."   The pastors of the Reformed
faith being superior to the monks in taste and education

formed to courtly men, indifferent about religious strife, agreeable associates. La Place, therefore, had been a frequent guest at the houses of the neighbouring gentlemen; but the stern, rough, earnest artisans who formed the little Church, had doubts concerning the propriety of this arrangement; and Bernard, with manifest pity for the next pastor, who was over-zealously controlled, goes on to relate how, " fearing lest that might not be the means of corrupting our ministers, they advised M. de la Boissière not to leave the town, except with permission, to attend upon the nobility, even though it might be upon urgent business. By such means, the poor man was shut up like a prisoner, and very frequently ate apples, and drank water for his dinner ; and for want of tablecloth he very often laid his dinner on a shirt, because there were very few rich people who joined our congregation, and so we had not the means of paying him his salary."

The laws against heresy were so stringent, that the life of any man who was a known heretic depended wholly on the sufferance of his neighbours. In the early years of the Reformed Church at Saintes, it was necessary for the members of the little flock to slip at midnight through the streets, and hold their mutual exhortations under cover of the darkness. But with time, in many parts of France, the manifest contrast between the orderly and upright lives of the new pastors and the abuses of the priesthood, caused the power of the heretics to grow. The sympathies of the people, the desire of relief from Church burdens which were cruelly unjust, caused many bold, unruly spirits to enter the ranks of the Calvinists, and assume an external show of much ascetic virtue. Many such men, who had thought of political reform alone, afterwards changing sides, let loose the passions which they had so long affected painfully to curb, and were among the wildest spirits in the storm for which the clouds had long been gathering.

There were few places in which the heretics multiplied so rapidly as in Saintonge. Passions were nowhere stronger, no place was more trampled by combatants—it was the scene of many of the maddest contests in the subsequent religious war. The timid beginning, the rapid increase, and, finally, the bold predominance of heretics in Saintes, are all described by Palissy.

" The Church," he tells us, " was established in the beginning with great difficulty and eminent perils ; we were blamed and vituperated with perverse and wicked calumnies . . . Notwithstanding all these things, God so well favoured our affair, that although our assemblies were most frequently held in the depth of midnight, and our enemies very often heard us passing through the street, yet so it was, that God bridled them in such manner that we were preserved under His protection. And when God willed that His Church was manifested publicly, and in the face of day, He fulfilled in our town an admirable work ; for there were sent to Toulouse two of the principal chiefs, who would not have permitted our assemblies to be public, which was the reason why we had the hardihood to take the Market Hall."

Throughout France there was a division among magistrates with respect to the interpretation of the penal edicts against heresy. Men are not by nature devilish, and the extreme severity of law in very many places being odious to its administrators, was either left in the dead letter, or interpreted into a milder spirit. The absence of the two men whose zeal was to be feared, gave a boldness indicating already considerable strength, when it encouraged the reformers to hold their meetings in the Market Hall. The absence of these men was long. Palissy tells us : " God detained them for the space of two years, or thereabout, at Toulouse, in order that they might not hurt His Church, during the time that He would have it to be manifested publicly."

These last events were subsequent to the year 1557. The remarkable prosperity of the Reformed Church of Saintes, which was of brief duration, dates from about 1560. Of Saintes, during this period, Bernard says : " In that way our Church was established: in the beginning, by despised folk ; and when its enemies arrived to waste and persecute it, it had so well prospered in a few years, that already the games, dances, ballads, banquets, and superfluities of head-dress and gildings, had almost all ceased; there were almost no more scandalous words or murders. Actions at law were beginning greatly to diminish; for so soon as two men of our religion began an action, means were found to bring them to accommodation; and even very often before commencing any suit, one man did not begin to proceed against another until first he had caused him to be reasoned with by members of the Church. When the time came for Easter preparations, many engaged in hatreds, dissensions, and quarrels, were reconciled. The question was not only about psalms, prayers, canticles, and spiritual songs, any more than it was only a quarrel against dissolute and lewd songs. The Church had so well prospered, that even the magistrates had assumed the control of many evil things which were dependent upon their authority. It was forbidden to innkeepers to have gaming in their houses, or to give meat and drink to people who inhabited houses in the town, in order that the debauched men might be returned to their families. You would have seen in those days, on a Sunday, fellow-tradesmen rambling through the fields, groves, and other places, singing in troops psalms, canticles, and spiritual songs, reading and instructing one another.

" You would have seen the daughters and virgins seated by troops in the gardens, and other places, who, in a like way, delighted themselves in the singing of all holy things. On the other hand, you would have seen the teachers, who had so well instructed youth, that the children had even no longer a puerility of manner, but a look of manly fortitude. These things had so well prospered, that people had changed their old manners, even to their very countenances."

Children so well instructed that they lose their puerility of manner, fellow-tradesmen who sing hymns among the fields and groves, would promise little good in our own day. But when a child of fifteen was not too young for the stake, when the daughters and virgins might be stabbed for their singing, and fellow-tradesmen broken on the wheel for exercising liberty of conscience, then it was fit that people should " change their old manners, even to their very countenances;" that they should sternly sing their hymns in the free air of heaven, and defy, when they could, the law that made itself a God over the soul.

CHAPTER XV.

AFFAIRS OF FRANCE.

PALISSY THE POTTER was extremely busy when King
Francis the First died. The affairs of Palissy, at that
time, concerned us more than the affairs of France; we
simply nodded acquiescence to the fact when the state
went into mourning, if we were not even perhaps so
disrespectful as to neglect it altogether. We have arrived
now, however, at a period when the affairs of France are
likely often to be the affairs of Bernard Palissy. The
Potter has succeeded in his art; he can make articles of
luxury which are to be had from no other hands in France;
he is a man, therefore, for the luxurious to patronise.
We shall find high and mighty personages soon connected
with the daily life of the successful artisan. For other
reasons also, some of the affairs of France will soon begin
to touch the interests of Bernard the Reformer.

We shall, of course, not trouble ourselves about affairs
of France, as they have to be told by the historian:

the wars we leave out altogether, and substitute for them
a word or two concerning the Fayence of Henry II.; in
other respects, our attention has to be confined to things
and people that can be common at once to a history of
France and to a history of Bernard Palissy.

Let us go back to the reign of the King Francis II., and
to the year 1545 (he died in 1547); there we touch upon
an exemplary slaughter, by the most Christian king, of
several thousand. heretical Vaudois, massacred horribly,
men, women, and children, on the confines of Provence
and Venaissin. Yet there were some who, looking at his
majesty's alliances with Protestant German princes, accused him of want of zeal against the heretics. " Want
of zeal!" cries Mezeray, " when every year heretics were
burnt by dozens, sent to the galleys by hundreds, banished
by thousands." Yes, indeed, want of zeal. They should
have been burnt by thousands, doomed to the galleys by
hundreds, and exiled by dozens, had King Francis been
in earnest. The Vaudois massacre was something, indeed;
but what credit is to be attached to a mere fitful gust of
goodness?

And what could be expected in the way of zeal from
the head of a court whose manners I dare not whisper
into the ears of the modest nineteenth century? The
gallant king, the hero of romance and ballad, partner in
the Field of the Cloth of Gold, presider at good-old-time
tournaments, the " Kaiser Franz" of Schiller's ballad
about the Proud Lady and the Glove, lived after a way

from which the pure heart turns with an unutterable loathing. He died in 1547, as kings used once to be fond of dying, with his family about' him, giving sage and prudent counsel to his heir, making his farewell bow to this world, with his hand upon the door that led into the next, in a most graceful and becoming manner. The Vaudois massacre rumbled, perhaps, a little in his conscience, but not much; he had already laid any blame connected therewith on the shoulders of his servants.

King Francis left his crown to his son Henry, who had not been always his heir; but the original dauphin, Francis, had been taken already from this world. He died by poison, some said; and so, most undoubtedly, he did. But the poison was of a kind well known to surgeons, and not unfamiliar to the court of France, which sometimes horribly destroys the men who give the rein too freely to their passions. Truly, there was no stake or gibbet in the country able to administer to man so vile a death as that which had deprived King Francis of his eldest son. Though, to be sure, there were not many courtiers in France who would at that time have thought it vile. Why should not scars of love be as well honoured as the scars of war, since there can be no doubt that, as war was understood in those days, they were the result of equally good service to mankind?

Henry, then, as King Henry II., at the age of twenty-nine, in the midst of a general—and, of course, deeply sincere—mourning, succeeded his great father, Francis.

The funeral oration over the late king was pronounced by a most learned man, Pierre du Châtel, latinized Castelan, Bishop of Mâcon. The bishop duly pronounced the said oration, which was, as such things ought to be, a tombstone-piece upon the grandest scale. Among other things, it was said by the bishop of the late king, " his death has been so pious, that I think his soul must have flown straight to heaven, without the need of any cleansing in the fire of purgatory." If his life had been pious, that would have been a better recommendation. The only field for ambition—the only luxury for self-love—left upon a death-bed, is to hang out as brilliant a show as possible of moral lights for the illumination of by-standers. I should have doubted, therefore, the bishop's plea for the deplored monarch's exemption from the taxes of the other world. Many worthy auditors not only doubted, but were greatly scandalised at the suggestion. Not that they honoured Francis less than the good bishop did, but that they honoured purgatory more. No man, however pure, however royal, could go into the next world, from this, without passing through the turnpike-gate of purgatory, as established by the holy Church. No doubt there was a carefully-adjusted scale of tolls, and the charge might be inconsiderable for the passage of an orthodox king; but still there would be some charge, and he must pay it. The doctrine of the Bishop of Mâcon was heretical and revolutionary. The auditors thus scandalised denounced the bishop to the university; the university regarded the question as a matter of so much importance, that it sent a solemn deputation to the young king, which was met at the door of the palace by Jean Mendoza, first maître d'hôtel, a witty Spaniard. Mendoza greeted in a friendly way the solemn embassy: " You are welcome, gentlemen; you come to discuss with the grand-almoner the travels of King Francis since he left us, and ascertain what stay he made in purgatory. Walk in, if you please. For my part, I can tell you, I knew our late master very well, and I am sure that he was not the man for stopping long in any place, or about anything. He was always for change in this world, and so he is, no doubt, in the next. If he did drop in upon purgatory, he could not do more than taste the wine and travel on; I know King Francis." Such banter strangled the discussion, and Du Châtel was made grand-almoner next year. That a question like this should have arisen ; that, having arisen, it could be destroyed by banter;—that a court like that of King Francis, upon the strength of religious feelings so artificial, should judge to be irreligious, and condemn to death men leading pure, ascetic lives, and mastered by religious feeling so sincere as, for example, that of Palissy;—is matter that suggests a painful aspect of the temper of those wretched times.

So in the year 1547 we have upon the throne of France Henry II., aged twenty-nine—a man with a feeble brain and a strong fist. He was at home in the licence of the court, and he was at home upon the field of battle; as he had been trained to arms under the Constable Montmorenci, it is not a bad point in him that he retained a pupil-like affection for his ancient leader. On King Henry's accession, the great crowd of nobles round the throne divided itself into four factions, each pledged to the interests of a distinct chief. There were the partisans of the Constable Montmorenci, and the partisans of his great rivals, the House of Guise—the Duke of Guise, a military commander of great skill, and his brother, Cardinal of Lorraine, the same Cardinal of whom we heard the Draper speaking in an early chapter of this narrative. Those were the two parties headed by men; the other two factions were devoted respectively to Diana of Poitiers and to the Queen Catherine of Medicis. As the story of the life of Palissy will shortly flow between banks peopled by the high and mighty of the nation, we shall find it necessary to refresh our memories concerning the position held in France by some of these great people.

The Constable Anne de Montmorenci was, during a large part of his life, next to the king the most important man in France. This personage possessed enormous wealth, and we are presently to see him standing in the first rank among the patrons of that skill which Bernard Palissy has won for himself through so much suffering. The constable, therefore, has a special claim upon these pages. He was born at Chantilli in 1493, and named after Anne of Brittany, his godmother. Godmothers, fortunately, do not often claim the privilege of christening

male children into the female sex. He was a year older
than King Francis I., and, having been his playmate when
his majesty was Count of Angoulême, had gained in early
years an influence over the mind of Francis which was
long retained. Young Montmorenci fought in the Italian
wars, and was created a marshal in 1522, that is to say,
when he was twenty-nine. It is always advisable to connect
a man's age distinctly with the events and actions of his life,
because their significance is at all times greatly modified
by considerations that arise from knowledge of that kind.
Montmorenci has been already mentioned as seen by
Montluc struggling on foot at the battle of Bicoque. At
Pavia he was taken prisoner, and carried with King
Francis, his friend, to Madrid. Francis would have retained him as a companion in captivity. Montmorenci,
however, having prudently suggested that it would be
better that he should return to France and labour about the
releasing of his master, this suggestion was thought good.
He did so release himself by ransom, and did so labour on
the king's behalf with good effect, since he was afterwards
made, in reward for his services, governor of Languedoc
and grand-master of France. With this last office was
connected the administration of affairs.

In 1536, Charles V. made an attempt to subdue France
by invasion. Montmorenci, then aged forty-three, commanding the army of defence, ruined the emperor by wise
delays, and forced him to retreat, avoiding a battle, the loss
of which might for a season have destroyed the monarchy.

The French, even in those days, had a taste for Roman parallels, and they called Anne, Cunctator, or the Fabius of France.

On the 10th of February, 1538, Montmorenci, aged forty-five, was appointed constable, being the fifth of his family who had attained that honour. He was then by far the greatest man in France, and received homage and presents from foreign states, not only of Europe but of Asia, being courted abroad as a man not less mighty than his king. He was an austere man, very much too rough to be agreeable at court; his wealth had become enormous, and he stood upon the pinnacle of power. There is not much room for a man's feet upon that pinnacle, and Montmorenci slipped, as they who are in his position generally do. He was disgraced in 1541, three years after he was made a constable; deprived, to be sure, of no office or possession, losing nothing but the royal favour; and he dispensed proudly with that, retiring to his birthplace of Chantilli, where he lived in a state of sullen grandeur till King Francis died. Why he was disgraced it is not easy to tell; some hold him to have been so rough a bear among the perfumed ladies who were powerful at court that they all set their wits against him; others say that the king was jealous of the close attachment between Montmorenci and his son Henry; certainly, among the death-bed advice of the king was an item, that Henry ought not to recal Montmorenci from seclusion.

Henry did not keep that precept, for upon the death of

Francis he lost no time in summoning his friend the constable to court, where he styled him Compeer, as a man
who was his equal, and received him with a manifest
affection. Constable Montmorenci, therefore, at the age
of fifty-four, returned to court, and was the head acknow-
ledged by one of the four court factions by which the
throne of the new king was surrounded.

In political affairs rivalry meant enmity, three centuries
ago. Therefore the Guises and their friends, rivals of
Montmorenci, used against and suffered at the hands of
the Montmorenci faction all the tricks and stratagems
which a court enmity dictates.

And then there were the two ladies and their partisans.
There was Diana of Poitiers, or of St. Vallier, widow of
Louis de Biézé, Grand-Seneschal of Normandy. She
bore the honourable title of King's Mistress, and was made
Duchess of Valentinois. This lady had made her first
appearance some time since at the court of King Francis,
in the interesting character of a distressed damsel pleading for her father. King Francis appreciated her beauty;
she went home affected by his knightly courtesy. After
her husband's death, she came to reside permanently at
the court of Francis; and there, seeing that the education
of Prince Henry was very much neglected, she undertook
to play the part of governess to the boy, after a fashion of
her own. She begged him of King Francis for her chevalier; the best way to touch the understanding, she said,
was through love. So, though she was a widow with

more than one marriageable daughter to dispose of, she took the boy Henry for her knight. The youth was pleased; the attention of a full-sized woman greatly flatters a three-quarter-sized man: the only curious part of the transaction is, that Henry clung as firmly to his mistress in love and peace as he had clung to his master in war. Diana of Poitiers maintained her ascendancy as well as Montmorenci maintained his, during the whole life of the king. Diana held a brilliant court, and was a little more to King Henry than his wife, though it is quite possible that she was king's mistress only according to the old knightly meaning of the word. Nothing opposes itself to that supposition but a knowledge of the intense grossness of court morals during Henry's reign. They had been licentious under King Francis; but under Henry, who had much of the camp breeding in himself, the film of outward courtesy, the elegant gloss and fiction of speech, the polite *double entendre*, and all such devices which at least make payment of a tacit tribute to the sense of what is decent,—these were laid aside, and the bare, hard brutality of a licentious camp furnished a model for the conduct of the court of France. Diana of Poitiers then was the head of the third faction of courtiers.

But the poor queen, the wife of Henry!—if it were only possible to pity her. She was twenty-eight years old when her husband succeeded to the throne. King Francis had allowed his son Henry to marry her, because in the first place he wanted money, and her father Lorenzo was rich; in the second place, because he did not greatly care for his son Henry, and did not mind throwing him away upon a girl who was an unequal match, for he did not then suppose that Henry would ever come to be a king, and make a queen of her. Thus Catherine of Medicis found herself looked down upon from all sides, as an insignificant person whose alliance conferred anything but honour on the royal blood of France. Pitiable as her position was, she needed no man's pity. She was not trained to very tender feelings, and she was diplomatist enough to show a smooth face to the world, though she knew that she was pretty widely hated, and that she had a pretty wide circle of hates to pay back in return. Petty princes are profound in all minor diplomacy, and Catherine's mind had been fed early with that kind of meat. So when her husband became king, and she was Queen Catherine, and had her own faction at court, she outwardly professed the gentlest feelings towards Diana of Poitiers, towards the Duke or Cardinal Guise, and towards Montmorenci, although their mutual hatreds and their factions were notorious. She was a pretty and a witty woman, and during the life of King Henry, she allowed him to pay what attentions he would to Diana, while she waited with a great appearance of placidity in the background, among all the overruling influences of the court. She caressed Diana, flattered the rugged constable, and so became, after all, a woman of great power before she was nailed down into her coffin.

In the midst of these factions lived King Henry, getting up at seven, and going to bed at ten; between those hours, one would think, not the happiest of men. The business at court of each faction was to get what it could, and to keep what it could out of the getting of the other three. Whenever a living, or estate, or appointment, however small, had fallen, or was about to fall, into the king's gift, there was a rush, not of obsequious beggars, but of tyrannical exacters. The small men of each faction formed a network of spies over the country, who reported to its chief any mouthful that they met with anywhere worth picking up. Of this the Draper has told us something in his eulogy upon the Cardinal de Guise. Perhaps the king had promised something to a friend of his friend Montmorenci ; then the next day there would come to him the Duke of Guise, with his proud, stern face of military command, and he would ask for it. The king would murmur, Montmorenci;—say the place was given. Whereupon the duke would so argue down his majesty, that in the end—and I relate what is recorded of one such occasion—the king did not dare to fulfil his promise to Montmorenci, because he feared the stern Duke of Guise, nor could he give the place to a Guise without enraging Montmorenci.

One of the first acts of the new king was to issue an edict confirmatory of religious penalties. A blasphemer was to have his tongue pierced with a hot iron, but all heretics were to be burnt alive.

VOL. I.   R

I hinted, some chapters ago, that the people of Saintonge did not very quietly endure the salt-tax. They broke out into a rebellion, about a year after the accession of Henry, in 1548. While Palissy was in the depth of poverty, labouring at his furnace, a scene of riot and violence was enacted for some months in Saintonge and the surrounding districts. It began in Angoumois, and extended to the Bordelais, Agenois, Perigord, la Marche, Poitou, Aunis, and Saintonge. The first insurgents were the country people, who took arms and expelled the officers of the gabelle. The people of Saintonge—this was in 1547—massacred eight of them. The people of Perigueux were content that theirs should be expelled. Henri d'Albret, governor of Guienne, sent troops against the insurgents, but his troops were driven back. Deserters and disbanded captains had been scattered by the constant state of war over the face of France; such men headed the bands of country people, and instructed them in martial ways. Pillage, fire, and massacre abounded, the revolt extended to Bourdeaux, which became the head-quarters of the disaffected. The garrison of Château Trompette endeavoured to subdue Bourdeaux; that was repulsed, and the commander, Tristan de Morienne, king's lieutenant in Navarre, coming out imprudently to address the people, was seized by them, killed, mutilated, and buried. His body before burial had been first powdered over with salt, in order that by some act, however rude and clumsy of invention, the people might connect this victim of their fury with a sign of their fierce hate for the gabelle.

The king was at that time with his troops in Italy, but he sent letters patent, promising that justice should be done, and these appeased the people. Justice was done, for the parliament immediately erected gibbets and wheels, on which they hung or broke the bodies of those ringleaders who were not sent to the galleys. La Vergne, a citizen, who had been first to sound the tocsin, was torn asunder by four horses. While this was being done, two bodies of troops sent by the king were on their way to complete the act of justice. One body was under the Duke d'Aumâle, the other was under Constable Montmorenci. The duke traversed Saintonge, Poitou, Aunis, &c., restoring order with the aid of few acts of severity. The constable marched upon Bourdeaux to be revenged for the outrage on Tristan de Morienne.

The keys of the town of Bourdeaux Montmorenci disdained to accept, and with drums beating, cannons rolling, lances pointed, and flags flying, he marched his troops into the town as a triumphant enemy. The people were disarmed, a grim tribunal was appointed, and the great square was crowded with scaffolding and gibbets. A hundred citizens were promptly sent to die upon them. Two leaders of the people were broken on the wheel, one of them wearing at the same time on his head a red-hot crown. The town was declared guilty of felony, and deprived of all its bells. The parliament, because it had been tardy in

its effort to suppress the tumult, was suppressed. The
magnates of the town were sent to dig up with their nails
the body of Tristan de Morienne. They were then ordered
to carry it before the windows of the constable, and go
down on their knees with it, beseeching pardon for the
deed that had been done. After this they carried in their
hands the putrefying corpse to the cathedral, where they
buried it beside the choir. Finally, they paid two hundred thousand livres for the expense incurred in giving them
their punishment. It was ordered also that the town-hall,
from which Tristan stepped out to be murdered, should be
razed to the ground, and that in a chapel built over its
site prayers should be offered every day for Tristan's soul.
This, however, was not done ; and all the other penalties
incurred by Bourdeaux were remitted during the succeeding year, only a few minor privileges remained lost
for ever to its parliament.

From Bourdeaux, Montmorenci went through the other
disturbed districts, Saintonge among the rest, and wherever
he went he built and furnished gibbets. This having been
done, the king allowed the people to buy off their salt-tax
at the price of two hundred thousand gold dollars, in addition to the cost of paying all the officers. That arrangement suited the king very well, for he was at all times
prompt to turn the crown revenues into capital, and so
consume them, without any care for what might be the
income left to his successors.

During the year 1551, Henry II. was taking a very

bold position of hostility towards the Pope, and fearing much lest this might give a false encouragement to heretics, he supplied them with the edict of Chateaubriant by way of counter-demonstration. This edict aggravated former penalties ; it forbade all presentation of petitions for the aid of heretics, all refuge to them; it offered rewards to their denouncers, and confiscated their goods when they went into exile. Public men, on their appointment to an office, or otherwise when called upon, were obliged to exhibit a certificate of orthodoxy ; and active inquisition into private opinion, with a view to the discovery of heretics, was recommended.

It should be remembered that this edict was in force, and this was the temper of the state, when Bernard Palissy besieged in their houses, with a bold expostulation, six of the chief men of Saintes, by whom his avowed friend and fellow-heretic, Philebert Hamelin, was held for death.

But as these judges leniently shut their ears to the rash words of Palissy, and kindly answered him, so also in many parts of France men had not heart to act up fully to the fiercest spirit of the law. The heretics grew stronger: heresy tainted a large part of the Montmorenci faction, the religious struggle heightened court disputes, and in the camps the soldiers often were prepared to come to blows together, because some were orthodox and some were not. Therefore, it was thought necessary that law should be more severe.

Rome had named an inquisitor for France; to him the
bishops made objection; they said, it sufficed that there
should be given to them absolute power to condemn heretics, and that the heretics should have no right of appeal.
To this the council of the king agreed, and the arrangement was submitted to the consent of the parliament of
Paris. The parliament denied consent, and through the
advocate-general, Séguier, they made the king's blood
tingle with a noble speech. " If heresy was to be suppressed," said Séguier, whose name is very honourable
for the bold utterance more than once at this period of
manly feelings—" if heresy was to be suppressed, let pastors be compelled to labour among their flocks. Commence, sire," said he, " with giving an edict to the nation
which will not cover your kingdom with scaffolds, which
will not be moistened with the blood or tears of faithful
subjects. Distant, sire, from your presence, bent under
the weight of labour in the fields, or absorbed in the exercise of arts and trades, they know not what is now being
designed against them. It is for them, it is in their name,
that the parliament addresses to you its most humble
remonstrance and its ardent supplication." The bold
orator then turned upon the counsellors with a stern apos-
trophe, reminding them of the uncertain future of all
subjects who were high in power. Montmorenci could
provide a comment from his past experience, the Duke of
Guise looked his sternest; but Séguier spoke to good pur-

pose, for the opposition of the parliament caused the new project to be set aside.

To provide the better justice for his people, or more offices for the friends of the friends of his courtiers, Henry II. greatly increased the number of lawyers and other officers throughout France. He established under the name of Presidial Courts a fresh spider's web over the country, for the catching of his subject-flies, and for the fattening upon them of such spiders as might have a friend at court. His abuse of the crown revenues I have mentioned. He was reckless in expenditure. He gave the seigneurie of Gannat, in the Bourbonnais, to a fiddler named Lambert, as a marriage-gift upon his leading to the altar nobody knows whom. The parliament reminded him through their mouthpiece, the honest Séguier, that he had only usufruct of crown revenues, and that if he must needs be wasteful, he should waste his own money, and not that which appertained to his successors. Henry listened, smiled assent, and went on as before. The disorder and lewdness that prevailed in his court were revealed about this time in a suit for what we should call " Breach of Promise of Marriage," by one Demoiselle de Rohan against the Duke de Nemours. Most of the chief men about the king were witnesses, and their evidence supplies a filthy picture of the court of France during that time.

In the year 1557 Montmorenci was captured by the Spaniards in an endeavour to relieve his nephew, Coligny, shut up in St. Quintin. This is the latest date we have

at present reached in any section of our narrative. It is
the date of the completion of Bernard's fifteen or sixteen
years of apprenticeship in pottery. Montmorenci being
absent in the power of the enemy, the Duke of Guise, after
his great exploit, the capture of Calais, was at court,
improving the occasion. In spite of the stern look of
commander which the weak spirit of Henry feared, Guise,
who was certainly a gallant soldier, was a handsome man
of polished manners, who could be agreeably persuasive
when he pleased. When Montmorenci heard through
some of his attentive spies how cleverly his rival was at
work, he obtained leave on parole to visit the French
court, and betook himself, in 1558, to Paris—he was then
a man sixty-five years old—to watch over his own interests. He was at first coldly received, but soon regained
his old ascendancy.

In the mean time Calvinism—heresy—was spreading,
and already numbered many great men in its ranks.
Among these men were Admiral Coligny, and his brother,
D'Andelot, Colonel-General of French Infantry. These
were two nephews of the constable, and Cardinal Guise
(Lorraine) resolved to strike at Montmorenci, and to
wound the adverse faction, by a blow aimed against them.
He denounced them as heretics, and they were summoned
to reply. D'Andelot boldly came, acknowledging and
justifying his opinions, while he attacked the abuses in the
Church with a freedom that incensed the king. D'Andelot, therefore, was imprisoned, and his office of colonel-

general was given to a soldier whom we knew in his youth, and who has since been rising in the world—Blaise de Montluc. Persuaded by his friends, D'Andelot consented to go through the form of hearing a mass, and was set free, but he could not forgive himself for having in that way obtained his freedom.

The brothers Coligny and D'Andelot thus came to be regarded as their chiefs by the great body of heretics in France, who admired their austere habits, honoured the sacrifice by them of worldly power and profit which the adoption of Calvinism had involved. The orthodox were proud of a defender like the Duke of Guise—the defender of Metz, the captor of Calais, a military genius, a man brave, eloquent, and liberal in gifts.

Montmorenci having regained his influence at court, went back to Spain, obedient to his parole. He had regained his influence very completely. The Guise party, having formed a coalition with the party of Queen Catherine de Medicis, had left the king's mistress anxious to retaliate upon them by forming a close alliance with the constable. Montmorenci, with Diana of Poitiers, gained not only the extension of his faction, but the completest hold upon the king. Diana and Montmorenci were the woman and the man who influenced King Henry most, who were his nearest friends, and when they ceased from rivalry and worked together with a common purpose, they were themselves the King. So thorough was the influence thus exercised, that after the constable's return to Spain, the king, enrolled among the number of his meanest spies, listened for court-tattle to report, watched all the tactics and manœuvres of the Guise faction, and sent details of them to the great head of the rival party. In this work of course Diana helped, and manuscripts remain to us containing information of this kind, written in one place by the king, in another place by his mistress,—one continuing the letter of the other, and the other then resuming,—with the signature of both affixed as, your old, best friends, Diana and Henry: " Vos anciens et meilleurs amis, Diane et Henri."

A conference having been appointed in 1558, for the discussion of some terms of peace, Montmorenci was sent by Spain to the meeting. King Henry, seeing him approach, ran forward and hung upon his neck; kept the constable in his tent, and caused him to share his bed, till he returned again. Soon afterwards the constable was ransomed, and laboured so industriously to bring about a peace, that in the year 1559, the war in Italy, which had endured then for six-and-seventy years, was ended. For the peace the constable received no benediction from the Duke of Guise, whose glory was in war, or from the people; it was termed the Unfortunate Peace, because it was obtained by yielding up all that had been filched in seventy-six years of disastrous contest. The contention ceased by a surrender of the bone.

I know no words that can depict the wretched state of the French people at this time. Incessant war had taken brave young men out of the fields, and left thousands of them dead on a foreign soil, or returned them to the country men of debauched life, bullies, cripples. The immense cost of these wars had been defrayed by oppressive taxes, recklessly imagined, cruelly enforced. The lust and luxury of a debased court had grown fat for years upon the money of the poor. Almost every year saw the creation of new salaried officials, whom the people had to carry on their backs, and pay besides for doing them the honour to be burdens. The morals of the people were perverted, they were impoverished, embittered, made litigious, and devoured by lawyers before judges of whom scarcely one in ten was unassailable by bribe. The Church was a machine for burning heretics and raising tithes. Against the debasing influence of a corrupt court, which extended among all ranks of the nobility, and through them was displayed before the ignorant among their fields, —against the vice bred in the camp and dispersed along the march of armies, or brought home by thousands of disbanded soldiers,—the Church, as a whole, made not one effort to establish Christian discipline. Pastors laboured only at the shearing of their flocks; bishops received in idle and luxurious abodes their own large portion of the wool. Instead of dwelling in their bishoprics, and struggling for the cause of Christ, no less than forty of these bishops were at this time in Paris, holding their mouths open like dogs for bits of meat, and struggling for the cause of Guise or Montmorenci.

The heretics grew bold, and made a demonstration in the Pré aux Clercs. The king grew more embittered against them, and on the 1st of June, 1559, he played off a sly trick at a meeting of a council called the Mercuriale, by inducing all the members to speak their minds about the demonstration, and then causing the arrest of those who spoke with any leaning towards its promoters. He then bethought himself concerning some new measures of severity ; but on the 28th of the same month a lance went through his skull while he was jousting at a tournament;—being strong-fisted, he was glad to show his skill;—and so King Henry died at the age of forty-one, leaving Catherine de Medicis a widow.   She was a good-looking widow of forty, with three daughters and four sons.   Her eldest son, a lad of fifteen or sixteen, on the 10th of July, 1559, became, while yet under his mother's tutelage, King Francis the Second.

There remain to us specimens of a beautiful kind of pottery which was made in France, under the patronage of Henry II. and Diana of Poitiers, while Palissy was maturing his discovery.   This ware is called Fayence of Henry II.,* sometimes Fayence of Diana of Poitiers ; it differs from Palissy ware altogether, but is quite as beautiful, and is the earliest fine fabric of the kind known to

* For my information on this subject, I am indebted to Mr. Marryat's excellent volume upon Pottery and Porcelain, to which I have in a previous chapter had some obligations to acknowledge.

have been made in France. Where it was made, or by
whom, are questions that remain unanswered; probably
by Italian artists, perhaps by descendants of Luca della
Robbia, several of whose family exercised his arts in
France. The fayence of Henry II. is of a hard paste—
that used by Palissy is soft. This fayence is made of a
true pipeclay, very fine and white, so that it does not
require any enamel, and the ornaments upon its surface
are covered only with a thin, transparent, yellowish var-
nish. The ornaments themselves are engraved patterns,
of which all the grooves are filled with coloured paste, so
that there results a smooth surface, of which the decoration is a fine inlaying. Of these inlaid ornaments, yellow-
ochre is a prevailing colour. In addition, however, to the
inlaid patterns, the fayence of Henry II. is adorned with
ornaments in bold relief—masks, escutcheons, reptiles,
shells, flowers, which abound in a pink colour. The
pieces of this fayence are mostly small and light, and their
exquisite workmanship equals the chiselling of famous
goldsmiths.

On the early specimens of this kind of fayence, the
Salamander and other insignia of Francis I. occur; but
upon most of the pieces, and upon all the best, are the
arms of Henry II., with his device of three crescents, and
the initial H., interlaced with the two D.'s of Diana,
Duchess of Valentinois. The emblems of Diana are as
common on the ware as those of her royal chevalier. Her
colours as a widow, black and white—which the king

wore at tournaments, and in which, therefore, he died—
had been created into fashionable colours at the court, and
are employed in some of the best pieces of this class of
pottery.   There occurs also her emblem—the crescent of
Diana, which King Henry carved upon his palaces, and
even had engraved upon his coins.

This beautiful fayence, which must have been first
made at the end of the reign of King Francis I., and the
making of which was continued under that of Henry II.,
then disappears.   Its maker, or its makers, died or left the
country.   It is a pleasant mystery.   It heralded the appearance of Palissy ware, different in its beauty, although
not less beautiful.   Its maker does not contend with Bernard for applause ; he quits the field almost in the same
moment that Bernard enters.   We hear of him no more,
nor is there any ware known that can claim affinity to the
Fayence of Henry II.

CHAPTER XVI.

PALISSY PUBLISHES A BOOK.

PALISSY published his first book during the first troubles, that is to say, most likely in the year 1557 or 1558, when he was forty-eight or forty-nine years old, and accounted himself to have reached the end of his great period of struggle as a potter. It is to this point that we have now brought the story of his life; and upon the question of the book, therefore—which is, perhaps, a lost book —it becomes necessary for us now to pause.

We may so far forestal our narrative as to say, that the only works bearing on their title-page the name of Bernard Palissy, and those on which his reputation as a man of sense and science must depend, were published, the first at Rochelle, in 1563, the second at Paris, in 1580. If the former of these publications were not called by Palissy himself, " this my second book," and if in the latter he had not made distinct and special reference to both the date and the contents of his first work, no known trace would exist in literature to indicate that Palissy had written more than the two books bearing date 1563 and 1580. This fact can be accounted for only by the supposition that the first attempt of Palissy to put his thoughts in print had either no name at all, or only an invented name, upon the title-page.

In the publication of 1580, at the commencement of a treatise on Potable Gold, Palissy thus speaks to his theoretical disciple: "And how is it that you are still cherishing these dreams? Have you not seen a little book which I caused to be printed during the first troubles, by which I have sufficiently proved that gold cannot act as a restorative, but rather as a poison, about which many doctors of medicine, having seen my arguments, were of my side: so that a short time since there was a certain physician, doctor and regent in the faculty of medicine, who, being at Paris in the chair, confirmed my statements,* proposing them to his disciples as a doctrine well assured? If there were only that, it would suffice for the confounding of your arguments."

Acting upon the hint given in this passage, MM. Faujas de St. Fond and Gobet, the editors of the quarto edition of the works of Palissy, in the year 1777, included in their volume a clever dissertation on the Ignorance of Doctors, in which they believed that they had dis-

---

* Probably this reference is to " Germani Courtini, Medici Parisiensis adversùs Paracelsi de tribus principiis auro potabili totâque pyrotechniâ portentosas opiniones, Disputatio." 4to. Paris, 1579.

covered Palissy's first work.   In support of their opinion
they produce a fair body of argument.   I doubt, however, whether they have made out a complete case of
affiliation.

Without committing myself to a decision on the question, I shall briefly enable the reader to decide or hesitate
for himself, as he may think fit.   We can then get from
the treatise a few sketches which may or may not be
drawn from the originals of Palissy, but which will, in
any case, depict an aspect of society from which Bernard
had taken views extremely similar.

At Fontenay le Comte, in Poitou, which is a district
adjacent to Saintonge, dwelt a physician named Sebastien
Colin.   This physician had translated Alexander Trallian
and other things, had written medically against Plagues
and Fevers, and Apothecaries.   His treatise on Apothecaries
became popular.   It is an old joke to regard the doctor
as one of the most fatal of diseases.   In the sixteenth
century the joke had a good deal of earnest in it.   When
the doctor falls under a joke, the apothecary falls under
a sneer, and an onslaught on apothecaries by a doctor
would of course be ably seconded as fun by the surrounding world.

Sebastien Colin's manifesto is entitled* " A Declaration
of the Blunders and Tricks of the Apothecaries, very use-

* Déclaration des abuz et tromperies que font les Apoticaires, fort
utile et nécessaire à ung chascun studieux et curieux de sa santé,
par Me Lisset Benancio, imprimé à Tours, par Mathieu Chercelé, pour
Guilleaume Bourgea, Libraire, demourant audict lieu. 16mo.

ful and necessary to every one studious and careful of his
health, by Me Lisset Benancio." Lisset Benancio is an
exact anagram of the author's name, Sebastien Colin.
The publication professes to have been printed at Tours by
Mathew Chercelé, but the printer's name is also feigned,
and the work probably was printed at Poitiers, like the
other writings of the same physician. The tract was frequently reprinted, and has been translated into German
and into Latin. It was reprinted at Lyon " by Michel
Joue," in 1557.

This Michel Joue, with his punning motto of " Cuncta
juvant à Jove," is, we are told, an imaginary person. The
reply to Colin, said to be the work of Palissy, proceeded
in the same year from the same imaginary publisher,
whom MM. Faujas de St. Fond and Gobet, by a comparison of types, vignettes, tail-pieces, and so forth, identify
with Barthelemi Berton of Rochelle. It should be observed, that the second book of Palissy was printed at
Rochelle, the printing-presses of which town were those
that were most conveniently accessible to an inhabitant of
Saintes.

Let us now assume, for a moment, that it was really
Palissy who lent his shrewd intelligence to the apothecaries, and retorted in their behalf upon the ignorance of
doctors. The act itself appears to be very consistent with
his character and habits. He knew well the pretensions
of the faculty, and the unsoundness of the little science
they possessed; he had some contempt for the belief that
knowledge lay in Greek and Latin. He had lost six

children, and been so brought into melancholy contact with physicians. As professed men of science, he had sought them in his travels, and must very commonly have found them little worth his search. Since he improved in his art as a potter, and gained more extended patronage, he had again been called upon often to pass far beyond the limits of the town of Saintes. In one of his known works he tells a contemptuous story of a doctor in Poitou, who founded his reputation on trickery connected with a subject which we know Colin to have made one of his strong points, and upon which he wrote a book. If it be Colin to whom Palissy in that passage alludes, it is very certain that Bernard must have looked upon the assaulter of deceit in apothecaries as a man who was himself an arch-deceiver. Colin's pamphlet had attracted a good deal of notice; in it the physician was to be seen thundering down out of his sublime height a storm upon the heads of the apothecaries. It would be quite consistent, there-fore, with the mood of Palissy to make a work like this the text for a short exposition of what seemed to him some very gross delusions prevalent among the doctors of his day.

The reply to Colin, which has been supposed to con-stitute the maiden work of Bernard Palissy, has its title framed upon that of the attack to which it is intended to reply. It is called* " A Declaration of the Blunders

* Déclaration des abus et ignorances des Médecins, œuvre très-utile et profitable à un chacun studieux et curieux de sa santé, com-

and Ignorances of the Doctors, a work very useful and
profitable to every one studious and careful of his health,
composed by Pierre Braillier, trading apothecary of Lyon,
in answer to Lisset Benancio, physician." It professes to
be published at Lyon, by Michel Joue. It is dedicated
to the Seigneur de Boissi, in an epistle dated from Lyon,
on the 1st of January, 1557. That means, in our present
language, January, 1558, since January was at that time
reckoned one of the last months of the old year, and not
the first month of the new.

It is necessary to state that this quarrel between doctor
and apothecary produced another crop of fruit in the
succeeding year. Jean Surrelh, a physician, published a
tract,* also at Lyon, in May, 1558, which was opposed
equally to the productions of Colin and Pierre Braillier.

Soon afterwards Pierre Brallier, either the former
writer or some other who assumed that name, re-entered
the lists with a violent attack against Surrelh,† whose
antecedents laid him very open to annoying personalities.
This Brallier called himself scholar of the college of M.
Jean de Canapes, one of the most celebrated physicians
of Lyon. It will be observed, that the second Braillier
retains the sound of the old name, but makes a variation

posé par *Pierre Braillier*, Marchand Apoticaire de Lyon, pour reponce
contre *Lisset Benancio*, Médecin. Lyon, par *Michel Joue*, 1556.
16mo.

* Apologie des Médecins contre les calomnies et grands abus de cer-
tains Apothicaires, par *Jean Surrelh*, Médecin. 8vo. Lyon, 1558.

† Les articulations de Pierre Brallier, Apothicaire de Lyon, sur
l'Apologie de *Jean Surrelh*, Médecin à Saint Galmier. 8vo. Lyon, 1558.

in the spelling. Much stress cannot be laid upon this fact, but it assists to some extent in confirmation of a belief that the two publications were not written by one author. It is quite certain, that if they were, that author could not have been Bernard Palissy.

It is suggested by MM. Faujas de St. Fond and Gobet, that as the author of the attack upon apothecaries, printing at Poitiers, had affected for disguise to publish his book at Tours, so Palissy, having transformed himself, for convenience both of disguise and satire, into an apothecary, dated his book from Lyon. It is suggested that the initials of Pierre Braillier, " P. B." are, when inverted, " B. P.," and so stand for Bernard Palissy: perhaps it would be an almost equally valuable coincidence to observe that neither of the names contains an " x."

The main reason, however, for assigning to Palissy the authorship of the treatise in question, arises from the fact that it is the only publication, anonymous or pseudonymous, which has been found answering at all to the account given by Bernard himself of his first work. A work was wanted written during the first troubles, that is to say, in or very near the year 1558, manifesting an enlightened spirit, having its author's name unknown,—unless indeed it had upon its title-page the name of Palissy,—and containing arguments against belief in the efficacy as a medicine of metallic gold. After a diligent search, no other treatise against this use of gold, written in French, and answering to the required description, could be found to have been published between the years 1540 and 1560. Nothing presented itself but this Dissertation upon Doctors. It is declared by the discoverers, that not only in opinion, but also in style, the treatise thus suggesting itself conforms closely to the known writings of Bernard Palissy.

Dismissing from consideration those resemblances which are produced by the common use of modes of writing proper to the age, one cannot but think the identity of style between the work assigned to Palissy, and works known to be his, extremely doubtful. In his second book, for example, published four or five years after the first, there is a quaint habit, evident on almost every page, of carrying a sentence on by the use of such phrases as "le dit," "audit," &c. Thus Palissy tells us, that, while labouring at the enamels, "I was so wasted in my person, that there was no form nor prominence of muscle on my arms or legs ; also *the said legs* were throughout of one size, so that the garters with which I tied my stockings, were at once, when I walked, down upon my heels with the stockings too." This quaint habit is entirely absent from the Dissertation upon Doctors.

It is to be admitted, however, that there occur passages of some length here and there among the works of Palissy wherein the said "saids" do not occur, and the whole style has a good deal of conformity with that of the Apothecary's Dissertation. The said Dissertation does in clearness of thought, in boldness of opposition to prevailing errors, and in constant production of experience against absurdities of theory, resemble very much the works of Palissy. To its opinions Palissy would have certainly subscribed, and many of them were enforced by him in later writings.

The treatise is not written in the form of dialogue, and in that respect it differs from all Bernard's other writing.

It ought also to be stubbornly remembered, that Bernard Palissy refers to his first work as "a book by which I have sufficiently proved that gold cannot act as a restorative, but rather as a poison, about which many doctors of medicine, having seen my arguments, were of my side." This being remembered, at the same time it is to be observed, that the Dissertation upon Doctors is by no means a treatise specially devoted to the errors touching gold. Errors of this kind are only displayed in it incidentally, among a list of other blunders. The subject of gold occupies, in fact, only two pages out of fifty. In these two pages it is only said: that the author had fed a cock with gold, because a doctor had declared cocks could digest it; that he had found the statement of the doctor false; also, that he had exposed gold to fire for eight-and-forty hours without producing diminution of its substance. Therefore the writer holds that gold could never be digested, and must act as an impediment only in the stomach. "If I were to say that gold was not restorative," he adds, "that would be false; because through gold one may get capons, partridges, quails, pheasants, and all good things to rejoice and renovate a man; as houses, castles, lands, possessions." No more is propounded on the subject in this treatise. Colin himself, in the Declaration against which it was a counter-manifesto, had written against the medicinal use of gold, and had said more than is here said in condemnation of it. If any merit was due, therefore, to the few paragraphs of Pierre Braillier, a little more than the same merit was due to the preceding paragraphs of Colin. The reference of Palissy to his first work is gravely made, as to a work containing an elaborate argument upon the use of gold in medicine, which had exerted influence upon the minds of some physicians, and had been confirmed by a professor in his chair at Paris. The Declaration against Doctors, containing no more than had been said just before in the Declaration against Apothecaries, cannot be said to verify this reference in a convincing manner.

Again, the Dissertation upon Doctors contains, as a work of Palissy would contain, scriptural allusions; it was written, very likely, by a member of the Reformed Church. But it was written with good faith, in the true vein of an offended apothecary fighting for the honour of his order. It may be said that, if so, the cleverness of personation was only so much the more creditable to the wit of Palissy. But it is very questionable, indeed, whether his deeply religious spirit would have suffered him to carry

his humour beyond certain bounds; I doubt whether
Palissy would have written as Pierre Braillier puts it, of
" the state of pharmacy, *to which God has called me.*"

Pierre Braillier, in his epistle to the reader, begins
with a scriptural allusion to forgiveness of injuries, which
slides rapidly into recrimination upon doctors who are
jealous of apothecaries. Of all states in the world, he says,
that of the apothecary is the worst ; he is the worst paid,
made the most servile, and the least esteemed of men. He
does not wonder that apothecaries combine other occupations with their calling; for their own is so much trampled
down by surgeons and physicians, that patients expect to
be attended by them for the honour's sake : " saying
(when they are healed) what did you send me ? herbs :
and that is how the poor apothecaries come to be paid."

" As for the physician, he is paid upon the spot ; or if
he be not paid he will not return to a place, though he
spends nothing but his trouble there ; and the apothecary
spends much more trouble than the doctor, for he must
apply all blisters, clysters, and the like, supply the use of
his drugs, his time, his servants, and sometimes get
nothing at all, losing his time, his trouble, and his drugs.
. . . . It is well of Lisset to say that the apothecaries
sell the virtues of drugs and plants which God has supplied
to us gratis, without cultivating them, which they ought
not to do, and tell us that it is a great sin against God. I
would beg him to take the trouble, he and his friends, to
go and look for herbs, flowers, roots and seeds, gums,

fruits, &c., and conserve and store them with great care
and diligence, pay house-rents, wages, and keep of servants, buy the drugs that come from distant lands for
large sums of ready money, and then supply them gratis.
How would they sell their drugs for nothing, when they
will not even furnish a simple visit without being paid,
and sell their presence and their words. Yet their visit
and prescription sometimes do more harm than good. . . .
I leave you to judge, when they have conscience to take
a dollar for feeling a pulse and ordering a simple julep,
while the apothecary shall find trouble to get paid two
sols, which is the greater thief, apothecary or physician?"

Pierre Braillier reasons here like an apothecary of the
good old times. Let us, however, call to mind the doctor
a hundred years after the publication of this treatise, as he
appeared, and deserved to appear, in the works of Molière.
Pierre Braillier had vulnerable matter to attack. In our
own day, what is called address will assist much more than
intellectual ability in the creation of a thriving practice.
In the time of Palissy, Pierre Braillier writes of the physicians—" I think that they have studied mumming more
than medicine; it is in that, at any rate, that they are
wisest; and they might more fairly call themselves incor-
porated mummers than physicians, for it is the chief perfection that they have."

Pierre then dwells upon doctors who cannot cure themselves, and upon doctors who prescribe absurdly, so that

it is necessary for apothecaries quietly to rectify their blunders. He then turns specially to Lisset Benancio, and ends his preface with this paragraph: "Here are not blamed the learned and the wise, and not to be prolix, I will pray to God very heartily that He will give us grace so well to exercise our estates and vocations into which it has pleased Him to call us, that it may be to His praise and glory, so that we may have no just occasion to blame and abuse each other, to the great prejudice and debasement of our professions."

The Declaration of the Blundering and Ignorance of Doctors then begins in a religious, philosophic tone. Presently it defines the doctor's duty. "In the first place, the doctor should consider, before prescribing, the acrimony of the disease, its strength, the strength and age of the affected person, his temperature and habit, the quality and temperature of the existing season; then he should know and recollect the virtue and properties of the medicament with which he designs to heal: and all this having been well considered and recollected, he has still many difficulties to encounter, and sometimes cannot effect his purpose." This being defined to be the physician's duty, he proceeds with much shrewd sense, and a little acrimony, through a catalogue of the physician's blunders.

"Do you not think," he says, "that it is a great blunder on the part of doctors to keep an unhappy patient shut up in a room, the windows close, the bed close, and forbid any one to give him air? When already the poor patient cannot get his breath by reason of his malady, except with a great deal of trouble, you cause him to be furthermore shut up and smothered. See how you blunder: first you rob him of his breath, and render him more melancholy than he would be made by his disease, through the foul odours which cannot escape, which pierce his brain and aggravate his illness: and if you grant to me that air aids the expulsive virtue, and that no animals having lungs can live without air, then man, however whole and cheerful he may be, cannot live without air, still less can he do so when he is sick: wherefore I say that you blunder in forbidding air to patients when it is good, and not too cold, or moist, or windy. . . . . I should like to ask whether if you were shut up alone for six days in a chamber without air, you sound and not sick (as you shut up your patients), whether you would find it a good thing, and whether you could live as you now do?"

Although the writer was, of course, like all the men of his day, ignorant of the real use of air to animals, and accounted for its obvious necessity upon a theory belonging to the physiology of his own time, yet it is worthy of remark, that, in spite of our own better science, there are doctors enough in the present day who take great care to keep the sun and air out of a sick room, and make of it a place in which they could not themselves live without decided injury to health.

The writer then combats the cruel and fatal practice of

forbidding any drink to persons suffering with fevers.
Then he passes on to other matters.

" How many times," says Pierre Braillier—and if Pierre
be really Palissy his thoughts are prompted by the recollection of dead children of his own—" how many times
have I been in company with the physician seeing patients of an evening, when he has said to the parents—
' The child will do well, and certainly will soon recover;'
and in the morning we have found it dead upon the
table. Several times that has happened with physicians
who were in the best repute, at which I have been
astonished greatly. And if an apothecary dresses a poor
man's wound without their ordering, he will be blamed
for it; and if the patient die, people will say, ' The
apothecary has killed him by his ignorance;' why do
they never say the same of doctors when their patients die
under their hands?"

The next attack is on a blunder of which the medical
profession is only freeing itself in our own day, the belief
that there is wisdom in a long prescription. The long
prescription of three centuries ago, arranged after an
orthodox sentiment in triacles, was, of course, eminently
open to attack; but I suspect that at this day there is
many an old physician, surgeon, or apothecary, who
might adopt with advantage to his patients the good
doctrine of Pierre Braillier. Whether " P. B." be Bernard
Palissy or not, I will not venture to determine; but it may
be seen that his shrewd sense has a Palissian character.

" Our Master Lisset," he says, " blames us, saying that we
cause many drugs to be used by the sick, in order that we
may get more money; it is very much the contrary, for
the sensible apothecary will take heed how he gives to
the sick anything about which he is not assured by
experience, and of which he does not clearly know the
properties. He will not be like many doctors who prescribe confusing recipes, that is to say, great triacles, a
quantity of drugs, to make believe that they are very
wise, where two or three things, having good relation to
the malady, would be of more use than all the triacles.
If anybody would examine the physician who prescribes
them, he would find him pretty well puzzled to explain
the use of half, and would find his prescription an inex-
tricable knot: for it is impossible that so many drugs can
produce one action favourable to the malady, without
setting up another which is hurtful or obstructive, and
which may have some occult virtue that is out of place.
Therefore I hold that practitioner to be wise who com-
bines into one prescription few medicaments."

Discussing also other matters, such as distillations and
essential oils, with equal good sense, Pierre comes to the
use of gold in medicine, which he dismisses with the
arguments we have already seen. From gold he passes
to electuaries of pounded glass, to the use in medicine of
sapphires, rubies, emeralds, and laughs at coral dust in
ointment as it used then to be applied over the region of
the stomach.

The patients of those days really have to be admired for not rising in general rebellion against the faculty. They were denied drink when they were thirsty, and when they were hungry were denied young capons, and directed to eat only the oldest cocks and hens. Young meat was forbidden; old and tough meat was the diet of the sick. As they, moreover, paid a heavy price for drinking gold and rubies, when they could afford such costly dirt —for in the mouth they were precisely dirt—sickness must have been, more than it is now, a thing to dread. Pierre Braillier defends the wholesomeness of a young capon fat and tender, and argues against the theory by which an old hen is pronounced to be a "warmer diet." He then proceeds to demonstrate the folly of giving distilled meat to the patients. There was a plan of putting a fowl, partridge, or quail with marrow, and a quantity of water, into an alembic, and then distilling. The fowl of course boiled, but only the pure water evaporated and distilled over into the receiver, where it was caught as the distilled essence of quail or partridge, to be prescribed to the sick in measured quantities, as a nutritious food.

Pierre Braillier dwells with not less sense upon other matters, and manifests a correct knowledge of the materia medica of his own day, with sounder views upon it than were often to be met with in the sixteenth century. He says: "I hope, with time, to write of medicaments, as well as of distillation, more amply;" a promise which Palissy would scarcely have thrown in for the sake of strengthening the impression that the book was written by a real apothecary. Upon the reverence for Greek and Latin, Pierre writes as Bernard might have written. " Lisset says that the apothecaries are no grammarians, and that therefore medicine is in great danger. I can find apothecaries who will talk physic in French, that many a physician shall not know how to answer in Latin. It is easier for every man to study in his mother-tongue, than to borrow of strangers languages to study in.

" Galen wrote in his own language, and has not borrowed a tongue of any other country for the writing of his books ; so also Hippocrates and Avicenna, each wrote and studied in his own language. The apothecaries of France can study in French, without borrowing either a Latin or a German tongue; for all that concerns pharmacy has been translated into French, so they can be wise without being grammarians—ay, to be sure, and wiser than the doctors: for their books are in Greek and Latin, very choice, and half the doctors understand Greek not at all, and Latin hardly; so they do not comprehend what they are studying, and the poor patients run great risk under their hands, for then at the best they physic us according to the manner of the Greeks and Arabs, and with Greek and Arabian drugs ; but we are neither Greeks nor Arabs, have not the same complexions, are not born or bred in the same climate. It is altogether opposite to ours: for their country and climate is twice as hot, and their medicaments much stronger and sharper, a great deal more active."

Of this Declaration of the Blunders of the Doctors we

need say no more. We have obtained from it some curious illustrations of another aspect of society in France during the life of Palissy ; but we probably quit it with the impression that it was in simple truth the works of an apothecary, who proved himself well fitted to stand forward as the champion of his order.

If we reject the suggestion made by MM. Faujas de St. Fond and Gobet,—upon the credit of whose assurance this treatise upon doctors finds its way into encyclopædias as first in the enumeration of the works of Palissy—if we reject this suggestion, there exists no other at present to supply its place. We must content ourselves with knowing, that in about the year 1558, when Palissy was forty-nine years old, he published his first work. That in this work he reasoned against the use of gold in medicine, and employed arguments which attracted some attention from enlightened men. Finally, that the first work of Palissy is a lost work ; and that we have yet to hope for its discovery among the dusty pamphlets stored up in old libraries. Certainly, whenever it shall be discovered, its dry skin will be found to cover sound muscle and sinew, bone and marrow, a heart throbbing warmly with rich healthy blood, and brains astir with vigour and vivacity.

CHAPTER XVII.

PALISSY IN SUNSHINE, AND FRANCE UNDER A CLOUD.

WHATEVER ignorance was manifested in the treatment of sick bodies during that portion of the miserable old times in France with which we are concerned, the treatment of a sick state by its politicians was no less to be declared against. If doctors hungered after dollars, and dwelt upon the fee as the grand aim of a prescription, kings and princes were no less rapacious, and the profit at which laws and edicts aimed when they were put forth nominally for the nation's good, was the profit of a man or party. The people of France entered only then into the calculation of their rulers when they made a declaration against blunders, and shaped their arguments in some form of revolt.

In our own time and country, there are only a few men whose lives we are unable to narrate without especial reference to state affairs. In France, during the sixteenth century, there did not live a clown, perhaps, the current of whose life was not distressed and troubled by the course of state affairs, who had not been, or was not yet destined to be, at some time of his life heavily bruised by a hard-fisted government. There is a blow at hand for Bernard Palissy, and we must now, therefore, pursue the narrative of court intrigue and national misfortune.

Palissy had prospered in his art, and had fulfilled his utmost expectations of success. His beautiful designs in pottery, completed with much labour, and sold at a price which only the rich could pay, presented a new luxury to the great people of his neighbourhood. Antoine Sire de Pons, the Count of Marennes and his wife Anne de Partenay, Baron de Jarnac, and the Governor of Rochelle, became acquainted with his skill and supplied him with commissions. The Seigneur de Burie and the Count de Rochefoucault, men of much influence, became his patrons. The Constable Montmorenci, who filled up seasons of forced leisure in the luxurious employment of his vast wealth, found out the Frenchman who had learned to stamp his genius indelibly on clay, and soon established himself as head patron of Palissy the Potter. Bernard was bidden to employ himself on behalf of the great constable in the adornment of his Château d'Ecouen, about four leagues from Paris. Among all the business that flowed in to keep his furnace active and his wits at work, the decorations of the Château d'Ecouen took the first place.

The Château d'Ecouen, which had been built by the

constable, was carefully adorned by him with costly works of art. Much time was occupied by Palissy in the painting and enamelling of decorated tiles which were to pave the galleries and portions of the chapel. The designs were all of subjects taken from the Scriptures, very highly finished, and so well contrived that they gave to the whole pavement a rich effect of beauty that cannot be equalled by the best of Turkey carpets. In one part of the sacristy the Passion of our Lord was represented upon pottery by sixteen pictures, in a single frame, copies from Albert Durer, by the hand of Palissy. The other Scripture pieces were designed by Palissy himself.

Let us now call to mind the picture we have had of the Reformed Church of Saintes in the days of its prosperity, when " you would have seen the daughters and virgins seated by troops in the gardens, and other places, who delighted themselves in the singing of all holy things." Let us think of the good minister, M. de la Boissière, so prosperous that he is no longer obliged for want of table-cloth to lay his dinner on a shirt. Let us think of Bernard Palissy, so well supplied with patronage, that he might be rich if his restless energy were not expending ever time and toil and money on new efforts to improve his talent. If not rich, Bernard was now, at any rate, exempted from the cares of poverty. So let us think of him at ease, rejoicing in the religious aspect of his town, frequently travelling abroad to Ecouen and elsewhere, as his business required, and coming home to wander thoughtfully and tranquilly among the rocks and fields. While he delighted in the water, earth, and air, he was revolving in his fertile brain quaint schemes which had but small connexion with his daily business, revolving also delicate designs, dreaming ideal heads of Christ, and penitents and pharisees. At the same time there were old fables to be thought about—Psyche, Proserpine, the Banquet of the Gods—which were to be painted upon glass for Montmorenci; and there was the rustic grotto for the gardens of Ecouen—an ingenious contrivance of his own, of which, " if men inquire into it, they will find that such a work had not before been seen." Let our thoughts dwell for a short time on Palissy thus cheerfully at work. Having eyes, he saw that clouds were gathering about his country; having ears, he heard the rising of the storm that was hereafter to beat down pitilessly on his head. But let us picture him now with a sunbeam on his face and on his furnace, while the shadow of the storm is out of doors.

The shadow is a dark one. The eldest of the young sons of King Henry the Second and Queen Catherine of Medicis, under the name of Francis the Second, succeeded his father on the 10th of July, 1559. He was then less than sixteen years old, and already a married man. His wife was Mary, Queen of Scots.

During the eleven days of suffering which intervened between the wound received by Henry at the tournament and its result in death, the court factions were all busily at work sorting their cards for the next game. The

battle for ascendancy would be between the Guises and
the Constable Montmorenci. Montmorenci had lost no
time, while the king lay sick to death, in sending couriers
out at all hours and in all directions. He gave notice to
the princes of the blood, and especially to Antony of
Bourbon, King of Navarre, that their affairs were at a
crisis, and that they must at once claim their supremacy
in the councils of the new king, or the boy would be
stolen from them by the Guises.

The Guises, however, happened to be uncles to the boy's
wife, and made themselves a way into his confidence
through her. They also took care to propitiate his mother;
for Queen Catherine was now a person to be courted in
the state. The Guises won the favour of the queen-
mother by sacrificing her antagonists, and chief of all, her
rival Diana of Poitiers. The great men had caressed
Diana while she had the means of paying them for their
caresses, but when her crescent waned, none scrupled to
abandon her. All persons distasteful to Queen Catherine
were banished from the court, and forced to leave some
portions of their property behind them.

It was to no purpose that Montmorenci sent his couriers
out to noblemen and princes of the blood, while his astute
rivals had quietly secured their game by the assistance of
a pair of women. When the parliament came to salute
the new king, after his father's death, he bade them understand that he had requested his good uncles, the Cardinal
of Lorraine and the Duke of Guise, to govern his states,

and advised the parliament in future to refer to them upon all matters of public business. Montmorenci made an effort to convince the queen-mother of the impropriety of this arrangement, but he wasted his breath upon an angry woman, who reminded him that he had been too friendly with Diana to be any friend of hers. Therefore, Montmorenci took the advice of Master Francis, the young king, and retired to his own domain of Chantilli.

The noblemen and princes of the blood who had been baulked in this way, came together at the court of Antony of Bourbon, the good-humoured and not at all energetic King of Navarre. They held a meeting at Vendôme, the constable not being there present to the eye, though he had sent his wits thither, and prompted the whole of the proceedings through Dardois, his secretary. It was resolved at this meeting that the Guises had no right to supersede the claims of princes of the blood and ancient officers of state. Resolved also that the King of Navarre should go to court, win over the queen-mother, open the king's eyes, and obtain public office for himself and for his friends. So King Antony went to court, where he was befooled by the Guise party, and whence he was presently sent on a wild-goose chase to Madrid.

The Guises, being now as kings, assumed the pride belonging to their power. The cardinal especially maintained the reputation of his calling; and, as Brantôme tells us, " was in his prosperity very insolent and blinded." The duke, being himself a worldly man, felt that he owed

to the world courtesy and moderation.   Cardinal Charles
was quick and clever, with some literary taste.   He carried the grave face of a rigid ecclesiastic, while he quietly
indulged the passions of a libertine.   Duke Francis was
a handsome man, with a majestic presence, and an easy,
affable address.   His pride never degenerated into scorn-
fulness; he was a brave and skilful general, honest and
frank in his dealings, a firm friend, but a remorseless
enemy.   That last characteristic was shared with him by
the cardinal, his brother.   But when the duke had satisfied
his enmity by seeing an opponent humbled at his feet, it
gratified his pride to raise him up again; the cardinal,
when he had a victim prostrate, was impatient for a scalp.
War is cruel, Christianity is meek; so we will endeavour
to suppose this the only instance known to the world in
which the soldier was less cruel than the priest.

Duke and cardinal took equal pains to strengthen the
foundations of their power, by the multiplying of sub-
servient partisans.   To surround themselves with a high
bulwark of human rottenness, they laboured to corrupt
men on all sides, and devote them to their uses by gifts,
pensions, benefices, orders of St. Michael.   The collar of
St. Michael was so much debased in social value by too
lavish distribution, that it came at last to be called
among the people, with a happy sarcasm, " Every Beast's
Collar."

The people did not look with love upon the heads of the
Guise faction.   It did not please the people that the duke

should heap on his own head the honour of an office snatched from Montmorenci, that of grand-master of the house to the king. Still less did it please them that the same brave duke, after inducing Admiral Coligny to resign the government of Picardy, under the belief that he was doing so in favour of the Prince of Condé, should have bestowed that dignity on one of the hungry dogs that fawned on him for morsels—one of his creatures, Brissac.

But if men shook their heads in talking of the duke, they ground their teeth over the doings of the cardinal. The cardinal took care of the finance, and had found many retrenchments necessary. King Henry had left money matters in a state of terrible confusion. Then there came to the new court, when it was at Fontaine-bleau, a number of men petitioning for payment of contracted debts, or for arrears of neglected salary, or asking indemnity for loss sustained by the new minister's reforms in the exchequer. The court at Fontainebleau was, in fact, beset by duns. The cardinal then built a gibbet near the palace, and proclaimed by sound of trumpet that all men who had come to Fontainebleau to ask for anything were to depart within four-and-twenty hours, on penalty of being hung. That measure of course got rid of the petitioners, but they did not go back to their homes blessing the cardinal, or spread content by the roadside on their homeward journeys.

It has been said, that in the last month of the reign of Henry II., certain councillors were tricked into a free expression of unorthodox sympathy, and then arrested. Against these men, five in number, the Guises set on foot the prosecution which had been delayed a little by King Henry's death. One of them, Anne du Bourg, a deacon, was eventually hung and burnt. From that time there was a cry given to political malcontents, to the oppressed people, the party of the princes of the blood, and Montmorenci. To secure the alliance of the large body of Calvinists, Montmorenci and his friends, who had, moreover, other claims to Calvinistic sympathy, had only to dwell upon the persecuting spirit of the Guises. The retainers of the house of Guise, on the other hand, sought friends by pointing to the rigid orthodoxy of the cardinal, and so endeavoured to swell the ranks of a court-faction by identifying it with the welfare of the dominant form of religion. The Guises carefully stirred up religious zeal, and encouraged orthodox processions in the streets, intended to annoy the Calvinists, which commonly resulted in the mobbing of some Huguenot, who had refused to take part in the sacred demonstration.

Whoever might head the great party of malcontents, created by what was called the usurpation of power by the House of Guise, the men to whom the Huguenots looked up as their own chiefs were the three brothers Coligny, D'Andelot, and Châtillon. Of Coligny and D'Andelot we have already spoken. Admiral Coligny was a man stubborn, taciturn, and inflexible of purpose ; D'Andelot was not less steadfast and intrepid, and only a few degrees less sombre and reserved. Both, says Brantôme, being so formed by nature that they moved with difficulty, and on their faces never any sudden change of countenance betrayed their thoughts. Very useful to them, therefore, was the alliance of their brother, who possessed, by nature, a more pliable surface to his character, and had increased its elasticity by education. This brother, Cardinal de Châtillon, Bishop of Beauvais, had a mild, engaging way, and so much tact in addressing those with whom he had to deal, that he knew how to avoid all those disagreeable collisons of opinion which would have checked the course of his more hard-minded associates. When negotiation was required, therefore, Châtillon, with his insinuating, courtly habits, proved a most efficient helper to his party.

At La Ferté, on the frontier of Picardy, the malcontents assembled at a château belonging to the Prince of Condé, who was a Bourbon, brother to Antony, King of Navarre. The Prince de Condé was a man given to ease and pleasure, who did not keep one mistress the less for having adopted the Reformed opinions in religion. At this meeting, Coligny showed that there were in France two million of reformers capable of bearing arms. It was resolved to strike a great and final blow at the dominant Guise faction. Troops were to be levied secretly throughout France, captains were to be appointed over them, and they were to be brought quietly from all parts to concentrate at Blois, for there the king would rusticate in the succeeding spring, and endeavour to recruit his feeble health. The exact service to be done by them, and their precise destination, were to be kept secret from the troops; but Calvinists were to be levied on the understanding that they were to strike a sure blow for the freedom of their religion, political malcontents were to be told that they were to secure the triumph of their party. The real intention was to break out suddenly at Blois with overwhelming force, to drag the Guises—the king's uncles and his chosen, though obnoxious, ministers—out of the royal presence, to imprison them, and institute against them public prosecution. The princes of the blood and the ancient officials, with Montmorenci of course at their head, were thus to be placed where they believed they had a right to be, at the head of the state affairs, and the party of the Guises would be most effectually crippled.

This plot, which is called the conspiracy of Amboise, was kept duly secret by its first promoters. None of them would venture to commit himself by assuming the post of leader in an enterprise which, even when seen through the mists of faction in those days of enterprise, could not have appeared very noble to an honest man. An ostensible leader was required, also, who should be notoriously bold and able, while at the same time he was not provided with a set of principles too inconveniently definite. Captains and soldiers were to be tempted out of many regions of opinion, and a leader was required who should be distasteful to none. The required chief was found in a reck-

less, roving soldier, named La Renaudie, a man sprung
from a good house in Perigord. La Renaudie received a
detailed plan of the whole enterprise, in which provision
had been made beforehand for a long series of contin-
gencies. He was instructed to say that when the time
should be ripe, the Prince of Condé would assume the lead
of the movement, to which the people were invited. The
name of the queen-mother was by some unfairly used as
a consenting party to the enterprise, and she, it was said,
would certainly have never sanctioned treason. Finally,
to prop all sinking consciences, theologians and juriscon-
sults, chosen judiciously, were requested to supply, and
did supply, attestations that no law, whether divine or
human, would be violated by the proposed move in the
game of politics.

La Renaudie wrote to his associates, requesting them to
meet him on the 1st of January, in the year 1560, at
Nantes. The parliament of Bretagne there held its sit-
tings, and as feasts were also to be held on the occasion of
certain weddings among great families of the province, a
large collection of conspirators might pass unnoticed in
the throng of holiday-folk gathered there together from
surrounding districts. At Nantes, on the appointed day,
the whole plan was finally arranged, and the 15th of
March appointed for the capture of the ministers at Blois.
All went well. The Duke and Cardinal of Guise went
with the pallid young king to Blois in due time. A
throng of people, wholly unobserved by the Guises, was

marching from all corners of France steadily on, prepared
to meet each other on the 15th of March. A dim
hint of some danger reached the court, and though but
slight importance was attached to it, the king was removed
by his uncles from Blois to Amboise, a small town more
easily defensible, in case defence at any time should be
required. This change did not much disconcert La Renaudie.

I need not dwell upon the failure of the scheme. La
Renaudie betrayed the secret to a friend, Avenelles, with
whom he lodged. Avenelles gave information to the
Guises, who heard with consternation of a danger close at
hand upon so large a scale. There was time, however, for
self-preservation. They succeeded in frustrating the whole
design. La Renaudie being killed, was hung upon a gibbet,
with a superscription " Chief of the Rebels." Amnesty,
against the will of the Guises, was offered by the Chancellor Olivier to all those misguided men who would return home peaceably, and upon this promise large num-
bers immediately retired. A party of those who remained
having attacked Amboise by night and been repulsed, the
Guises became violent in their revenge, and sending in
pursuit even of those who had departed on the faith of
peaceful promises, committed all to indiscriminate imprisonment and massacre. The Prince of Condé was
arrested, but was afterwards set free upon his own denial
of complicity. Castelnau, a faithful servant of the state,
died on the scaffold. He had quitted the castle he de-

fended to plead before the king his quarrel against the
Guises, and to clear himself of treason to his sovereign,
at the instance of the Duke de Nemours, and after receiving from the duke a written pledge that he should be
suffered to go and return in safety. The Guises, however,
arrested their opponent instantly, and the duke in vain
implored them to enable him to keep his word. This, says
the Marshal Vieilleville in his memoirs, " vexed the duke
much, who was concerned only about his signature; for if
it had been his mere word, he would have been able to give
the lie at any time to any one who might reproach him
with it, and that without any exception, for the prince
was brave and generous." Such used to be good ethics
for a knight in armour.

The immoderate, indiscriminate vengeance taken by the
Guises after the failure of this plot heaped up terribly the
measure of the public discontent. " I saw Huguenots,"
Brantôme tells us, " who said, ' Yesterday we had no part
in the conspiracy, and would not have approved of it for
all the gold in the world; but to-day we will own it for a
dollar, and say that the enterprise was good and pious.' "

The Constable Montmorenci was maliciously selected by
the Guises as the narrator to the parliament of Paris of the
failure of a scheme in which many of his own adherents
had been implicated. He was then sixty-seven years of
age, an old man not yet feeble; and to the disappoint-
ment of his political opponents, he fulfilled his mission in
a most becoming way. He simply narrated the facts,

abstained from all comment on the conduct of the Guises, confining his expression of opinion to a statement that the conspirators were clearly in the wrong; for, he said, if a private man is bound to protect friends under his roof, much more is a king bound, under the same circumstances, to protect relations who are at the same time his appointed ministers.

It has been said that the name of the queen-mother was used by certain members of the unsuccessful party. They may not have spoken wholly without grounds in claiming her as an ally. Catherine of Medicis had, at that period of her career, no settled plan of action ; and as she flattered equally men opposite in party, each might sometimes carry home a tale of favour. She could listen to a tale of grievance, and interject such sympathetic words and syllables as were agreeable to the narrator; but she had not, at that time, attached herself as a true partisan to any faction. She was forty-one years old, and still a handsome woman. In the midst of the gloom which overspread society, through all the plots and tumults of which we have just been speaking, the queen-mother held a gay and brilliant court of ladies, who employed themselves in frivolous amusements. She favoured and protected artists, as a matter of elegance and taste, rather than settled purpose. At a time when the foulest stratagems were fair in love, she did not vex her ladies by too strict a care about their morals. They all fished and hunted, sang, danced, and embroidered, while the storm of civil war was gathering.

The darkness deepened over France. The Prince of Condé retired to the court of his brother of Navarre. An assembly held at Fontainebleau produced, and was intended to produce, no healthy result. The king, a most pitiable youth of seventeen, desperately sick, entered Orleans in October, to assist at the meeting of the states that was to take place there. Throughout his brief reign he had lived in the wild centre of a contention that he could not understand. Sometimes he drooped, and felt that, young as he was, and little good or harm as he had done yet in his feeble days, all those conspiracies and murmurs of the people, which had their centre in his chamber, could not be directed against him. But he was in the power of his uncles, and with them he entered Orleans, pale and unhappy, surrounded by armed troops, and looking through them at stern, discontented faces on the pavement.

The princes of Bourbon had been bidden to attend at Orleans on this occasion. Charles, Cardinal de Bourbon,* had been sent out to reassure them with a message from the queen, declaring that they had no treachery to fear. On the 30th of October, therefore, they entered Orleans. But there was a pitfall laid for them. At the moment of his appearing in the young king's presence, the Prince of Condé was arrested. His papers afterwards were seized, and his accomplices imprisoned. He was destined to be

* Among other things, Bishop of Saintes.

tried by a commission, and not, according to the preroga-
tive of his rank, by peers and parliament under the presi-
dency of the king. He asked for counsel to defend him,
and his wish was granted, but only in order that the
private instructions which he drew out, and the information which he gave for use in his defence, might be
seized and directed against him as instruments in favour
of the prosecution. The King of Navarre pleaded in
vain for his brother before the proud Cardinal Lorraine,
the king standing and bare-headed, abjectly pleading
before the cardinal, while the priest, seated and covered,
scornfully rejected his petition. His young wife wept in
vain before the throne; the Prince of Condé was found
guilty, and condemned to die on the 10th of December,
the day on which the states were to be opened.

Several commissioners had already affixed their names
to this decision, when rumours of the rapid waning of the
king's life suspended their proceedings. The rumours
were well founded. On the 5th of December, 1560, the
poor boy—the French monarch—died. A child succeeded him.

CHAPTER XVIII.

THE OUTBREAK OF THE STORM—PALISSY WRECKED.

BERNARD PALISSY, on whom the sun was shining still, continued busy in his workshop. The Reformed religion had gained strength in Saintes, and Palissy was prominent in his own town among its firm and peaceable supporters. He assumed to himself the right of free inquiry, and did not scruple to make bold confession of his faith ; while doing this he quietly pursued his studies in the fields, and laboured in his prosperous vocation as a potter.

The chief work upon which Bernard Palissy was at this time engaged had been committed to him, as we have seen already, by the Constable Montmorenci. Perhaps Montmorenci had become acquainted with the skill of Palissy when his mission to quell the revolt against the salt-tax had brought him, after punishing the town of Bourdeaux, through Saintonge. Perhaps the constable, whose ears were open to all useful hints for the promotion of his famous building-works at Ecouen, had heard of

Bernard Palissy through courtly friends residing in or
near Saintonge, whose homes the Potter had already
decorated with examples of his skill.   The patronage of
Montmorenci must have gone far to assist the artist's
worldly fortunes.   A man who had been entrusted with
important charges in the decoration of one of the most
famous architectural works of France during his own
time, was recommended by his position to a large circle of
seigneurs who had castles to build or to improve.

The building of the Château d'Ecouen was commenced
as one of the chief amusements of the wealthy constable,
when he was forced into political inaction by the loss of
royal favour.   The architect employed upon it was Jean
Bullant, who afterwards enjoyed the patronage of Catherine of Medicis, and commenced the building of the
Tuileries in conjunction with Philibert de Lorme.   In the
history of French architecture, the reputation of Jean Bullant is founded principally on the Château d'Ecouen, with
which we are now concerned.   Bullant, a strict disciple
of Vitruvius, had studied in Italy the remains of ancient
art, and was among those who introduced into France
Greek principles of architecture, which were often at first
curiously grafted on the heavy Gothic character that belonged to the buildings of the period then closed.   So it
happens that the château at Ecouen displays a quaint
mixture of old Gothic associations with the doctrine of
Vitruvius, and exhibits classic outlines, Doric, Ionic, and
Corinthian, with high roofs and church windows.

The château, distant about four leagues from Paris, over-looks from a hill the little country-town of Ecouen. It was built in the quadrangular form, and surrounded on three sides by a moat, in accordance with that fortress style of architecture which had not yet become unsuited to the wants of the French nobility. In its main plan there was much to remind one of the Luxembourg. On the fourth side, overlooking Ecouen, there was, and is, a terrace famous for the pleasant prospect it commands. The four corners of the building are slightly elevated in the form of towers, having cupola roofs. The château surrounds three sides of the quadrangle within, these being the three sides guarded by the moat. On the fourth side, corresponding to the terrace, the square is completed by a wall, having a plain massive gate, through which a visitor must pass into the quadrangle before coming to the grand front of the château itself. The entrance to this is quoted among architects for its majestic peristyle, with four Corinthian columns and as many pilasters, as the best specimen remaining of the works of Jean Bullant. The whole style of architecture in the Château of Ecouen is said to be characterised by that simplicity belonging to a work of genius, which produces in the student's mind, according to its humour at the time, a sense either of elegance or grandeur.

The altar of the chapel at Ecouen, by Bullant himself, is preserved now in a museum. There are carved on it in bas-relief the four Evangelists and the theologic Virtues; there are also spaces on it, formerly filled by statues of the constable and of his wife, Magdalen of Savoy, both chiselled by Prieur. Of the work contributed by Palissy towards the decoration of the building, nothing remains in the present day but the beautiful pavement in the chapel and galleries. Of the history of Psyche, painted on glass by Palissy, after the designs of Raffaelle, and of his large piece from the designs of Albert Durer, there remain only representations upon paper.*

A brief record of a visit paid to the Château d'Ecouen, not very long after the death of Bernard, supplies to us a few particulars which will assist in defining to our minds the scheme of decoration in which Palissy performed his part. " We saw," says the writer,† " a dozen heads and many beautiful figures in marble antiques ; there is one of a hero, in white marble, which is excellent; and above all, there are two drooping captives, from the hand of Michael Angelo, which are not finished, but the design of them is marvellous. In the chapel we saw beautiful pictures, and among others a copy of the Last Supper, by Raffaelle d'Urbino, drawn on the piece of Papal tapestry which M. the Constable gave to the late Pope Cle-

* They occupy forty-five plates in vol. vi. of the Musée des Monuments Français.

† Nicholas-Claude Fabry de Peiresc, whose visit was paid in the year 1606, and whose account of it is quoted from MS. in a note to the edition of Palissy by MM. Faujas de St. Fond and Gobet.

ment VIII. The court is almost precisely square, forty paces in breadth, and forty-five paces long. The galleries and the château contain many precious marbles, and of those beautiful articles of pottery invented by Master Bernard of the Tuileries.* There are two galleries entirely painted with great skill by one Maestro Nicolo, who had been in the service of the Cardinal de Châtillon. On the glass, the fables that are represented best are that of Proserpine, on one, and that of the Banquet of the Gods; that of Psyche on the other; the pavement of these galleries is also the invention of the above-named Master Bernard."

In the peristyle before the chapel was a round table of great size, of black and white stone, polished, full of shells. The château contained works of taste executed in black Egyptian marble, verd antique, and other curious material. The walls of the chapel were adorned with figures of the Apostles in mosaic, and among other pictures, besides that of the Last Supper from Raphael, was the Woman taken in Adultery, by Jean Bellin. The font was a vase of Italian jasper, on antique bronze feet. The sacristy included among its contents a map of the Crusades, and was paved, as we have seen already, with the exquisite pottery of Palissy, covered with paintings of his own design, on subjects taken from the Scriptures. Of all the windows at Ecouen Bernard Palissy is said to have been the painter. In a grove of the garden there

* We shall find this name first attached to Palissy when we have reached a later chapter in the story of his life.

was formerly a fountain called FONTAINE MADAME, to
which was attached the rustic grotto, of which Palissy
speaks always with pride as one of the chief triumphs
of his ingenuity. The formation of the fountain, and
the arrangements made for its supply, were also, most
probably, suggested by the Potter, whose study of nature,
as we shall hereafter see, had already by this time led
him to discover the true theory of springs, and whose
shrewd wit instructed him in many ways by which he
could make useful application of his knowledge.

Happily occupied with such work, and declining all
part in the turmoil of the day, Palissy prospered still,
while France was falling into trouble. Far removed from
the old days of solitary struggling, he had now two
sons, Mathurin and Nicolas, cheerfully taking their part
of the labour in the well-appointed workshop. The
trouble of France was being felt at Saintes. The hymns
of the triumphant Huguenots, who had reformed the
town, had begun already to fall into discord. Many who
had put upon themselves reform as a garment cut to
the prevailing fashion, had found the dress not loose
enough to suit them, and returned to their old clothes
again. Since orthodoxy had endured a summary eject-
ment from the town, it had found time to make a formid-
able muster of its forces, and a contest was imminent.
Still Palissy worked tranquilly at his vocation, exercising,
however, openly a right to act on his own convictions,
and to speak what he thought to be the truth. He

zealously supported the ministry of M. de la Boissière, and he did not spare his censure upon men of the old school, who enjoyed themselves on the revenue of the Church, and took no part in the performance of its duties. "They are accursed, damned, and lost," he used to say. "And I can tell you this with certainty, because it is written in the Prophet Ezekiel, chap. 34; for the prophet says, 'Woe be to you, shepherds, who eat the fat and clothe you with the wool, and leave my flock scattered upon the mountains; I will require it at your hands.' "*

The free speaking of Palissy created no goodwill towards the honest Potter through a large circle of men against whom his shafts were pointed. Any frivolous young noble of the neighbourhood would not much relish the good Potter's humour for applying common sense to the details of dress. " Brother," Bernard asks of an ideal courtier, " who has moved you to cut in this way the good cloth you are wearing in your breeches and other habiliments? Do you not know very well that it is a folly? But this insensate wished to make me believe that breeches so cut would last longer than others, a thing I could not believe. Then I said to him, 'My friend, assure yourself of this, and do not doubt it, that the first man who had holes cut in his breeches, was a fool by

* When I quote Palissy in this chapter, it is either from the *History of the Troubles in Saintonge*, or from a part of the *Jardin Delectable*, translated complete in the Appendix, under the title of *The Naturalist looking out on Evil Days*.

nature; and though, in general matters, you may be the wisest person in the world, yet in this particular you imitate and follow the example of a fool.' True it is, that a folly transmitted from our ancestors is esteemed wisdom; but for my part, I cannot agree that such a thing is not a direct piece of folly."

So from the highest to the lowest matters, Bernard freely exercised his judgment on the wisdom of his ancestors. He tested by a rule of common sense the absurdities of feminine attire. "You have got to yourself," he tells us in his lively way, after the form of an address to a high dame—" you have got to yourself a farthingale in order to dilate your dress in such a manner, that your garments barely escape exposing what you ought to hide. After I had made her this remonstrance, instead of thanking me, the silly woman called me Huguenot; seeing which, I left her."

Of the trader he desires to know what he has put into his pepper, that enables him to buy it in Rochelle at thirty-five sols the pound, and to make a great profit by selling it again in the fair of Niord at seventeen sols, "in consequence of the adulteration added to the said pepper. Then I asked why he was so foolish, and without judgment, as to deceive thus wickedly the customers; but without any shame, this rascal maintained that the folly of which he was guilty was a piece of wisdom; and I urged upon him then that he was damning himself, and that he could afford better to be poor than damned; but this

insensate said that poor men were of no esteem, and that
he would not be poor, follow what might; then I was
constrained to leave him in his folly."

These, and other examples of his style of criticism on
the follies and the vices of his time, occur in a book published by Palissy immediately after the events narrated
in the present chapter. His criticism takes the form of
an inspection of different heads, for the purpose of dis-
covering what they contain. "In this way," he says,
"I took the head of a presiding judge who called himself
good servant to the king; the same had greatly persecuted certain Christians, and had favoured many wicked
men; and having subjected his head to examination, and
separated its parts, I found that there was one part fattened
by a morsel of benefice which he possessed; then I knew
directly that this was the reason why he had made war
against the Gospel, or against those who desired to lay it
open to the light. Seeing which, I left him to his folly,
knowing well that I should have no power of argument
over him, since his kitchen was fattened with that kind
of pottage.

"Then I came to examine the head and the whole body
of a counsellor of parliament—the slyest fellow one might
ever meet with; and having put his parts into the retort
and furnace of examination, I found that he had in his
belly many bits of benefices, which had fattened him so
much that he could not confine his belly in his breeches.
When I perceived such a thing, I entered into dispute

with him;" but Palissy adds, when he has made remonstrance against his folly, " I had no sooner finished my
discourse, than this foolish and insensate man used all his
efforts to put me to shame, and gain a victory upon the
proposition that I had maintained; and said to me with a
loud voice: ' What, is that your argument ? If I were,
indeed, a fool for holding benefices, the number of fools
would be terribly great.' Then I said to him, quite gently,
that all those who drink the milk and wear the wool of
the sheep, without providing for their pasture, are accursed;
and alleged to him the passage that is written in Jeremiah
the Prophet, chapter 34. Then he attempted a bravado,
and a marvellously high-flown fury, saying, ' What?
According to your account there are a great many whom
God has cursed. For I know that in our sovereign court'
(of parliament), ' and in all the courts of France, there
are few counsellors and presidents who do not possess some
morsel of benefice, which helps to support the gildings
and accoutrements, banquets and common pleasures of
the house, necessary to acquire in time some noble place,
or office of more honour and authority. Do you call
that folly? It is the most consummate wisdom,' said he.
' It is a great folly to let oneself be hung, or burnt, for the
maintenance of the authorities of the Bible. *Item*,' said
he, ' I know that there are many great lords in France, who
take the revenue of benefices ; nevertheless, they are not
fools, but very wise; for such things help them greatly in
the maintenance of their estates, honours, and fat kitchens;

and by such means they get good horses for their service during war.'" The war-horse, it will be observed, makes a shrewd climax to the list of worldly goods.

Plain-speaking, of the character here indicated, must be added to the list of Bernard's occupations during the period of his prosperity at Saintes. The same originality and force of intellect which procured patrons for the Potter, was serving at the same time to multiply enemies about the austere Reformer who indulged so freely in the luxury of truth. The affairs of the Potter prospered, and after all, the wife of Palissy perhaps would have been well content if pottery had been her only care.

The child who succeeded Francis II. upon the throne of France was six years younger than his predecessor; he was a little more than ten years old, and Charles IX. was his title. On his accession, the Prince of Condé had one foot upon the scaffold, and the King of Navarre was not many steps therefrom; they being the two first princes of the royal blood. The old four factions of the time of Henry II. had decomposed by this time into two great parties, and involved in their dispute the passions of the whole French nation. At the head of one party, which included all the Huguenots, were the slighted members of the high French nobility; at the head of the other party, which included all the Catholics, were the Guises, aliens in blood, who had then their advantage in a tight grasp of the reins of power. The parties to the great dispute upon theology, the Huguenots and Catholics, had been respectively invited to ally themselves to opposite sides in a fierce quarrel among great men for court influence: they fell accordingly into opposing ranks, and with their strong, deep passions, overwhelmed the mean first cause of the dispute, which rapidly resolved itself into a civil war upon the angriest of topics.

Queen Catherine of Medicis, who, by the elevation of her second son, was now continued in her title of queen-mother, had for a long time been troubled by the clang of parties, and the quarrel of court factions for predominance. Wisely advised, she determined, when her boy Francis was released by death from the dominion of the Guises, to preserve her next son, Charles, if possible, and France at the same time, in a more tranquil state. The heads of each faction, even while Francis shifted restlessly upon his death-bed, lavished promises of faithfulness upon the mother, and endeavoured to secure her as a close ally. She repelled neither, she embraced neither, but she reconciled all to herself. The King of Navarre, renouncing his claim to a regency in favour of Catherine, was made lieutenant-general of the kingdom, ostensibly reconciled to the Guises, who continued powerful at court. The Prince of Condé came with honour from his prison. The court smiled upon the discontented nobles, who returned to favour, the great Constable Montmorenci among the rest. The veteran, when he first knelt before the little king and kissed his hand, was moved to tears: " Sire," he said, " do not fear the present troubles. I will sacrifice

my life, and so will all your faithful subjects, for the pre-
servation of your throne."

The constable, according to his conscience, kept his
word. Every act tended to conciliation. The policy of
the queen-mother prevailed, and the monopoly of power
was taken from the Guises. The Bourbon party lost no
opportunity of causing their old enemies to feel the change;
the Guises maintained a proud front, and as they still
enjoyed much manifest favour, complaint grew against
them even in their humbler state. At last the King of
Navarre, Coligny, D'Andelot, Cardinal Châtillon, and the
chief nobility, with Constable Montmorenci to support
them, carried the old dispute so far as to call out their
horses for a ride to Paris, from the court at Fontainebleau,
declaring that if the Guises were not banished, they would
cause the parliament of Paris to declare Antony, King of
Navarre, the regent of the kingdom. At the critical
moment, Montmorenci was summoned to the presence of
the young king, who commanded him to remain about his
person. The old constable was not prepared to be disloyal,
and remained; his friends, unable to get on without him,
sent their horses back into the stables, and all stopped at
Fontainebleau to play a round game at negotiation.

The object of Queen Catherine was, if possible, to
offend neither of the contending parties, and to hold them
so well balanced that she might sway either as she pleased,
and it was her desire to exert all her influence for the
maintenance of peace. The Guises, following their own

ends, and not confiding greatly in the queen, allied themselves with the ambassador of Spain, whom Philip II. had
sent over to maintain his interests, and who was disposed
to meddle actively in the affairs of France. This dan-
gerous alliance boded so much the ascendancy of Catholic
intolerance, that Catherine considered it her policy to set
the balance right by showing favour to the Calvinists.
She carried her tolerance to the point of an apparent pre-
ference for the Reformed religion, and in that way very
much shocked the orthodox old constable, who bade her
pay more pious heed to the appointed fast days of the
Church.

At the same time the parliament of Paris was propound-
ing counsels of political and financial reform. The King
of Navarre was to be regent, the Guises and all priests
were to be dismissed from participation in state business.
Account was wanted of all gifts made by the late kings
to the Guises, to Diana of Poitiers, to the constable, the
Marshal of St. André, and others.

The Marshal St. André and Diana had aforetime been
very active in procuring the confiscation of property belonging to the Huguenots. They were of course, therefore, fair subjects for retaliation. Uniting their interests
in self-defence, they combined to alarm the constable by
making him believe that the orthodox religion was to be
abolished in the first instance, and after that there was to
be confiscation of his property. The old man, possessed
with such ideas, was obstinately deaf to the re-assurances

of his eldest son, the marshal, and of his nephews, the Châtillons, and making common cause with his old political opponent, the Duke of Guise, and with the Marshal St. André, he formed with them what was entitled a triumvirate. A Catholic league was planned, with Philip of Spain at the head, and plots were laid to win over to the Catholic cause the easy-minded Bourbon of Navarre. His relations with his neighbours of Spain caused that task to seem by no means difficult. The queen endeavoured still to maintain peace, but as the chancellor informed the parliament of Paris, " The Devil had taken care of the religious contests," and there was no peace to be had.

In July, 1561, the Chancellor L'Hôpital addressed an edict of tolerance to all the presidial courts. Outbreaks of intolerance were the immediate result. In every district where the Huguenots prevailed, they triumphed in their privileges; where the Catholics prevailed, the edict was rebelled against. New tactics being requisite, the parliament in the next place decreed that punishment of death should be abolished in the case of those condemned for participating in heretical assemblies. It was ordained also that there should be peace throughout the kingdom, and that no levies should be made without the king's permission. Priests and ministers were respectively commanded to cease from abusive language. Calvinists were not allowed to hold assemblies ; bishops were to punish heresy, but with no penalty more grave than banishment. The edict was not well observed. The queen's favour

enabled the Huguenots to meet even at court, and in
some places they wrested even the churches of the orthodox to their own use.

Then there were assemblies. There was the colloquy
of Poissy, an elaborate theologic wrangle, held on the 9th
of September in the same year. Good never came of
theologic wrangle, whether two men or two hundred
were the parties to it ; and so no good followed from the
colloquy of Poissy. Each side, of course, confidently
claimed the victory. To win the pleasure-loving King
of Navarre to the side of the Catholics, it was proposed
that he should divorce his old wife, Jeanne d'Albret, for
heresy, and take as a new one Mary Stuart, with the
crown of Scotland. The king was not tempted, however,
either by Mary on the one hand or by Margaret of Valois,
the king's sister, whom Catherine offered him by way of
counter-bribe to Mary. The King of Spain knew better
how to bribe, by promising the island of Sardinia, at the
same time that Antony was reminded of the subordinate
position he would hold among the heretics, who regarded
as their leader, not the King of Navarre, but the Prince
of Condé. Antony then formed alliance with the Duke
of Guise, and openly espoused the faction of the orthodox,
celebrating the event with a grand procession.

While these intrigues took place among the leaders,
tumults and riots were increasing throughout the country. Queen Catherine and the Chancellor L'Hôpital still
laboured to promote peace by edict ; and as the last

edicts had been unavailing, deputies from all the parliaments assembled at Saint-Germain, in January, 1562, contrived another. Usurped churches were to be restored, and orthodoxy honoured; but the heretics were to be allowed to meet for worship, unarmed, and outside the towns. Their ministers were to abstain from all invective against the ceremonies of the Established Church, but to promote kind feeling to the utmost of their power. In places where the heretics were weak, this edict was rejected; where parties were balanced, the opposition of the orthodox had to be put down by force of arms; in some places, as at Barjols, the heretics displayed that furious and cruel temper which is by no means the peculiar attribute of any one sect of contending Christians.

The edict of January was attributed by the heretics to the success of their representatives—Beza the chief—in the colloquy of Poissy. They thought that all doubts were removed ; and in some places, fortified by the edict and the favour of the queen, they shared the temples with the priests, who yielded to them sometimes out of fear, and sometimes half disposed to take part with the ascendant doctrines. As for the king, by whom of course the edict had formally been issued, songs were made in his honour ; he was claimed as a reformer, and significant anagrams were found to be connected with his name, Charles de Valois : Va chasser l'idole—Chassa leur idole.

The Guises had at this time quitted the court. The Pope's legate and the Spanish ambassador, remaining near

the king, worried the queen-mother, who repaid them
with cold looks. The King of Navarre, enamoured of a
maid of honour, Rouhet de la Béraudière, could not
patiently find time to spare for other topics. The veteran
Montmorenci and the Marshal St. André seemed to be
the only active heads of the great Catholic party; while
the Prince of Condé was drilling Huguenots, and Coligny
and D'Andelot rejoiced at court in the smiles of Catherine
of Medicis.

But the Guises had left the court not to seek rest, but
to employ themselves in active preparations for a struggle.
The King of Navarre being impatient of the ascendancy
obtained by his brother, the Prince of Condé, in Paris,
the Duke of Guise was summoned to exert himself. He
left Joinville for Paris, with his brother the cardinal and
a numerous suite, at the end of February. In passing
through Vassy, on the frontier of Champagne, his attendants disturbed the service of a Huguenot congregation
with disputes that mounted very soon from words to
blows, from fists to stones. The duke, coming to calm the
riot, was struck with a stone. The flowing of his blood,
say Catholic accounts, produced a rage among his people,
and resulted in a massacre. Huguenots told that the
whole matter was premeditated, and that the townspeople
were charged upon to the sound of the duke's trumpets.
The duke declared upon his death-bed that the massacre
was accidental, and we take his word, for certainly he was
not a dishonourable witness. Three hundred, of every age

and either sex, were slaughtered at Vassy. The Huguenots brought their remonstrance to the queen, and were
heard with favour ; the King of Navarre, the lieutenant-
general, declared them to be factious heretics. The Duke
of Guise and Montmorenci at the same time made a
triumphal entry into Paris.

The massacre of Vassy was being imitated at Cahors,
at Sens, at Auxerre, and at Tours, in which places more
than a thousand perished. Three hundred of these were
shut up in the house of God to starve for three days
before they were taken two by two for slaughter on a river
bank. There were little children, who had not been murdered with their parents, sold for a dollar apiece. There
was a beautiful girl killed naked, that vile eyes might
contemplate the paling of the skin, and the whole sudden
change of beauty to the ghastliness of death. Such
cruelties there were that dotted with a deeper black the
massacres in Aurillac, Nemours, Grenades, the new town
of Avignon, Marsilagues, Senlis, Amiens, Abbeville,
Meaux, Châlons, Troze, Bar-sur-Seine, Epernai, Nevers,
Châtillon-sur-Loire, Gien, Moulins, Yssoudun, le Mans,
Angers, Cran, Blois, Mer, and Poitiers. In all these
places, massacres succeeding that of Vassy preceded the
first outbreak of the civil war.

The Prince of Condé, finding it impossible to recover
Paris from the hands of the Guises and Montmorenci,
their new ally, endeavoured to collect at Meaux all forces
that were available for action. He wrote to summon to

his aid Coligny and D'Andelot, telling them, in reference
to the events at Paris, " Cæsar has not only crossed the
Rubicon, but he has taken Rome." Cardinal Châtillon
and D'Andelot, with Senlis, Boucard, Bricquemant, and
others, were assembled in the dwelling-place of the admiral, at Châtillon-sur-Loire. The admiral shrunk from the
step which pledged him to a part in civil war, and for
two days resisted the arguments of his companions. To
the complaints of his wife, however, uttered in the mid-
watches of the night (her important curtain-lecture is on
record*), Coligny yielded. As the Sieur d'Aubigné relates, " The persuasions of a well-beloved voice and of a
proved faith were so violent that they set the admiral on
horseback to ride in search of the Prince of Condé and
his friends at Meaux."

Catherine, fearing violence, carried the king from
Monceaux, an undefended country-house, to Melun, and
again to Fontainebleau, after having written to call Condé
to her aid. The triumvirs, with a troop of cavalry, followed to Fontainebleau, where they told the queen that
they required the presence of her son, and that she might

---

* D'Aubigné relates it, from the evidence of the parties concerned.
"We lie here a-bed in luxury," the lady said, in the course of her
discourse, "and the bodies of our brothers, flesh of our flesh and bone
of our bone, are some in the prisons, some in the fields, where they lie
at the mercy of the dogs and crows; this bed is a tomb to me, because
they have no tombs; these Curtains reproach me, for they sleep without
a shroud." The discourse was delivered to Coligny, with the usual
preface of sobs, two hours after he had said "Good night." So D'Aubigné
informs us.

accompany him or leave him, as she pleased. Menaces
and prayers were in vain, and the queen-mother, clasp-
ing the boy in her arms, travelled away among the soldiers. The king, being then taken to Paris, was received
with joy, and as the triumvirate now had, at least in a
literal sense, the royal countenance, their acts against the
Calvinists assumed a more determined character. The
constable in Paris, at the head of troops equipped as for a
severe campaign, charged into the suburbs among the
churches used by heretics, broke open their gates, and
dragged their pulpits and their benches out to make great
bonfires for the delectation of the people. This exploit
amused the wits of Paris, who forthwith honoured Montmorenci with the name of Captain Burn-a-bench (Le
Capitaine Brûle-Bancs). "Burn-a-bench," however, reads
to our eyes much better than "Burn-a-man." The constable
was versed in war, but had no appetite for massacre, and
the complete equipment of the troop he led to perform
so trivial a work, precisely served its purpose, by dis-
couraging resistance, in preventing bloodshed.

The Prince of Condé, at the head of three thousand
horsemen, was on his way to Fontainebleau, obedient to
the urgent missives of the queen, when he had tidings
of the capture of the court, and its removal into Paris.
"The plunge is made," he said to Coligny, "and we
have gone so far that we must drink or drown." He
hurried with his troops to Orleans, where D'Andelot
was with some difficulty holding the town against the
Catholics. The troops brought by Condé decided the

struggle, and the heretics, possessed of Orleans, established their head-quarters in that town. Thither they
summoned all good Frenchmen to repair, and aid in the
deliverance of the king and the queen-mother out of the
hands of the triumvirs.

The Guises were accused in manifestoes as the authors
of all mischief and all intolerance. They replied that
whatever was imputed to them, must be imputed also to
the King of Navarre. As for the accusation of intolerance, had not the king, while in Paris, confirmed that
very edict of January which had pleased the Huguenots
so much? It was only in Paris and the neighbourhood
of the court that heretics were denied the right of preaching. Manifestoes were in fashion, issued from both sides,
and taking every shape of threat, complaint, promise
to lay arms down on condition. Each side was in the
mean time occupied in raising troops and finishing its
preparations for the contest. Since the conspiracy of Amboise, minor struggles, levies of soldiers, besieging of towns,
wasting of crops, had been perpetrated by such private
adventurers as Maugiron in the Dauphiné, Montbrun
in the Comtat-Venaissin, and the brothers Mouvans in
Provence. These, however, were mere drops before the
storm. The fury of the storm itself was on the point of
breaking, when the great mass of the French people became divided into two great factions, represented by two
armies, one within the walls of Orleans, and one within
the walls of Paris.

The leaders looked abroad for aid, and in so doing

employed the usual devices: when the orthodox sought Protestant allies, they said that they were preparing to subdue not heretics, but rebels; and when the heretics laboured abroad for orthodox assistance, they pleaded that they did not fight to subdue the old religion; but to release the king and queen from their audacious captors.

Queen Catherine, meanwhile, who attempted to supply the want of masculine vigour by substituting for it in the management of public affairs feminine tact, accepted the new position that was forced upon her, and endeavoured to act in it, still in pursuance of her old desires. When there came from the Duke of Guise letters to the provinces, commanding death to all the malcontents, there came in the same packets letters from the queen, commanding that mercy should be shown to all. Both wrote in the king's name; and when the puzzled magistrates went, as they sometimes did, to court for definite instructions, they could get no satisfactory answer.

The confederates of Orleans, having formed a league in opposition to the league which bound their enemies together, having sworn to deliver the king, to put down profanity, uphold the edict of January, and obey the Prince of Condé as their lawful chief, incited a rising throughout France of their adherents. Troops were brought into Orleans from all the provinces by the brothers Châtillon, La Rochefoucault, Rohan, Genlis, Grammont, and other seigneurs. The army in Paris, having the king to show, called itself royalist; but the greater number of the nobles was attached to the cause headed by the Prince of Condé. In the beginning of June, the two armies, each numbering eight or ten thousand, took the field, the one bent on delivering the king, the other eager to lay siege to Orleans.

Before the contest, at the intercession of Queen Catherine, a last discussion, a last attempt at reconciling differences, was demanded. In it the heretic chiefs promised for themselves and for their followers, by way of oratory, more than they intended to perform; and being unexpectedly and inconveniently taken at their words by the queen-mother, they escaped only by the breaking of their pledge. Instead of marching like heroes into voluntary exile for the sake of peace, they suddenly marched down upon the royalists to give them battle unexpectedly. The orthodox, however, were not to be taken by surprise, and the heretics turned off to besiege Beaugenci, which town they took and pillaged. The Huguenot soldiers sang psalms in their camp, and had many hours of prayer from sunrise until sunset; but the sack of a town, never a pious scene, will not endure description where all evil passions that belong to it are heightened by fanaticism. Whatever inhumanity the Huguenots displayed in Beaugenci, was equalled by the royalists in Tours, Poitiers, and other towns which they succeeded in delivering to pillage.

The queen, by letters, urged the Prince of Condé to submit to a conciliatory policy, and warned him that an edict was preparing of the utmost severity against the

heretics, that the king himself would be placed at the head
of the royalist army, and that reinforcement was expected
from abroad.

The time for conciliation was, however, past. The
declaration foretold by the queen was made at the end of
July, wherein the king declared all those who were in arms
against him guilty of treason, condemned them to death,
confiscated their property, and deprived all their posterity
of title to bear charges or honours in the kingdom.
Only the Prince of Condé was excepted from the condemnation, because it was thought prudent not to drive him
to despair. The confederates replied that they were no
traitors, but that they refused submission to the house of
Guise ; and the old work of civil war, tumult, massacre,
battle, and siege, went on.

Every town in France was filled at that time with the
riot of contending factions. In Saintes, as Palissy has
told us, M. de la Boissière had won an ample congregation,
and the heretics of Saintonge had made their voices
potent. " In those days," says Palissy, " the priests and
monks were blamed in common talk, that is to say, by
enemies of the religion, and they said thus : ' The ministers make prayers which we cannot deny to be good.
Why is it that you do not make the like?' which seeing,
Monsieur, the theologian of the chapter, betook himself
to making prayers like the ministers; so did the monks,
who were paid salaries for preaching; for if there was
a shrewd brother, awkward customer, and subtle argu-

mentator among the monks in the whole country, he must
be had in the cathedral church. Thus it happened, that,
in those days, there was prayer in the town of Xaintes
every day, from one side or the other." This constant
prayer is a fearful preface to a bloody contest. Palissy
describes also very pithily the alarm of the tithe-owners
at the refusal of the country-people to pay for church
service, unless preachers were provided for them, citing
the odd case of an orthodox attorney who got into the
pulpit and preached heresy himself, in order that he might
receive his money. " In those days," he tells us, " deeds
were done worthy enough to make one laugh and weep
at the same time; for certain farmers, hostile to the religion, seeing these new events, betook themselves to the
ministers to pray that they would come and exhort the
people of the district which they farmed, and this in
order that they might be paid their tithes. I never looked
so merry, though I wept the while, when I heard say
that the attorney, who was criminal-notary when suits
were brought against those of the religion, had himself
made the prayers, a little while before the devastation of
the church in the parish of which he was farmer. It is
to be decided whether, when he himself made the prayers,
he was a better Christian than when he made out the
indictment against those of the religion; *certes*, he was as
good a Christian when he made out the indictment as
when he made the prayers, provided that he made them
only to get out of the labourers their corn and fruit."

" The fruit of our little Church," says the Potter, speaking, it is to be remembered, of a Church which he himself had founded—" the fruit of our little Church had so well prospered, that they had constrained the wicked to become good; nevertheless, their hypocrisy has been since then amply made manifest and known; for when they had license to do evil, they have shown outwardly what they kept hidden in their wretched breasts. They have done deeds so wretched that I have horror in the mere remembrance, at the time when they rose to disperse, engulf, ruin, and destroy those of the Reformed Church. To avoid their horrible and execrable tyrannies, I withdrew myself into the secret recesses of my house, that I might not behold the murders, cursings, and indecent deeds which were done in our rural glades; and being thus withdrawn into my house for the space of two months, I had warning that hell was loose, and that all the spirits of the devils had come into the town of Xaintes : for where I had heard a little while before psalms, canticles, and all honest words of edification and of good example, I heard only blasphemies, blows, menaces, tumults, all miserable words, dissoluteness, lewd and detestable songs ; in such wise, that it seemed to me as if all virtue and holiness on earth had been smothered and extinguished : for there issued certain imps out of the Château of Taillebourg, who did more ill than the demons of antiquity. They, entering the town, accompanied by certain priests, with naked sword in hand, cried, ' Where are they ?' They must cut

throats immediately; and so they did to those who walked
abroad, well knowing that there was no resistance; for
those of the Reformed Church had all disappeared."

This disappearance of reformers from the town of
Saintes is explained to us in a contemporary chronicle.
The Count de la Rochefoucault had held at Saintes a little
synod to assert the justice of the Huguenot cause, and
with the troops thus augmented had made a vain attempt
on Rochelle, then taken Pons by assault, and attacked St.
Jean. Before St. Jean he heard that Duras, an ally,
whom he expected on the way to join him, had been
attacked near Vers by our old friend Montluc, and had
been thus compelled to change his course. The march of
La Rochefoucault to join Duras was joined by nearly all
reformers of the district able to bear arms, " especially,"
says the historian, " by those of Saintes;" which town,
being thus deprived of its soldiers, was taken by Nogeret,
a hostile leader, " who rudely treated all those who remained, in execution of a decree from Bourdeaux, by
which the lives of the reformers were abandoned without appeal to the mercy of any royal judge whatever."
Among those who remained was Palissy, who thus describes to us the horrors that made part of his experience
while he continued for two months secretly persevering
in his labour as a potter, and avoiding prudently the dangers of the street:

" In any case to find evil, they took a Parisian in the
streets, who was reported to have money; they killed

him without meeting any resistance, and exercising their
accustomed trade, reduced him to his shirt before life was
extinct. After that, they went from house to house, to
seize, sack, gluttonise, laugh, jest, and make joy with all
dissolute deeds and blasphemous words against God and
man; and they did not content themselves with jesting
against man, but they also jested at God; for they said,
that Agimus had beaten the Eternal Father.

" In that day there were certain persons in the prisons,
to whom the pages of the canons, when they passed before
the said prisons, said, jesting, ' The Lord will help you;'
and they said to them again, ' Now say, Avenge me,
espouse my cause.' And some others, beating with a
stick, said, ' The Lord be merciful to you.' I was greatly
terrified for the space of two months, seeing that the link-
boys and blackguards had become masters at the expense
of those of the Reformed Church. I had nothing every
day but reports of frightful crimes that from day to day
were committed; and it was of all those things the one
that grieved me most within myself, that certain little
children of the town, who came daily to assemble in an
open space near the spot where I was hidden (exerting
myself always to produce some work of my art), dividing
themselves into two parties, and casting stones one side
against the other, swore and blasphemed in the most
execrable language that ever man could utter; for they
said, 'By the blood, death, head, double-head, triple-head,'
and blasphemies so horrible, that I have, as it were, horror
in writing them. Now, that lasted a long while, while

neither fathers nor mothers exercised over them any rule. Often I was seized with a desire to risk my life by going out to punish them; but I said in my heart the seventy-ninth Psalm, which begins, ' O God, the heathen are come into thine inheritance.' "

The children playing in the street at Catholic and Huguenot, and cursing one another, form indeed a feature of the civil war more horrible than massacres themselves.

The workshop of Palissy, which had been erected for him partly at the expense of the Constable Montmorenci, did not long shelter him from harm. It was thrown open to the feet of a wild rabble, supported by the officers of justice, and all the pottery on which he had been employed was broken. Palissy held for his protection a safeguard from Louis de Bourbon, the first Duke of Montpensier, and nearly all the great men of Saintonge were his patrons and his friends. But he had been too bold an advocate of heresy to be omitted from the list of the proscribed. There were friends who in the daytime might have interfered on his behalf. At night, therefore, the trampling of the officers of justice at their door awoke the family of Palissy. Under the starlight he was hurried to a dungeon at Bourdeaux, the waiting-chamber to the scaffold.

END OF VOL. I.

WHITING, BEAUFORT HOUSE, STRAND.

CPSIA information can be obtained at www.ICGtesting.com
Printed in the USA
LVOW11s0845220315

431427LV00001B/59/P